Early Psychological Thought

Early Psychological Thought
Ancient Accounts of Mind and Soul

CHRISTOPHER D. GREEN

AND

PHILIP R. GROFF

PRAEGER

Westport, Connecticut
London

Library of Congress Cataloging-in-Publication Data

Green, Christopher D.
    Early psychological thought : ancient accounts of mind and soul / Christopher D. Green
and Philip R. Groff.
      p. cm.
    Includes bibliographical references and index.
    ISBN 0–313–31845–X (alk. paper)
      1. Psychology—History.   2. Philosophy of mind—History.   3. Philosophy, Ancient.
I. Groff, Philip R., 1966– II. Title.
BF91.G74   2003
150′.9—dc21   2002029760

British Library Cataloguing in Publication Data is available.

Library of Congress Catalog Card Number: 2002029760
ISBN: 0–313–31845–X

First published in 2003

Praeger Publishers, 88 Post Road West, Westport, CT 06881
An imprint of Greenwood Publishing Group, Inc.
www.praeger.com

Printed in the United States of America

The paper used in this book complies with the
Permanent Paper Standard issued by the National
Information Standards Organization (Z39.48–1984).

10 9 8 7 6 5 4 3 2 1

Copyright Acknowledgments

Acknowledgment is made to the following for permission to quote from their copyrighted works:

De Anima (On the Soul): Reproduced by the permission of Penguin Books Ltd., London.
   Translation copyright © 1986 by Hugh Lawson-Tancred.
Galen: Selected Works: Reprinted by permission of Oxford University Press. Translation copy-
   right © 1997 by P.N. Singer.
Greek Medicine From the Heroic to the Hellenistic Age: A Source Book: Reproduced by permis-
   sion of Routledge, Inc., New York, part of the Taylor & Francis Group. Copyright © 1998
   by James Longrigg.
Hellenistic Philosophy: Introductory Readings: Reprinted by permission of Hackett Publishing
   Company, Inc., Indianapolis, Ind. All rights reserved. Copyright © 1988 by B. Inwood and
   L.P. Gerson, Eds.
The Iliad: Reproduced by the permission of Penguin Books Ltd., Harmondsworth, U.K.: 1950.
   Translation copyright © 1946 by the Estate of E.V. Rieu.
"Medicine" in *Hippocratic Writings*, edited by G.E.R. Lloyd. Reproduced by permission of
   Penguin Books Ltd., New York: 1978. Translation copyright © 1950 by J. Chadwick and
   W.N. Mann.

Contents

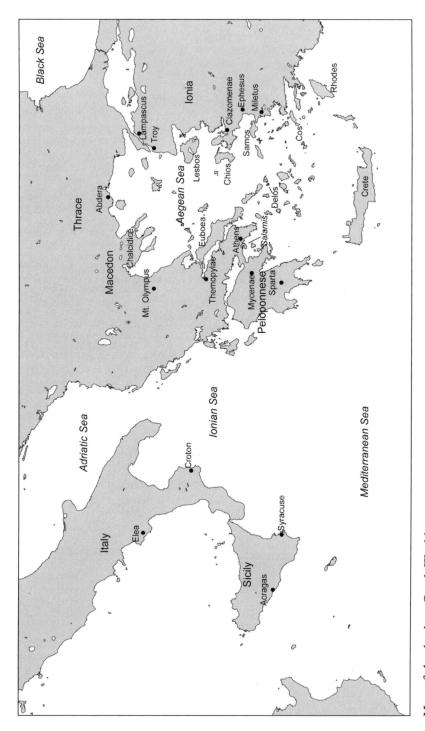

Map of the Ancient Greek World

Introduction

WHY STUDY EARLY PSYCHOLOGICAL THOUGHT?

Among the first questions one might ask as one begins reading this book is, "Why study the Greeks?" Why, indeed, should contemporary psychologists be particularly interested in what the Ancient Greeks thought about the mind? One possible answer can be found on the opening page of a classic study of Greek psychological thought by the German classicist Bruno Snell: "They discovered the human mind" (1953/1982, p. v).

What Snell meant by this claim is probably not immediately apparent. On the one hand, the Greeks did not undertake investigations we would consider to be scientific and as a result discover something called "the mind." Nor were they by any means the first to be aware that there existed various aspects of "mental life" such as memory, emotion, and thought. Surely the Egyptians, Sumerians, Babylonians, and even earlier peoples had their own understandings of these things.

What Snell meant, then, is that the concept of mind, *as we now conceive of it,* was a development of Greek thinkers. The "we" in the previous sentence, however, requires some explication, for Snell was writing at a time when many of the important sociological and cultural questions that profoundly inform historical studies of the present day were not so salient to historians. Snell began his book *The Discovery of the Mind in Greek Philosophy and Literature* by claiming, "European thinking began with the Greeks. They have made it what it is: our only way of thinking; its authority, in the Western world, is undisputed" (p. v). Thus, Snell believed that the traditional Western European way of thinking about mind originated with the Greeks. Although it may have been undisputed in Snell's day, that way of thinking about the mind is anything but undisputed in today's world. With the advent of various forms of "new history," cultural history, social history, and postmodernism more broadly, it is precisely these traditional assumptions that are now under attack. Many postmodern thinkers (e.g., Gergen, 1985, 1991, 1994, 2001; Rorty, 1979; Sampson, 1985) would dispute that there is, indeed, any single way the mind is for all people at all times. Thus, we might be inclined to retort to Snell that the Greeks did not discover the mind; rather, they merely invented or constructed the foundations of the way that we in the modern West conceive of the mind.

In one sense at least, the present authors would go even further than this. A main aim of this book, as the reader will see, is to show how alien the Greek view of what we now call the mind was to the ways in which we now conceptualize the topic, at least in some ways. Not only does the meaning of the Greek term *psychê* corresponds only extremely roughly to the meaning of its modern English cognate, it also changed radically over the course of the millennium or so covered in this book—Homer's *psychê*, Plato's *psychê*, and the early Christian *psychê* were quite different sorts of beasts.

Nevertheless, Snell had a point that is not without merit. Although he conceded that "the discovery of the intellect cannot be compared with the discovery of, let us say, a new continent" (p. v), he specifically defended his use of the word "discovery."

> The intellect was not "invented," as a man would invent a tool to improve the operation of his physical functions, or a method to master a certain type of problem. As a rule, inventions are arbitrarily determined; they are adapted to the purpose from which they take their cure. No objective, no aims were involved in the discovery of the intellect. In a certain sense it actually did exist before it was discovered, only not in the same form. (p. vi)

This, then, is the key to Snell's argument. It is not that people before the Greeks were not acquainted with various mental functions such as perception, thought, emotion, and the like but, rather, that it was only with the Greeks that these various functions came to be seen as "going together" in some important sense—as forming a unity of sorts, one that bears a close resemblance to what we now call "the mind." Whether we think of this unification as a "discovery" or as a more conceptual achievement—a "construction"—matters fairly little for present purposes. It was with the Greeks, during the half-millennium running from about 800 BC until about 300 BC, that this unification seems to have taken place.

The story we will be tracing in this book is, naturally enough, framed in the history of philosophy. As noted, it is in the writings of the early Greek philosophers, as well as their literary and medical contemporaries, that the first theories of what we would anachronistically call psychology are first encountered. Thus, many philosophers will have previously had access to this material in many other forms, presented to them throughout their professional training, but it is relatively rare for all of it to be brought together in this way, covering across the ancient European world the material pertaining to what we now call the mind.

This book has, however, been written primarily for psychologists who have an interest in the history of the discipline. Of course, in ancient times there existed no discipline called "psychology." (Consequently, we have instead tried to use the circumlocution "psychological thought" throughout.) Nevertheless, many of the questions that initially draw people to the field of psychology are among the earliest questions asked in our Western cultural tradition—what are the underpinnings, whether material or divine, of thinking and feeling, and how do they relate to our conduct? The intellectual frameworks within which such questions have been asked in the distant past, however, and the areas of knowledge and belief from which answers have been drawn, have often been quite different than they are today. Thus, we hope that the present volume draws the attention of psychologists by examining questions that remain interesting to them today, but that it also presents as answers to these questions material of which most modern psychologists remain largely unaware. It is also our hope that the modern reader will begin to appreciate anew the debts that current investigations owe to their theoretical forbears; that they will, in addition, see that psychology's present state of affairs is the result not simply of a steady march of progress but of many philosophical, religious, and broader historical contingencies as well. Although much of the material in this book is written in the mode of "history of ideas," we have made an effort to provide a good deal of general historical background as well so that the reader can see the connections between events in intellectual history and those in political, military, social, and cultural history.

Although this book is primarily for psychologists and philosophers, we hope that it will be of value, as well, to students of the arts and humanities more generally, or indeed to anyone with an interest in human beings. Rarely before has the material presented here been collected together in one place, offering a unique perspective on familiar texts and an opportunity to trace particular threads through the complex tapestry of classical writing.

The first chapter traces the beginnings of the unification of the various mental functions from the time of Homer through the writings of the lyric and tragic poets. As will be seen, in the beginning they were regarded as relatively disparate or heterogeneous entities. Yet, distinctions that seem quite clear to us, such as that between history and myth, had not been fully developed in Homer's time. Thus it is that we begin our investigation of psychological thought with these works of poetry. Indeed, it is in the very first line of the very first work of European literature.

Chapter 2 considers the transformation that took place in archaic Greek poetic thought that gave rise to the earliest forms of philosophy. Here we trace the story of the founding of philosophy, as distinct from poetry, on the Ionian coast, through to the challenges raised by Greek colonists in southern

Italy, and then to the responses of the thinkers of Athens and northern Greece. During this period early philosophers first began to develop accounts of nature as a whole, and it is within these early writings that the first glimmer of a theory of the mental began to emerge. In some sense it is the positions of even these very early thinkers that set the terms of debate in philosophy and science for centuries afterward, setting out various logically coherent possibilities for ways in which the world might be structured: Is matter continuous or made of particles? Are there only a few basic substances or many? Is the *psychê* a part of the body or a separate thing?

Then we examine the developments of more fully developed philosophies—the Sophists, Socrates, and Plato—in chapter 3. Often ignored or openly decried as mere orators, the Sophists transformed philosophy into a formal discipline of argumentation and highlight moral issues and social behavior as topics worthy of consideration alongside nature. Although opposing the Sophists in fundamental ways, Socrates extended their interest in the philosophical examination of the person and the person's role in society, raising it in prestige to a point higher than the consideration of nature that had dominated the thought of the earliest philosophers. It is in the writings of Socrates' student Plato that what we might consider a full psychological theory was presented.

Aristotle, the most famous of Plato's students, is the subject of chapter 4. Although interested in many of the same subjects as his mentor, Aristotle took a naturalistic approach to many issues. Consequently, his work was both a revival of the earlier work of the Ionians and simultaneously a point of contact with the modern reader who has been raised in a "scientific culture." His approach to the *psychê* was, too, in many ways strikingly naturalistic.

Following Aristotle, the Hellenistic philosophies of Stoicism and Epicurianism, rarely treated in much depth until recently, are presented in chapter 5. The modern reader will find much that is familiar in both the ordered world of the Stoics and in the chaotic world described by the Epicurians. For those with an interest in modern cognitive science, it is interesting to note that it was the Stoic writers who first presented a theory of mind based upon what appear to be logical functional relations. The behaviorist and psychodynamist alike will be intrigued by the discussion of the role of desire in all Hellenistic thought. We conclude the chapter with a brief overview of the oft-neglected schools of Skepticism and Cynicism.

In chapter 6 we temporarily leave the story of philosophy and turn to the ancient medical views of the mind and soul from some of the earliest ancient medical texts, through the teachings of the Hippocratic schools, and on to Galen. Tracing a history from early animistic and shamanistic practices through to the first great writings in the history of neuroanatomy, we see much the same subject matter as in earlier chapters but examine it from an entirely different perspective.

Finally, in chapter 7 we address the impact that the rise of Christianity, as well as that of its major philosophical competitor, Neoplatonism, had on ancient psychological thought. We conclude our story at this point, for here the philosophical world of the ancients had come to an end and the transition to the medieval world had already begun.

This volume lends itself to use as a course text either alone in a short course about ancient psychological thought or as part of a longer course on the history of psychology. Whether such a course is ultimately one or two semesters in length, the use of this text over the course of the first several weeks, especially in combination with primary source texts, should provide students with a firm grasp of the antecedents of psychology in the ancient world. The material in this book is also presented in sufficient depth and with sufficient detail with regard to context, citation, and acknowledgment of scholarly debate to serve as a reasonable reference volume for instructors and scholars who seek a general introduction to the subject.

Chapter 1

Early Greek Poetry
of Mind and Soul

PSYCHOLOGICAL THOUGHT IN HOMER'S
EPIC POETRY

The very first sentence of the very first work of European literature still left to us contains the Greek word *psychê*.[1] The book is the *Iliad*, by the poet Homer (fl. 8th c. BC[2]), and the sentence reads: "The Wrath of Achilles is my theme, that fatal wrath which, in fulfillment of the will of Zeus, brought the Acheans so much suffering and sent the gallant *psychês* of so many noblemen to Hades, leaving their *autous* as carrion for the dogs and passing birds."[3] A number of issues have to be explicated for this sentence to be fully understood. Achilles was the great Greek warrior who, having been insulted by the Greek king Agamemnon refused to fight against the city of Troy (also known as Ilium, thus the title, the *Iliad*), thereby extending the war and costing many lives. Zeus was, of course, the king of the Greek gods, and he favored the Trojans in the war. *"Acheans"* is one of the names the Greeks used for themselves. Hades is the place that *psychês* of people were thought to go after death. *Autous* is usually translated as "bodies" in this passage, but it literally means "themselves."[4] The usual words for "dead body" were *soma*[5] and *nekros*. Interestingly, the Greeks of Homer's time seem to have had no single word to refer to a live body; they spoke only of the various parts of living bodies—legs, arms, and so forth (see Snell, 1953/1982, pp. 5–8).

So the sentence implies that when one is killed (in war, anyway) something called the *psychê* goes to Hades, but oneself, seemingly identified with the body, remains on the battlefield. Obviously, at work here is an understanding quite alien to our own conception of what constitutes a person. One purpose of this section is to explore what the *psychê* was thought to be in Homeric Greece; another purpose, just as important, is to look at other words the Homeric Greeks used for processes that today we would call "psychological" to see how they fit together. In other words, we are looking for the pieces that constituted what might be called the Ancient Greek proto-theory of the mind. In doing this we must be careful not to impose too much of our own conceptual structure on their thought. As mentioned earlier in discussing Snell's work, the Homeric Greeks seem not to have had a unified concept of mind, although they did know about various mental functions, as we would call them now, so it would be misguided to go looking for a concept that didn't really exist for them. Rather, we will try to discover the conceptual structures corresponding to what *we* call "mind" as *they* saw them. In the limit, of course, this is an impossible project. We simply do not have the same worldview as the Greeks had, but the exercise is valuable nevertheless and will lead to a better, if still imperfect, understanding of their thought on the matter.

What exactly was the *psyche* to the Greeks of Homer's time? An obvious way to proceed is to examine the passages in which the word appears, to pick out commonalties. Using popular literature as a historical source can be a tricky business. As Bennett Simon (1978, p. 61) has pointed out, Homer was not so interested in articulating a *theory* of psychology as in writing an exciting heroic poem. Consequently, the language he uses is liable to be metaphorical and evocative—the way a modern sports announcer might extol the "guts" and "heart" and "wits" of the players rather than, say, the specific activities of their frontal lobes or their cerebellums. This having been said, the Homeric Greeks did not make the distinction between poetic and scientific discourse that we do, so even if the material found in the *Iliad* cannot be properly said to constitute a theory, it is still likely to be closer to what people of that time believed to be true than a poem of today is: The distinctions between literal and metaphorical, between logic and rhetoric, between myth and history, had not yet been fully formulated.

Before examining the uses of *psyche* in the *Iliad,* however, it is worth considering background on the story itself so that we have a context to work with. The *Iliad* is the story of a small part of a very long war between the Achean Greeks and the Trojans. The war is said to have lasted ten years, and the events surrounding it form the basis of a large number of the poems and plays of Ancient Greece. In brief the story is as follows. Paris, a prince of Troy, visits the house of the king of Sparta, Menelaus. While Menelaus is gone, Paris either kidnaps or seduces his wife, Helen. Menelaus demands justice and convinces his older brother, Agamemnon, the king of Mycenae, to gather up the Greek forces and make war on Troy. Agamemnon does this, but he is told by the goddess Artemis that he must sacrifice his daughter, Iphigenia, if he is to get good winds to take the war contingent to distant Troy. He agrees, much to the consternation of his own wife, Clytemnestra (although in one version of the story Iphigenia is spirited away by Artemis at the last minute). The force then sails for Troy and begins ten seasons of war. As the last year begins, Agamemnon is ordered by the god Apollo to return a woman he has taken hostage because she is the daughter of a priest of Apollo's temple. He does this, but in recompense he demands the slave girl of his best warrior, Achilles. Achilles is outraged, but under the influence of the goddess Athena he does as he is told and then vows to stop fighting for the Achean Greeks against Troy.

This is where the *Iliad* begins. The battle rages on, back and forth, influenced by gods and goddesses at various crucial points. When things are going particularly poorly for the Greeks and it looks as though they are about to be defeated, Achilles' best friend, Patroclus, asks Achilles if he can take to the field wearing Achilles' much-renowned armor, since Achilles is not using it. Achilles allows him to do this, but he puts specific limits on the sort of fighting in which Patroclus may engage. Patroclus agrees, but he becomes so impressed by his own newfound skill while wearing the armor that he oversteps Achilles' limits and is killed by Hector, the older brother of Paris and heir to the Trojan throne of their father, Priam. An enraged Achilles erupts against the Trojans who have killed his lifelong friend and finally kills Hector in one-on-one combat. His anger is so great that he refuses to return Hector's body to King Priam, as is the custom, but disgraces it by dragging it around the city behind his chariot. Priam's grief is so great that he finally deigns to visit Achilles' tent in person, and the body is returned. This is where the *Iliad* ends.

Using the ploy of the Trojan horse, the Greeks eventually defeat and sack Troy, and Helen is recaptured. Priam is killed by Achilles' son, Neoptolemus. Paris is almost killed by Menelaus but is saved at the last moment by the goddess Aphrodite. Achilles, too, is killed, by Paris, and a great battle erupts between two Greek warriors—Aias (or Ajax), king of Salamis, and Odysseus, king of Ithaca—over who will inherit Achilles' famous armor. Odysseus wins and, in at least one version of the story, Aias goes mad and kills himself. After this the story splits off in many directions.

Odysseus takes ten more years to return home because of the many obstacles set in his way by the god Poseidon, whom he has offended. This is the basis of Homer's other great poem, the *Odyssey*. Among his many adventures, Odysseus is forced to travel to Hades itself, where he meets the *psychês* of Achilles, Aias, and others, including his mother, who has died during his long absence from home. Upon finally arriving home, he finds his wife, Penelope, besieged by a number of suitors who have come to demand her hand (and Odysseus' property) in marriage. With his son, Telemachus, Odysseus is able to kill them all and return to his life as king of Ithaca. Agamemnon, by contrast, returns home much more quickly than Odysseus, only to be murdered by his wife, Clytemnestra, and her new lover, Aegisthus, in retribution for having sacrificed Iphigenia. Agamemnon's son, Orestes, in turn, seeks revenge by killing the couple, including his own mother, with the help of his sister, Electra.

With this context in mind, we can now fruitfully return to the question of what sort of thing the *psyché* was in Homeric thought. Below are several sentences from the *Iliad* in which the word *"psyché"* appears. Rather than advancing any particular interpretation preemptively, first we simply present the data, as it were, to let the reader try to work out what *psyché* meant to the Greeks of Homer's time.

1. "But you cannot steal or buy back a man's life once the *psyché* has left his lips" (IX, 408–409).[6]
2. "Conquered by my spear, you shall yield up your *psyché* to Hades of the Fabled Horse, and the glory to me" (XI, 443–445).
3. "Tearing its way in, the bronze [of the spearhead] let out his entrails; his *psyché* incontinently fled through the gaping wound; and darkness came down on his eyes" (XIV, 517–519).
4. "Patroclus put his foot on [Sarpedon's] chest, and withdrew the spear from his flesh. The diaphragm[7] came with it: he had drawn out the spear-point and the man's *psyché* together" (XVI, 503–505).
5. "Death cut Patroclus short and his disembodied *psyché* took wing for the House of Hades, bewailing its lot and the youth and manhood that it left" (XVI, 855–857).
6. "[Hector] hurled his spear [at Achilles]. But Athena, by a miracle that cost her but a little *psyché*,[8] blew the spear away from the illustrious Achilles, so that it flew back to Hector and fell at his feet" (XX, 438–440).
7. "'I beseech you,' said Hector of the golden helmet in a failing voice, 'by your knees, by your own *psyché* and by your parents, not to throw my body to the dogs at the Achean ships, but to take a ransom for me'" (XXII, 338–343).
8. "[Achilles] had no sooner fallen into a sleep that soothed and enfolded him, resolving all his cares, than he was visited by the *psyché* of poor Patroclus, looking and talking exactly like the man himself" (XXIII, 62–66).
9. "Achilles held out his arms to clasp the *psyché* [of Patroclus], but in vain. It vanished like a wisp of smoke and went gibbering underground" (XXIII, 99–101).

What is one to make of these references to the *psyché*? What sort of thing was it thought to be?

First notice that the *psyché* is never said to be doing anything in particular in the *living* human body. It is once mentioned in connection with effort expended by the goddess Athena (passage 6). *Psyché* is what leaves one's body when one dies. (There are a few instances, however, when unconscious people are said to temporarily lose their *psychés*.) It is the thing that keeps one alive; it is a life force, so to speak.[9] It is not the force supporting *all* life, however. Only humans and gods are said to have it. When animals are killed, *psychés* are not said to leave their bodies (except for one anomalous reference to pigs at *Iliad*, XIV, 426).

In short, the *psyché* seems to do little work that we would now consider to be "psychological": no cognition, emotion, will, or the like. When it leaves the body at death, it goes immediately to Hades—except in the case of

Patroclus, whose *psyché* haunts Achilles until his body has been properly disposed of. One important observation is that despite some superficial appearances, the *psyché* is not very much like the Christian soul. Most important, it seems to be a mere remnant of the dead person rather than his or her "essence," as Christians would have it. Further, as we find out in the *Odyssey* (XI), the "afterlife" of *psychés* in Hades is not like that of Christian souls, either in hell (as "Hades" is sometimes loosely translated) or in heaven. *Psychés* in Hades are unable to speak or act effectively. They are said to "flutter" and "gibber" and "squeak." If not strictly immaterial, they are vaporous, like wisps of smoke. They are mere shades or shadows of the people from whom they have come. In the *Odyssey* (X–XI), however, Odysseus is taught by the goddess Circe and by the *psyché* of the Theban seer Teiresias how to use of a kind of blood-magic to enable the *psychés* of his dead mother, Anticleia, as well as Agamemnon, Achilles, and others, to "hold rational speech" with him (XI, 148–149). They are described as "flutter[ing] to and fro . . . [and producing] a moaning that was horrible to hear" (XI, 42–43). Under the spell of the blood, however, they are able tell him the stories of their respective deaths. Odysseus' attempt to console his mother with an embrace is thwarted, though, because "like a shadow or a dream, she slipped through [his] arms" (XI, 207–209). She explains this as

the law of our mortal nature, when we come to die. We no longer have sinews keeping the bones and flesh together, but once the *thumos* has departed from our white bones, all is consumed by the fierce heat of the blazing fire, and the *psyché* slips always like a dream and flutters on the air. (XI, 217–224)

So if the *psyché* is not psychological in the modern sense, what terms, if any, did the Greeks of this era use to refer to processes that we might think of as psychological? The most important of these terms were *thumos*, seen in the passage immediately above, and *noos*. Bremmer (1983) says that *thumos* is "the source of all emotions. Friendship and feelings of revenge, joy and grief, anger and fear—all spring from *thumos*" (p. 54).[10] Typically, the *thumos* is the source of an impulse to action, or the impulse itself, usually of a courageous type. In the *Iliad* a battlecry to the troops from the wise old soldier Nestor, for instance, is said to have "put *thumos* and daring into every man" (VI, 72). Sometimes the *thumos* has a quasi-intellectual aspect. For instance, it is said that "Zeus must decide in his own *thumos* between the Trojans and the [Greeks]" (VIII, 429–431). Also, a warrior is sometimes described as arguing with his *thumos* about a plan of action (Odysseus in XI, 401–403). This latter example, however, may simply be Homer's way of depicting the warrior's efforts to resist a strong, but unwise, emotional impulse, such as quick revenge. *Thumos* is strongly connected to the idea of motivation and will: For example, why did the fighter lunge into battle? Because his *thumos* told him to. The *thumos* seems to be able to infuse the whole body—*thumos* can move into the limbs and muscles—but its source is the *phrenes,* or diaphragm. Upon death, *thumos* leaves the limbs, but unlike the *psyché* it does not then continue its existence elsewhere; it seems merely to dissipate. Also unlike the *psyché,* the *thumos* is characteristic of animals as well as humans; and so when animals die, they are often said to lose their *thumos* (as when Agamemnon sacrifices lambs in III, 292–294).

The *noos* (or later, *nous*), by contrast, is much more intellectual in character. Snell (1953/1982, p. 9) calls it the "cause of ideas and images." Bremmer (1983, p. 57) calls it "the mind or an act of mind, a thought or a purpose." It is often connected with a relatively abstract plan or idea. As such, it is not a term that appears often in Homer, who was writing about warriors, not thinkers. Thought to be located in the chest, it was never given a material form.

Other important psychological terms include *menos* and *até*. *Menos* is similar to *thumos* in many ways: It is the rage of the warrior about to launch into or resume battle, but it is most often something *put into* the warrior by a god, like a divine "second wind" when despair or fatigue has worn down the warrior's resolve (see Dodds, 1951, pp. 8–9). *Até* is a kind of folly or madness, but again, one that often finds its origin outside the person with the gods. For instance, when Agamemnon finally relents and returns to Achilles the slave without whom Achilles would not fight, Agamemnon blames his actions on *até* caused by Zeus, and Achilles accepts this explanation as plausible (XIX, 137–138; see also Dodds, 1951, ch. 1, for a classic discussion).

This belief that at least some mental states are foisted upon people by external forces seems not to have been uncommon in Homeric times. Snell (1953/1982, ch. 3) has argued that it was not until after the time of Homer, with the rise of the so-called lyric poets such as Archilochus of Paros (d. ca. 650 BC) and Sappho of Lesbos (fl. ca. 600 BC), that people began to write consistently as though they were the "owners" of their mental states.[11] Until this time, according to Snell, the trend was to attribute mental states to interventions by the gods. Although this a far more sweeping claim than is supported by the texts (and far more blunt than Snell actually puts the matter), there is a certain amount of truth to it.

Julian Jaynes, a psychologist by training, took an even more radical position with respect to this matter. In his book *The Origin of Consciousness in the Breakdown of the Bicameral Mind* (1976), he made the provocative claim that the Achean Greeks of Homer's *Iliad,* as well as their contemporaries in other cultures, were actually *preconscious* by modern standards. Specifically, he argued that the people of the *Iliad* had no sense of self in the way that modern humans do, instead believing themselves to be motivated by external forces of a divine nature. Thus, according to Jaynes, the psychology of the *Iliad* is not a psychology of the individual at all, or at least it is a selfless psychology in which preconscious humans—in effect, pre-human hominids—act without awareness or, indeed, without any organized mental life.

Such an extraordinary thesis requires extraordinary evidence. Jaynes relied on two major lines of argumentation. First is the seeming lack of description of a unified mental life in texts such as the *Iliad,* compounded by the inclusion of motivating forces personified as gods, which would seem to overdetermine the actions they motivate. Second, he argued for an analogy between descriptions of events in texts such as the *Iliad* and current theory and clinical work in human abnormal psychology and neuropsychology.

Jaynes quoted passages from the *Iliad* in which people's behavior is depicted as externally motivated. For example, he made much of the passage in which Achilles prepares to attack Agamemnon in anger but is deterred by the goddess Athena, who holds back his arm and counsels patience. Jaynes' argument was that Achilles' decision to curb his anger and refrain from striking his kinsman and king seems to be made not by Achilles but, rather, by a force external to him. Jaynes also pointed to passages that seem to indicate an inner struggle or deliberation but localize the conflict in the *thumos* or *phrenes* rather than in the *noos*. Thus, according to Jaynes, the description is not one of conflicting ideas but, rather, of conflicting actions.

For modern psychological models of people functioning in an apparently similar way, Jaynes invoked description of schizophrenic patients who report hearing voices, often voices demanding that they perform some action. Drawing on traditional neuropsychological literature, in which perception and interpretation of speech are localized in the left temporal lobe of the brain (at least in most right-handed individuals), Jaynes argued that the homologous area in the right hemisphere may possess similar receptive powers that are generally suppressed but that are occasionally disinhibited by stressors, causing the hallucinations experienced by schizophrenics. According to Jaynes, the threshold for psychological stress was much lower in the late Bronze Age than it is now, and thus Homeric humans may have often heard voices they couldn't identify making demands of them that they interpreted as instructions from the gods. Thus the people of the *Iliad* acted on the basis, not of conscious self-awareness, but of these phantom voices in their heads.

Even ignoring Jaynes' dated and highly speculative neuroscience, several counterarguments can be made in response to his view. First, there is the very real possibility that Jaynes is taking a literary device and raising it to the level of a psychological theory. After all, the *Iliad* is a war story, not a psychological treatise. It was meant to be heroic, dramatic, and evocative rather than philosophical. Thus Homer may have created vivid portraits of the interaction of gods and men in this, the greatest of the Greek myths, without actually believing the literal causal sequence of events. When a repentant televangelist reports that he sins because "the Devil makes him do it," we may question his sincerity, but we rarely question his status as a self-conscious human. Jaynes felt he had an answer to this objection. If the gods were only literary devices, why do they seem to overdetermine the actions of the characters in the story? One obvious response might be that the literary device is a somewhat clumsy one (by today's sensibilities, anyway), which later writers abandoned.

A second, perhaps worse, problem is the extreme selectiveness of the texts Jaynes reports. Although it is true that it is Athena who stays Achilles' hand and prevents his murder of King Agamemnon, there is no mention of a divine motivator for the aborted assault in the first place.

Finally, there are passages that, though making no mention of the psychological terms described above, nonetheless give vivid descriptions of people not altogether different from ourselves. Consider, for example, the following passage in which Achilles grieves for his lost friend and mentor Patroclus, for whose death he considered himself responsible:

> Achilles went on grieving for his friend, whom he could not banish from his mind, and all-conquering sleep refused to visit him. He tossed to one side and the other, thinking always of his loss, of Patroclus' manliness and spirit, of all they had been through together and the hardships they had shared, of fights with the enemy and adventures on unfriendly seas. As memories crowded in on him, the warm tears poured down his cheeks. Sometimes he lay on his side, sometimes on his back, and then again on his face. At last he would get up and wander aimlessly along the salt sea beach. (*Iliad*, XXIV, 3–13)

It is difficult to imagine a modern description of a man grieving the loss of his best friend that could better capture the flood of emotions and memories playing over him at such a time. Certainly, this is not a picture of a preconscious individual, someone who has no sense of himself or others and responds only instinctively to the demands of hallucinated voices. Consequently, we are inclined to regard Jaynes' theory, interesting as it is, with a degree of scepticism.

THE LYRIC POETS

Archilochus of Paros (ca. 675–ca. 635 BC) is often regarded as the first lyric poet, but because of his often biting, sometimes insulting, satirical content, he is sometimes put in the more restricted category of iambic poet (note, for instance, that he does not appear in the widely used Loeb volumes on *Lyra Graeca*). He was a soldier, and thus his writings were about the hardships of war as often as about the more common lyric themes of love and sex. Of the fragments of Archilochus' poetry still available to us, the term *psychê* only rarely appears and is there used metaphorically in describing a depressed character in the poem as being "lifeless." *Thumos* and *phrenes* appear much more frequently and are clearly his key psychological terms. *Thumos* was typically used in the way we might metaphorically use the English *heart*, as in "don't lose heart" and "you gotta have heart." Losing one's *thumos* was to become depressed or despairing. *Phrenes,* by contrast, seems to have acquired somewhat more intellectual connotations—when someone was said to lose his *phrenes,* he had "lost his wits" or "gone mad," rather than simply feeling in "poor spirits."

Consider the following passages from Archilochus' poetry:

1. "Although you consumed a large quantity of unmixed wine, you did not contribute to the cost . . . nor again did you come invited . . . as though a friend, but your belly led astray your *nous* and *phrenes* to shamelessness" (124b).
2. "*Thumos, thumos,* confounded by woes beyond remedy rise up(?) and defend yourself, setting your breast against your foes(?) as they lie in ambush(?) and standing steadfastly near the enemy. Do not exult openly in victory and in defeat do not fall down lamenting at home, but let your rejoicing in joyful times and your grief in bad times be moderate" (128).
3. "Father Lycambes, what did you mean by this? Who unhinged your *phrenes* which previously was so sound? Now you seem to the townspeople a source of much laughter" (172).
4. "A monkey was on his way alone in the outback, apart from the animals, when a crafty fox with guileful *nous* met him" (185).
5. "For such a desire for sex coiled itself up under my heart [*kardiên*], poured a thick mist down over my eyes, and stole the weak *phrenes* from my breast" (191).
6. "I am in the throes of desire, miserable and without *psychê* [*apsychos*], pierced through my bones with grievous pangs thanks to the gods" (193).
7. "But if you are in a hurry and *thumos* impels you, there is in our house one who now greatly longs for [marriage?]" (196a).[12]

Shortly after Achilochus there lived a writer named Alcman (fl. ca. 630 BC). He was probably from Sparta and in a tenth-century Byzantine encyclopedia (the *Suda*) was declared the "inventor of the love poem." Although he was well known in ancient times, very few fragments of Alcman's work have survived, and what does remain contains little of psychological import. One significant exception is a passage in which he asks rhetorically, "Who may with ease read the *nous* of another?" (fragment 55 of Loeb's *Lyra Graeca,* J. M. Edmonds, ed., 1928).

The best known of the lyric poets today is Sappho of Lesbos (b. ca. 612 BC). She has become an icon of contemporary lesbians, who have adopted the name of Sappho's home for themselves. Hers is one of the few women's voices we can still hear from the ancient world. Her poetry was mostly about love, but not as explicit as Archilochus' sexual writings, for she wrote for religious festivals and weddings in addition to composing more personal pieces. She often tells us of her feelings toward, and relationships with, other women, though occasionally about men as well. Although Sappho's work was famous in the ancient world, because of its content it has been censored many times over the centuries. As a result, her name has been continuously known through others' accounts; only in 1879 was most of what we now have of her actual work rediscovered. She was from a wealthy family and seems to have been married. She had at least one daughter, Kleïs, apparently named after her grandmother.

Naturally enough, Sappho says little about psychology directly, but her use of language is revealing about the psychological assumptions of her time and place. In one of her most famous poems, "A Prayer to Aphrodite," she repeatedly referred to her *thumos* as the location of sorrow and desire.

> On your dappled throne, Aphrodite,
> sly eternal daughter of Zeus,
> I beg you, do not crush my *thumos* with grief. . . .
> What does your mad *thumos* desire?
> Whom shall I make love you, Sappho,
> who is turning her back on you? . . .
> Then come to me now and free me
> from fearful agony. Labor
> for my mad *thumos,* and be my ally.

In another poem, "To Herself," she attributes her poetic gift to her *thumos:*

> Let the depths of my *thumos* be dumb
> for I cannot think up
> a clarion song about Adonis.

More frequently, however, *phrenes* was used for the seat of emotional life. In another of her most famous poems, "Seizure," she writes:

> To me that man equals a god
> as he sits before you and listens
> closely to your sweet voice
> and lovely laughter—which troubles
> the *phrenes* under my ribs.

In "A Letter to Atthis I," she writes:

> Now while our darling wanders she remembers
> lovely Atthis' love,
> and longing sinks deep in her *phrenes.*

In "Homecoming":

> You came. And you did well to come.
> I longed for you and you brought fire
> to my *phrenes,* which burns high for you.

In "A Child of God":

> Gold overpowers
> a man's *phrenes,*
> even the strongest man.

And in "Yielding":

> No more. Do not try
> to bend a hard *phrenes.*[13]

The overall impression we get is that the *phrenes* and its associated *thumos* were the "organs" of emotion for Sappho. Whether her emphasis on the *phrenes* represents a shift from the time of Homer or just the preferences of her Aeolic dialect of Greek is not clear. The other terms we have discussed, *psyché, noos,* and *menos,* do not figure in the writings of Sappho still extant, but they were not, in any case, traditionally affiliated with the main object of her concern, love. Perhaps even more psychologically important than these changes in the nuances of individual terms, however, is what Snell (1953, ch. 3) termed the "rise of the individual" in lyric poetry. The authors—or at least the characters they portrayed—speak in the first person. In an epic, the narrator relayed the acts, thoughts, and even feelings of others. In lyric poetry, by contrast, one speaks directly of one's own feelings, desires, and other psychological states.

The greatest of the Greek lyric poets after Sappho is commonly acknowledged to have been Pindar (ca. 520–ca. 438 BC), of whose work a great deal has been preserved, most famously his *Hymn to Zeus,* from which comes a great deal of our knowledge of the myths of the Olympian gods. Important as it is from a literary standpoint, however, it reveals little that is novel psychologically. Thus, we move on to the last of the literary forms covered in this chapter—tragedy.

PSYCHOLOGICAL THOUGHT IN GREEK TRAGEDY

Although the word "tragedy" is now widely applied to any sad event, it derives from the Greek *tragodia,* literally meaning "goat song." No one is quite sure of the source of this term, but it seems likely that it was originally grounded in the religious rituals of the time. Although there were many tragic poets in the fifth century BC—great festivals were held at which the plays were pitted against each other for prizes—complete plays of only three of the greatest have come down to us: Aeschylus (525–456 BC), Sophocles (ca. 496–406 BC), and Euripides (ca. 484–406 BC).

One significant psychological innovation of tragedy was an increased distinction between the emotional and intellectual demands in the mental economy of its characters. People are frequently depicted as being torn between emotional commitments, such as to family and friends, and intellectual judgments of right and wrong. Indeed, often the writers created paradoxical situations in which characters could not be true to one without violating the other. Consider, for instance, the most famous of the tragedies, Sophocles' *Oedipus Rex*. To review the story briefly, Oedipus was abandoned to die as an infant by his parents because of a prophecy that he would murder his father and marry his mother. He was found alive, however, and raised by another noble family. Not knowing he had been adopted, upon hearing of the prophecy as an adult, he left what he believed to be his home so as to prevent its coming true. On his travels, however, he fell into an altercation with a stranger—unbeknownst to him, his biological father—and killed him, thus fulfilling half of the prophecy. He then arrived at the place of his birth and wed the local queen—again unbeknownst to him, his mother—thus completing the prophecy. In the very act of making an apparently "rational" though undoubtedly emotionally difficult decision to leave forever the only home he had ever known, he unknowingly set himself on the doomed course fate had set for him. When he finally discovered what he had done, even though it was through no fault of his own, he was unable to live with the abomination and attempted to destroy himself. Note especially that the prophecy itself played a crucial role in its own fulfillment, for if it had never been made, Oedipus would never have been abandoned, never have been adopted, and never have left home in order to avoid the prophecy, thereby putting himself on the path to fulfill it.

Perhaps the most psychologically important aspect of tragedy, however, is its detailed treatment of madness, which is a recurring theme of the plays. There are many examples, but here we will examine two treatments of a single story stemming directly from the conclusion of the Trojan War. It will be recalled that King Agamemnon sacrificed his daughter Iphigenia to the gods when setting off to Troy in order to ensure favorable winds. Upon his return he was murdered by his wife, Clytemnestra, in retribution. Their son, Orestes, was thus immediately caught in an ethical bind: He was morally bound to avenge his father's murder by killing the perpetrator, but in doing so he would be killing his own mother, itself a moral outrage. Urged on by Apollo, he kills Clytemnestra, but as punishment he is haunted by the Erinyes (or Furies), three dark, snake-headed goddesses of vengeance who drive Orestes mad.

The story was first rendered for the stage by Aeschylus, the earliest of the three great tragedians whose work is still available to us, in his trilogy of plays—*Agamemnon, Choephoroi* (*The Libation Bearers*), and *The Eumenides*—collectively know as the *Oresteia*. In Aeschylus' telling of the tale, Orestes' madness is caused by a conflict of moral duties, or more specifically by the reflection of these duties in the world of the gods and goddesses. Apollo's demand that he kill Clytemnestra is real, as would undoubtedly be his displeasure if disobeyed. So too real are the Erinyes and their attack on the brain and soul (*Eumenides*, 343–345). As Simon puts it (1978, p. 104), the conflict leading to Orestes' madness is an "external" one, having it roots in the social world and the divine world of justice.[14]

The story was retold, however, about a half-century later, by Euripides in his play *Orestes*. Here we find an account that is quite different, at least from a psychological standpoint. The Erinyes' torments are described as having been hallucinated by Orestes, a *manifestation* of his madness rather than its cause. The conflict that drives Orestes insane has a strongly internal, mental component rather than being simply a case of external forces acting upon him. This represents an important shift in the understanding of madness. By the time of Euripides it seems that madness was no longer popularly seen simply as the result of divine displeasure—though there was still a divine component, to be sure—it could also arise from profound intrapsychic conflict, especially from paradoxical conflicts that are effectively irresolvable.

In this chapter we have examined the psychological background of ancient Greek society as expressed in its popular artistic forms over a period of about four hundred years. Over this time we have seen some important developments: an increased emphasis on individuality, an increasing distinction between emotional and intellectual life, and the growth of the idea of intrapsychic conflict as an explanation for madness. But in all these cases it is important to remember that the elucidation of a psychological theory was never the main intention of the authors. The account of their psychological thought has been extracted from writings with quite different aims. It was only with a major revolution in Greek discourse—the invention of philosophy—that we find individuals attempting to come to terms *directly* with the nature of the mind and soul. It is the purpose of the next chapter to begin the examination of this important intellectual development.

NOTES

1. Throughout this book we will use the Latin transliteration *psychê* or the Greek term ψυχη in order to distinguish it from its English cognate, "psyche." As we shall see, the Greek and English terms have quite distinct meanings. The circumflex over the letter *e* is used to distinguish the Greek letter η (eta) from the Greek letter ε (epsilon). For ease of English reading, we use *psychês* as the plural throughout, instead of the Greek plurals *psychai* or *psychas*. We have also rendered the Greek letter υ (upsilon) variously as *y* or *u*, depending on the spelling of modern English cognates.

2. Debate rages on about whether a single man, named Homer, wrote both the *Iliad* and the *Odyssey* (or either), or whether indeed such a man existed at all. Consensus now seems to be that each epic was written by a single person, on the basis of oral traditions spanning over four hundred years, but that the *Odyssey* was written somewhat later than the *Iliad*. Both texts were "standardized" in the sixth century BC for presentation at the Panathenaic festival and then reworked by Aristarchus

of Samothrace in the second century BC. Aristarchus' is essentially the text we have today. Because nothing crucial turns on the issue for present purposes, we will assume the traditional attribution of both works to Homer here.

3. Adapted from the translation by E. V. Rieu (1950), Penguin.

4. See, e.g., A. T. Murray's (1924) translation for the Loeb Classical Library.

5. Only centuries later, in the so-called Classical Age of Greece, did the *soma* come to refer to a living body.

6. The translations are from Rieu (1950). The book numbers are given in Roman numerals. The Arabic numerals represent line numbers of the original Greek text (which are given in any good translation), rather than page numbers of a particular translation. This facilitates the finding of the passage in any translation.

7. Rieu's translation is "midriff," but "diaphragm" is the more common contemporary translation of *phrenes*. This term also carries some psychological connotations, which are discussed below.

8. Rieu translates this as "breath," recalling an even earlier meaning for *psyché*.

9. Simon (1978, p. 57) seems to dissent from this view for reasons that are not entirely clear.

10. Bremmer actually uses the transliteration *thymos,* but we have chosen to use *thumos* consistently throughout.

11. Madness, however, continued to be attributed to divine intervention up to the time of the great Athenian tragic poets of the fifth century BC—Aeschylus, Sophocles, and Euripides—about which more below.

12. All passages adapted from the Loeb Library's *Greek Iambic Poetry,* Douglas E. Gerber, ed. and trans., 1999. Reference numbers follow Gerber's ordering of the fragments. In each instance *psyché, thumos, phrenes,* and *nous* have been left uninflected for easy identification.

13. All passages adapted from Willis Barnstone's *Sappho* (1965). I have used the titles he provides. In each instance *thumos* and *phrenes* have been left uninflected for easy identification.

14. One need not adopt Simon's strongly psychoanalytic interpretation of the tragedies in order to agree with the distinction he makes between the external and internal conflict in the portrayals of Orestes given by Aeschylus and Euripides respectively.

Chapter 2

The Emergence of Philosophy

THE FIRST FLOWER OF PHILOSOPHY

Thales and the Milesian School

The great English philosopher Bertrand Russell (1945) once wrote, "In every history of philosophy for students, the first thing mentioned is that philosophy began with Thales, who said that everything is made of water. This is a discouraging start for the beginner" (p. 44). Russell—who was perhaps too eager to make early philosophers out to be, or at least *trying* to be, scientists in the twentieth-century mold—encouraged his readers to respect Thales by arguing that "the statement that everything is made of water is to be regarded as a scientific hypothesis, and by no means a foolish one.... The Greeks were rash in their hypotheses, but the Milesian school," which Thales founded, "at least, was prepared to test them empirically" (p. 45). True understanding of thinkers millennia past, however, is unlikely to be gained by attempting to assimilate them to our ways of thinking about things. On the contrary, we must attempt to comprehend the contexts in which they operated—what kinds of knowledge were valued, what sorts of resources and technologies were available, what problems presented themselves most forcefully—and judge the import of their thought on the basis of what can reasonably have been expected to make good sense, or any sense, to people in those situations.

Thales (fl. ca. 585 BC) lived on the coast of Ionia—present-day southwestern Turkey—in the then-Greek city of Miletus during the late part of the seventh century BC. Many intellectual feats, and a few foibles as well, are attributed to him. Most of these are probably apocryphal, but one that shows him to have been active in 585 BC is the report that he predicted a solar eclipse that we know to have happened in that year. He is widely reported to have claimed that "all is water," but it is doubtful that this was the straightforward scientific claim Russell would have had us believe. This should not lead us to dismiss him as insignificant, however. In addition to the claim that (1) "all is water," there are two other sayings of his that are of interest to historians of psychology, namely, that (2) the universe has *psychê* and is full of gods (*to theion*) and that (3) magnets have *psychê*. (Aristotle relates all three claims in Book I of *De Anima*.) The second of these statements, in particular, seems to put the lie to any claim that Thales was a straightforward scientist in anything like the contemporary sense. First, we will examine some of the interpretations some modern classicists have made of the fragments of Thales' philosophy that are left to us. Then we will look at the philosophies of his successors at Miletus—Anaximander and Anaximenes.

In 1912 the Cambridge classicist F. M. Cornford (1874–1943) published his book *From Religion to Philosophy*. It was a revolutionary account, derived in part from the work of the German philosopher Friedrich Nietzsche (1844–1900), of the astounding transition in Ancient Greek discourse from traditional myths and religions set down by poets such as Homer to early philosophy. This movement began at about the time of Thales. The central thesis of Cornford's book, which has since become a classic, is that "philosophy is the immediate successor of theology" (p. 135). In Thales, he argued, we see not a scientist of the type Russell envisioned but a man caught between a powerful traditional way of thinking about the world, couched in terms of divine agents carrying out actions prescribed by ancient myths, and an altogether new way in which the world, including whatever divine agents there might be, must finally fall under the scope of reason and understanding. This transitional period has been described by Stanley Rosen (1988) as the "quarrel between philosophy and poetry." The traditional account of this period is that philosophy was born when the Ancient Greeks began to distinguish *logos,* a word closely related to the concept of reason, from *mythos,* the traditional mythological accounts of how things had come to be as they were (see, e.g., Ehrenberg, 1968, p. 103). A wholly new kind of discourse was slowly being born, one that would ultimately overtake the authority of the traditional ways of thinking. Thales was among those at the forefront of the change, but had not yet made the transition completely himself.

Thales attempted to develop an account of the world grounded in a single principle—a substance from which all others derived. For reasons about which we can only speculate, he declared that water is the basic substance from which the others emerged. McKirahan (1994, p. 31) suggests that water was picked because it was believed by Thales to surround the earth—above in the form of rain; on the surface in the forms of lakes, rivers, and oceans; and the earth itself, which was thought by Thales to float on water. However he arrived at the conclusion that water is the primary substance, it seems to have constituted his basic theory of what the Greeks called *physis;* what we might call "nature."

Physis was not without its divine aspects as far as the Greeks of this era were concerned, and not without good reason. One of the primary phenomena to be explained was how *physis* moves. Every day the sun goes overhead. Every night the moon and stars follow it. The sea moves in and out, and the wind blows, carrying ships over the sea. The earth itself is subject to change in the violent forms of earthquakes and volcanic eruptions and in more gradual, but still perceptible, ways as well. What might explain all this movement? It suggested to the Greeks that the universe itself is alive. This "organic" view of the cosmos is crucial to correctly interpreting their philosophical claims about it.

The notion of *psychê* seems to have been extended since the time of Homer to account for life in general, not just that of humans. And just as *psychê* was thought to be responsible for the life of human beings, it seems to have been declared by Thales to be responsible for the movements of the universe as well. Thus, as Thales said, "the universe has a *psychê*." But what of its being "full of gods"? Cornford (1991/1912) argued, somewhat enigmatically, that in addition to the *psychê* that was thought to make ordinary earth, water, air, and fire move, Thales believed in a *special* original substance, WATER, which possessed a "superhuman *manna,* a daemonic energy, distinct from the natural properties of [ordinary] water" (p. 135). It was out of this special WATER that earth, fire, air, as well as ordinary water were said by Thales to have emerged. A somewhat less spectacular, but perhaps more plausible, answer is that each thing that moves—each star, planet, tide, volcano, animal, and plant—has its own individual bit of the universal *psychê*, a daemon or spirit that generates its individual movements. Thus we come to the claim that the magnet, in particular, has *psychê*. It has the strange power to cause other things—namely, pieces of iron—to move. Thus it must have been thought to have extra *psychê*, or at least a particularly strong *psychê*.

Anaximander (ca. 611–ca. 545 BC) was probably Thales' immediate successor at Miletus. Legend has it that he studied under Thales, though the so-called Milesian school, mentioned by Russell, may well have been limited to discussions among a very small circle of friends. If Cornford's interpretation is even approximately correct, Thales had connected *physis* and *psychê*, but he had never proposed a theory of what *psychê* might be made of or how it had come into being. As psychologists, we might hope that his most famous student, Anaximander, would finish his master's work by providing such, but alas he did not (although there is a report from the first century AD writer Aëtius—cited in Barnes, 1982, p. 472—that he thought *psychês* to be "airy"). Instead, he concentrated his efforts on elaborating the theory of *physis*.

Anaximander seems to have adopted Thales' suggestion that the elements must have all once been one, but he rejected the conclusion that water, or any of the four elements, had been the source. Instead, he proposed a fifth *ur*-element as the source of the other four. He called it *to apeiron*, "the un-bounded," because he believed it to have filled the whole of the universe. At some point, he said, the universe had begun to move in a circular fash-ion, becoming a vortex. The movement of the vortex could account for many of the universe's observable features. The evidence of such movement can be seen even today in the circular movements of the sun, moon, and stars. Why the universe began to move in this way is not explained, at least not in the fragmentary reports that are available to us of Anaximander's work, but it is likely that Anaximander inherited from Thales the belief that the uni-verse has *psychê* and is therefore capable of self-initiated movement. In any case, this spinning motion forced the elements of earth, water, air, and fire to precipitate out of the unbounded stuff of the universe. The heaviest—earth—moved to the center, and bands of successively lighter elements—water, air, and fire, respectively—surrounded it. He is said to have thought the world to be cylindrical in shape, with a depth of one-third its diameter (cited in J. M. Robinson, 1968, p. 29). People were said to live on the top circular surface of this cylinder, and he drew map of it, the first map of the world. Also, with astounding prescience, Anaximander declared that life had first arisen in the wet parts of the world, presumably because all living things contain and depend upon water for their survival, and he believed that the ancient progenitors of men had been fishlike.

Anaximenes (fl. mid-6th c. BC), also of Miletus, was a colleague of Anaximander's, possibly his student, but his dates are unknown. He rejected Anaximander's claim that the original element had not been one of the four known ones, but he did not agree with Thales' claim that it had been water. He believed the original element, out of which the others had come, to have been air. As the air became compressed at the center of the vortex, he be-lieved, it was transformed into water, and with more compression still, earth. As the air became rarefied at the periphery of the vortex, it transmuted into fire.

Why was air considered by Anaximenes to be the primary element? As did Thales and Anaximander, Anaximenes did not think the *physis* to be solely material. It had *psychê,* and this had to be explained. From time immemorial *psychê* had been associated with breath—air—and so Anaximenes may have concluded that to get things moving (quite literally) in the first place, a prob-lem that neither Thales nor Anaximander had dealt with adequately, there had to be *psychê* at the very beginning of all things. Since *psychê* was associ-ated with air, the natural conclusion may have been that air was there at the beginning; thus air must have been the original element.

Philosophy Moves to Italy: The Pythagoreans

Just as Greece possessed colonies on the coast of present-day Turkey, such as Miletus, so it also established colonies in what is now southern Italy. This region is also called Magna Graecia. Beginning in the middle of the sixth century BC, this region began to develop its own characteristic philosophical traditions, often attracting philosophers from Ionia, to which the Persians were then laying siege, to live and teach in this new prosperous and relatively peaceful region. (An excellent brief account of these changes can be found in Ehrenberg, 1968, ch. 4, pt. 3.) Chief among these intellectual immigrants were Xenophanes (ca. 570–ca. 480 BC) and Pythagoras (ca. 570–ca. 500 BC). For present purposes, the former can be dispensed with fairly quickly. Xenophanes was born in Colophon, near Miletus on the Ionian coast, but was forced to flee to the West when it fell to the Persians in 546 BC, eventually settling on the island of Sicily. He apparently had little or nothing to say about the *psyché*, although the late fifth century AD writer Macrobius credits him with the claim that *psychés* are made of a combination of æther[1] and water (cited in Barnes, 1982, p. 472). He was primarily a theological poet, but one who preached monotheism to the long-time polytheistic Greeks. He is worthy of mention here mainly for his remarks about some fossils of marine plants and animals that were discovered during his lifetime in the interior of Sicily. Hippolytus, the late second and early third century AD bishop of Rome (cited in J. M. Robinson, 1968, p. 51), reported that Xenophanes "says that these [fossils] were formed long ago when everything was covered with mud, and that these impressions were dried in the mud." What makes this noteworthy is that it is essentially the modern explanation of fossils. He also described the rain cycle—namely, that rain falls and runs into lakes, rivers, and seas, only to be evaporated into clouds and precipitate out as rain again—in strikingly modern terms as well.

More significant than Xenophanes for our purposes, however, was Pythagoras, who was born on the island of Samos, off the coast of Ionia, but was apparently forced to leave after a dispute with the local political leadership. According to legend, years of travel took him to Egypt and Babylonia, where he is said to have learned mathematical techniques far in advance of anything in the possession of his Greek contemporaries. However much of this is true, it is relatively certain that he ultimately settled in the city of Croton, in southern Italy, in about 530 BC, establishing a philosophical school that had a strongly mathematical orientation. He is even said to have invented the word "philosophy," meaning "love of wisdom," and to have been the first to refer to the universe as a *cosmos*—an "ordering" of the *chaos* that was thought to have been the original state of the universe. His continued involvement in political affairs apparently led to his becoming the victim of a popular uprising in Croton, from which he was forced to flee near the end of the sixth century BC.

Pythagoras has the distinction of having both the most and the least documentation of any of the pre-Socratic philosophers. He personally committed nothing to paper, or at least none of what he wrote has been preserved, but his teachings inspired a large number of students, who lived with their mentor in a semi-monastic scholarly community, which continued for centuries after his death and which produced numerous works, many of which claimed the authorship of Pythagoras himself. The accuracy of these claims is unknown, since none of the works of Pythagoras' original school survive either, at least partly because the members of this community were sworn to strict secrecy regarding their beliefs. The only contemporary or nearly contemporary sources we have for the original thought of Pythagoras, as distinct from that of his later followers, are a contemptuous fragment of Xenophanes, two even more inflammatory remarks from Heraclitus, a mention or two by Herodotus, and later commentary by Empedocles and Plato. In considering the impact of Pythagoras on intellectual history, then, it is critical that none of the information we have about this unique thinker is in its original form and that much of it has been preserved only by philosophical traditions quite hostile to it.

If the philosophical tradition of Ionia can be characterized by a conscious attempt to establish natural philosophy as a tradition distinct from theology and poetry, then in the work of Pythagoras and his followers we see the opposite trend—a syncretic fusion of mysticism and naturalism. Bertrand Russell characterized this unlikely combination by describing Pythagoras as "a combination of Einstein and Mrs. Eddy" (1945, p. 32).[2] Neither extreme is likely to be true, but at least as early as Iamblichus (fl. 4th c. AD) it was recognized that among the followers of Pythagoras there were two reasonably distinct factions: the *Akousmatikoi* (from the Greek "to listen"), who were primarily concerned with maintaining the doctrinal purity of Pythagorean religion, and the *Mathematikoi* (from the Greek for "study," not just of mathematics), who were concerned with enlarging the body of mathematical and scientific lore (DK58 C4).[3] For our purposes it is important, not to judge how much of Pythagoras was preserved in each of these traditions,[4] but to note what this division suggests about the breadth of his vision.

Whereas the Milesian school formulated a cosmology radically different from that of the epic poets, based upon evaluation of candidates for the principle upon which the universe is based, the Pythagorean school rejected all physicalist formulations and instead posited *number* as the first principle of existence. We are told that Pythagoras performed experiments on a monochord, a one-string instrument with a moveable bridge, allowing the player to vary the length of the string being played (see Figure 2.1).

By demonstrating that differences in the perceived tone of a string varied with the ratio of vibrating string above the bridge to the length of the whole string, Pythagoras managed to reduce a qualitative difference in experience—namely, pitch—to a quantitative difference in the physical world—namely, string length. This discovery is paradigmatic of the Pythagoreans' interest in whole number ratios as an explanatory scheme for the cosmos in general, and it ushered in a kind of psychophysics in a form not to be significantly

Figure 2.1

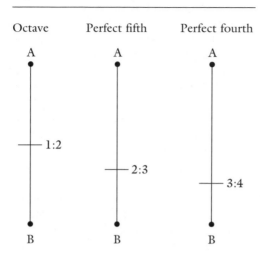

Octave   Perfect fifth   Perfect fourth

A   A   A

1:2

2:3

3:4

B   B   B

improved upon until Fechner's application of calculus to the field in the nine-teenth century.

In terms of his cosmology, Pythagoras concluded that the principles of number must be those on which the cosmos is based. He therefore tried to extend the notion of whole number ratios to his understanding of fields beyond simple acoustics. The most famous such work, which has made Pythagoras the only pre-Socratic philosopher to become a household word, was the geometric investigation, attributed to him, of the ratios of the sides of right triangles. When one takes a right triangle with two adjacent sides of equal length, no ratio of whole numbers will give the length of the third side. A perfectly exact result is impossible. Accordingly, Pythagoras concluded that his mathematical investigations had encroached upon fundamental se-crets of the universe, what are now called irrational numbers. This may help explain why his school took on such a mystical flavor. In any case, it is cer-tain that a major tenet of his philosophy was that the principles of number (unity vs. plurality, limitation, oddness vs. evenness, etc.) were thought to be the fundamental principles of which the universe is composed. Thus Aristotle tells us that

> [t]he Pythagoreans similarly posited two principles, but they have added some-thing that is peculiar to themselves, not that the limited and unlimited are dis-tinct natures like fire or earth or something similar, but that the unlimited it-self and the One itself are the substance of what they are predicated of. This is why they call number the substance of all things. (Aristotle, *Metaphysics*, 987a, 13–19)

The reduction of all objects in the cosmos to the principles of number would also include the *psyche*. For Pythagoras, the *psyche* was thought to be a mathematical entity, a ratio. We are told that Pythagoras stressed the study of mathematics as a means of purifying the *psyche* by contemplation of universal truths. Through the study of geometry the *psyche* is returned, however briefly, to the harmonies thought to be inherent in the cosmos, liberated from its "inprisonment" within the body. Whether or not the reference to the body as a prison for the *psyche* is genuine (this phrase is now widely thought to have originated with later Pythagoreans, not Pythagoras himself), it is interesting to note that for Pythagoras the *psyche* was no longer thought to be either the ghostly double of the Homeric epics or the impersonal animator of the Milesians, but something associated with the rationality and thinking.

The other major Pythagorean doctrine of interest to psychologists is his belief in metempsychosis. Briefly stated, the doctrine of metempsychosis holds that one's *psyche* is immortal and that upon one's death it migrates to inhabit a new body. It is important to note that Pythagoras did not restrict reincarnation to human *psyches*: We are told by Xenophanes that Pythagoras once ordered a man to stop beating a puppy because in the dog's yelps he recognized the voice (and thus presumably the *psyche*) of a recently departed friend. It is likely that his followers' belief in metempsychosis was responsible for some of the unusual religious practices of this sect, most notably their vegetarianism. Note that the doctrine of metempsychosis implies personal survival of bodily death, and thus for Pythagoras, the *psyche* was considered to be the essence of the person. What is more, Pythagoras is said to have claimed he could recall his past lives. Here again is an intimation that the *psyche* is cognitive, for it was thought to carry memories of past lives from body to body.

There appears to be an inconsistency in asserting that the *psyche* is both a particular ratio and that this personal *psyche* can survive one's death. It may be that Pythagoras believed that the correct relationships—in this case mathematical—constitute a mind regardless of the physical instantiation of this set of relationships. What seems more likely is that he, or at least his followers, held two distinct sets of beliefs about the *psyche*, one based upon his cosmology and the other upon his religious teachings. Certainly it is enough to note that at least Pythagoras tried to formulate a theory about the *psyche*, a theory containing some of the features that distinguish *psyches* from physical bodies, such as the capacity for thought and the basis of personality.

The origins of Pythagoras' beliefs concerning the immortality of the *psyche* are uncertain. Herodotus says that the origin of his belief in metempsychosis came from Egypt, presumably during his alleged stay there, but this seems unlikely. In all the vast and varied systems of religious and magical beliefs Egypt could boast, there is no reference to reincarnation. He may have been acquainted with the religious traditions of India, if indeed he visited

Mesopotamia, but there are many modern scholars who argue that his supposed stays in both Egypt and Mesopotamia are the inventions of later authors attempting to give an aura of antiquity and mystical authority to Pythagoras and his teachings. Theories of personal survival or, at least, psychic immortality were circulating freely in the Orphic religions of the time.

A younger contemporary of Pythagoras, Alcmaeon (ca. 510–440 BC), a physician from Croton, proposed a theory of the immortality of *psychês* that proved very influential on the thinking of later writers. Plato seems to have adopted his own theory of the immortality and transmigration of *psychês* from Alcmeon's theory and presented the details for this theory in his dialogues *Timaeus* and *Phaedrus*.[5] We are told from several sources that Alcmeon argued from mental causation to immortality, stating that if the *psychê* moves the body, it must itself be unmoved. As something able to move a body it must, however, be in motion and move itself. Thus, since the *psychê* is in ceaseless motion, it must itself be immortal and independent of any particular body.

Certainly the most important feature of Pythagoreanism is its focus on numbers as the chief explanatory elements in its theories. The belief that explanations couched in numerical form are to be preferred is, rightly or wrongly, still prevalent today and can be seen in modern psychology in diverse ways ranging from the ubiquitousness of psychological scales—such as IQ, MMPI, and 16PF—to the development of psychophysics and signal detection theory, to the prevalence of hypothesis-testing procedures in data analysis. Pythagoras casts a long shadow.

Heraclitus of Ephesus

Heraclitus (ca. 540–ca. 480 BC) lived in the city of Ephesus, of which substantial ruins remain still, on the coast of Ionia, about fifty kilometers from Miletus. His exact dates are not known. McKirahan (1994) reports them as 540–480 BC. Unlike Xenophanes and Pythagoras, he did not flee the Persian domination of Ionia; he survived it and even flourished under it. As with all other early pre-Socratics, none of Heraclitus' original writings remain, although like many others, he was said to have written a treatise on *physis*. What is known of Heraclitus' philosophy is contained in more than a hundred fragmentary mentions of him by his successors.[6] Many of these fragments are obscure, enigmatic, and even bizarre. Diogenes Laertius, a biographer who lived about AD 300, recounted a story (repeated by Barnes, 1987, pp. 57–58) that Socrates, upon reading a copy of Heraclitus' work, said, "What I understood was good. . . . But it would take a Delian diver to get to the bottom of it." Heraclitus frequently asserted the unity of opposites: "[T]he road up and down is one and the same road" (DK22 B60);[7] "while changing, it rests" (DK22 B84a); "in the case of a circle, beginning and end are the same" (DK22 B103); "cold things become warm, a warm thing becomes cold" (DK22B 126); and perhaps strangest of all, "immortals are mortals, mortals immortals: living their death, dying their life" (DK22 B62). Other comments made by Heraclitus are savagely critical of his contemporaries and immediate predecessors: "Pythagoras is the chief captain of swindlers" (DK22 B81a); "Pythagoras . . . practiced inquiry beyond all other men . . . artful knavery" (DK22 B129). Still others are astoundingly astute: "Poor witnesses for people are eyes and ears if they [the people] have *psychês* that do not understand their [the senses'] language" (DK22 B107). This latter statement was only one of many mentions of *psychê* in his sayings. Whether the sayings can be assembled into a coherent psychology is a question to be pursued here, but only after first briefly looking at what seems to have been his more general worldview.

Herlaclitus may have been one of the first victims of a major misquotation in philosophical history. No less an authority than Plato (*Cratylus,* 402a) said he had argued that "it is not possible to step twice into the same river," and this claim continues to be widely attributed to Heraclitus to this day. This misunderstanding may be attributable to a group of proto-Skeptics active in Ephesus in Plato's time, about a century after Heraclitus' death, who called themselves "Heracliteans." Arius Dydimus, a first century BC doxographer reported that Heraclitus had, in fact, said, "[A]s they step into the *same* rivers, different and still different waters flow" (DK22 B12, emphasis added), a very different sentiment indeed: The river remains the same, but its material composition changes as different water flows through it.

This calls into question the accuracy of another widespread belief about Heraclitus' philosophy, namely, that he claimed everything to be continually in flux (e.g., Plato, *Cratylus,* 401d). As T. M. Robinson (1987) has suggested, it seems that in using the example of rivers, Heraclitus was "stressing their *unity* amidst change, rather than simply their change" (p. 84). That is, what Heraclitus may have been trying to get at is that the material out of which a thing, such as a river, is composed does not alone define its existence. There is a constant underlying structure or organization that determines the thing's identity. This idea of an underlying structure governing the organization of the cosmos bears a remarkable resemblance to the meaning of a term that would later become, perhaps, the most important concept in Greek philosophy: *logos.*

McKirahan (1994) has called Heraclitus' invocation of *logos* his "greatest discovery" (p. 133). T. M. Robinson (1987, pp. 4–5), however, has warned that later Stoic philosophers,[8] themselves highly enamored of *logos,* may have exaggerated its importance in Heraclitus' thought. Many classicists now hold that in Heraclitus' time, *logos* still meant simply "something said" or "an account" of something. If so, when he began his treatise with the passage "all things come into being in accordance with this *logos*" (DK22 B1), he may have simply meant to say that his account of the world was true, not that he had discovered a cosmic organizing principle called *logos.* Several of the quotations discussed below with respect to the *psychê* seem to conflict with so conservative an interpretation, however.

In either case, so far was Heraclitus from holding the view that the world is in the throes of a continual wild, random flux, that he is reported to have once said, "[L]istening not to me, but to the *logos*, it is wise to agree that all things are one" (DK22 B50). He also believed that the truth about the world is available to all who care to apprehend it, a belief that was likely at the source of his sharp criticism of the Pythagoreans, cited above, who in their enforced secrecy acted "as though they had a private understanding of the cosmos" (DK22 B2).

With all this in mind, we can begin to make more sense of Heraclitus' seemingly paradoxical claim that "we step and do not step into the same rivers" (DK22 B49a). There is a sense in which we never step into the same river because the water of the river is undergoing continual replacement. There is another sense, however, in which the river remains the same despite this ongoing change in its material base. Extending the puzzle to human existence itself, Heraclitus continued, "[W]e are and we are not." Over 2,000 years later, the British philosopher Thomas Hobbes (*De Corpore*, II, 7.2) would discover the problem anew when he wondered if a ship remains the same ship if it continually has small repairs done to it over a period of many years, each replacing an original piece here or there with a new one, until finally it contains none of the material that went into the building of the ship initially. Again, in contemporary times psychological researchers who believe that the mind is simply a computer program that runs on the computing hardware we call the brain (e.g., Putnam, 1975/1960) have stumbled upon a similar problem. They argue that the mind is a function not so much of the particular brain in which it is grounded but, rather, of the *organization* of the information that the brain stores and processes. Because any brain—or in fact anything complex enough to be a computer—could store and process the same information, they claim that one and the same mind could be *transported* from brain to brain or even from brain to computer. Famed computer scientist Marvin Minsky has even gone so far as to suggest that we could make ourselves immortal by simply moving our minds to computers before our bodies die.

This is by no means to claim that Heraclitus was a proto-computationalist about the mind. That would be the worst sort of anachronism. It is only meant to show that some of the problems addressed by Heraclitus are still with us today. Snell (1953/1982, p. 17), who was discussed briefly earlier, argued that Heraclitus was the first to employ a concept of the *psychê* that unifies under its aegis the various functions we now call mental, including ones applicable to living people, not just dying ones. We have already seen, however, that this was anticipated by Pythagoras, or at least by the Pythagoreans, who attributed to the *psychê* intellectual powers that had not been associated with it before.

To understand Heraclitus' own view of the _psychê_, it is perhaps best to begin by simply reading what he is held to have said with respect to it.

1. "For _psychês_ it is death to become water, and for water death to become earth. Water comes into existence out of earth, and _psychê_ out of water" (DK22 B36).
2. "One would never discover the limits of _psychê_, should one traverse every road—so deep a _logos_ does it possess" (DK22 B45).
3. "For _psychês_ it is joy or death to become wet. . . . We live their death and they live our death" (DK22 B77).
4. "It is difficult to fight _thumos_,[9] for whatever it wishes it buys at the price of _psychê_" (DK22 B85).
5. "_Psychês_ sniff in Hades" (DK22 B98).
6. "Poor witnesses for people are eyes and ears if they have _psychês_ that do not understand their language" (DK22 B107).
7. "_Psychê_ possesses a _logos_ which increases itself" (DK22 B115).
8. "When a man is drunk, he is led along, stumbling, by a beardless boy; he does not perceive where he is going, because his _psychê_ is wet" (DK22 B117).
9. "A dry _psychê_ is wisest and best" (DK22 B118).

What are we to make of this collection? In several places he mentions that wetness is bad for _psychês;_ that it can even destroy them. This would imply that if _psychês_ are made of one of the elements, they are likely made of fire. As fire is extinguished by water, so the _psychê_ is extinguished by water. This has become the standard interpretation of Heraclitus' position on the matter (see, e.g., Barnes, 1982, pp. 472–474; Schofield, 1991, pp. 20, 29–30; McKirahan, 1994, pp. 140, 146). Indeed, fire was the most important part of the Heraclitean cosmology; he thought _it,_ rather than Thales' water or Anaximenes' air, to be the primary stuff of the cosmos (DK22 B90; see also Barnes, 1982, pp. 60–62). This would represent quite a break with tradition dating back to at least Homer, holding that the _psychê_ is airy and vaporous. There is some dispute about this, however. Kahn (1979), for instance, argues that the Heraclitean _psychê_ actually falls within the airy tradition. One is reminded here of Anaximenes' belief that water is just compressed air. Perhaps it is the compression of a _psychê_ to death that converts it into water.

Whatever else, _psychê_ for Heraclitus, contrary to Pythagorean claims, seems to have been regarded as part of the physical chain of being. It is important, however, to recall that _physis_ was not thought to be purely material by these Greeks, a point the noted Aristotelian scholar Jonathan Barnes (1982) seems to ignore when he describes not only Heraclitus' account of the _psychê_ but also those accounts of _all_ the pre-Socratics up to his time as having been "uncompromisingly materialistic" (p. 475). Marcovich (1967), too, has argued that Heraclitus believed the _psychê_ to be a fully physiological entity in the modern sense. But more conceptual subtlety than this is required. The conceptual schemes of the Greeks differed significantly from ours. As not only Cornford (1991/1912) but more recently McKirahan (1994, p. 31) noted, the universe was thought of as being made of *living* substance, a belief evinced every moment of every day by its constant motion. Thus, although it is certainly *possible* to do as Barnes insists and hold the theories of the pre-Socratics up against our category of matter for comparison—and they certainly are *not* materialistic in our sense—what is to be gained by such an exercise is not clear. The elements as understood by the Greeks fit with our contemporary concept of matter only very approximately. To attempt to reconstruct the conceptual schemes within which the pre-Socratics worked is of more interest, with the aim of finding out just what they thought they knew, what they considered to be knowledge of the *psychê*.

Another psychological issue to be grappled with is whether Heraclitus believed the *psychê* to be mortal or not. A few passages suggest to some (e.g., Kahn, 1979, p. 249) that Heraclitus believed at least some *psychês* to be immortal, namely, those of noble people. Others (e.g., Nussbaum, 1972, p. 169) reject this claim, arguing that Heraclitus believed that the *psychê* dies at the point of bodily death. McKirahan (1994, p. 146) argues that the fate of the *psychê* depends on how "fiery" it remains at the point of bodily death. Souls made "wet" by drunkenness or disease may die. Those that remain "dry," as that of the warrior is said to do, will survive.

In uncharacteristic harmony with the Pythagorean doctrine, Heraclitus also seems to have believed the *psychê* to be the source not only of life but also of reason and rational control—that which interprets (or fails to) the "language" of the senses (DK22 B85) and that which is lost in the face of desire or anger (DK22 B107). Physicalism with respect to the mind, then as now, has trouble accounting for the rational aspect of mind. Unfortunately, precise interpretative alternatives to the physicalist thesis are difficult to come by. Schofield (1991), for instance, offers only the commonplace that Heraclitus presented no determinate theory of the *psychê* at all. In light of this, perhaps the most telling of Heraclitus' comments on the *psychê* is that it has a *logos* that is constantly expanding, one so "deep" that no one will ever discover it fully.

Parmenides and the Eleatics

After Heraclitus, probably as a more or less direct result of the Persian takeover of Ionia, the philosophical center of the Greek world shifted to Italy. Although the first Italian philosophers had been refugees from Ionia, their native Italian students would soon become the principal flag-bearers for the next generation of philosophy as Ionia slipped into a series of wars.

Parmenides (ca. 515–ca. 445 BC) was the first, and probably best, of the major native Italian thinkers. He was from the city of Elea, and various reports say he studied with either Xenophanes (although Gallop, 1984, p. 3, thinks this to be a misreading of a remark of Plato's) or with the

Pythagoreans. The magnitude of the revolution he wrought in philosophical thought, however, enabled him to outstrip the significance of any teacher he might have had. Nevertheless, his inclusion in a history of early psychological thought is a little tricky to justify, since he had little or nothing to say on the issue of the *psyche* (but for the comment, attributed to him by Aëtius, cited in Barnes, 1982, p. 472, that *psychês* are fiery). His major contributions were in epistemology, the theory of knowledge itself, and in ontology, the theory of what, at the most basic level, can be said to exist. It is for these that he merits inclusion in any work that covers the intellectual life of fifth century BC Greece. Just to give an idea of how influential Parmenides' thought was, consider the following quotation from the opening of Gallop's (1984) book on the great Eleatic:

> The development of western philosophy was once said by A. N. Whitehead to have consisted in a series of footnotes to Plato. In a similar vein, and with hardly more exaggeration, Plato's own writings might be said to have consisted in footnotes to Parmenides of Elea. (p. 3)

Higher praise could hardly be given to a philosopher of any period.

Parmenides is the first philosopher from whom we have substantial portions of original work. This is thanks to the sixth century AD commentator Simplicius, who copied long passages of Parmenides' text into his own work, noting that copies of Parmenides' work were becoming difficult to find even in his day. Parmenides titled his primary work *On Nature*. It is written in verse and ostensibly tells the story of Parmenides' being brought to the abode of a goddess to have revealed to him two "Ways" of knowing: the Way of Truth (*Aletheia*) and the Way of Appearance (*Doxa*). Of the first of these, the more important in Parmenides' eyes—or at least in the goddess's—we have an almost complete copy. Of the second, which seems to have been a fairly typical pre-Socratic account of the origin of the world, we have only a few fragments.

What makes Parmenides so important is his recognition of an epistemological problem that has guided debate in philosophy and science throughout the centuries since and that remains unresolved to the present day. The problem is this: What we observe occasionally, and perhaps more than occasionally, conflicts with what we can reason to be true about the world. This means that at least one—either observation or reasoning—is not a reliable route to knowledge. Thus, it behooves us to figure out which one is unreliable and abandon it in favor of the other. In our own strongly empiricist age, the natural answer for many people is to favor observation over reason; but things are not as simple as that.

Consider the following problem. Look at the above figure, known as the Müller-Lyer figure. Which of the two line segments is longer? Almost everyone reports that the line segment on the right appears longer. If you measure them, however, you will find that they are the same length. Thus, your eyes deceived you; observation proved to be unreliable. You may want to argue that the measurements you make to determine that they are the same length are observations as well, but this is only part of the story. In addition to making the measurements, you also make an important inference: that if the segment on the left has a length of x, and the segment on the right also has a length of x, then the segment on the left must be equal in length to the segment on the right. That is, you favored your powers of reasoning about lengths over your simple observations that the two line segments are of different lengths.

Of course, we now believe that science works by a combination of observation and reason, but to Parmenides this was a new issue. When observation and reasoning conflict, what is to be done? Parmenides chose reason over observation, calling it the Way of Truth and relegating observation to the Way of Appearance. Interestingly, he did not reject the Way of Appearance utterly—it originally took up more than half his book. He believed, however, that the Way of Appearance has problems that are ultimately insurmountable and thus the Way of Truth is to be preferred.

He also arrived at some stunning conclusions because of his reliance on reason. The argument for which he became the focal point of Greek philosophy for the next century was, to a first approximation, as follows:

1. Everything that exists, exists.
2. Everything that does not exist, does not exist.
3. All change is just passing from nonexistence into existence, or vice versa.
4. But if nonexistence doesn't exist (by 2), then nothing can pass out of it or into it.
5. Therefore, all change is impossible.
6. Therefore there is no change in the world; all is as it always has been and always will be.

Now this is a truly stunning conclusion. We seem to see change around us all the time. Parmenides' argument led him to believe that change is impossible and therefore that perception only gives rise to illusion. If logic forces us to conclude that there can be no change, then we must reject as false the appearances around us—or we must reject logic itself. As if this were not enough, Parmenides went on to conclude that everything is a single homogeneous whole as well, that is, that there are no different parts to the world. The argument is straightforward enough: To say that some part of the world, A, is different from some other part, B, is to say that at least one of the properties of part A is not present (i.e., does not exist) at part B. But this is to try to assert something about what manifestly does not exist. And since what does not exist, to repeat, does not exist (by 2 above), there is simply nothing about it to be known. Thus, it is absurd to suggest anything at all with respect to it. Therefore, since no part of the world can be said *not* to have any property, there can be no distinct parts. Thus, all is one.

If this whole line of argument seems somewhat absurd, it is hardly surprising. The important point to keep in mind, however, is that if one accepts reasoning into one's theory of knowledge at all, as almost everyone does, then one cannot simply reject out of hand an argument that arrives at a counterintuitive conclusion. One must find the flaw in the argument and then convince others that it is indeed a flaw. The Greeks who followed Parmenides were impressed enough with his argument to realize that if it could not be logically refuted—either by showing at least one of its premises to be false or at least one of its inferences invalid—then it must be accepted.

Parmenides attracted a number of followers. The best known of these was Zeno of Elea (b. ca. 490 BC). He was famous for the paradoxes he developed in support of Parmenides' worldview and against the common-sense view that there are many distinct and changing things in the world. One of the most common forms of change is motion. Zeno argued that motion is impossible. If I shoot an arrow at a target, for instance, the arrow must first travel halfway to the target. But in order for it to travel halfway to the target, it must first travel a quarter of the way, and before that an eighth of the way, and a sixteenth, a thirty-second, and so on backward to zero. Thus, it seems, the arrow can never leave the bowstring at all. Why does it appear to fly through the air and into the target? Because our perceptions are illusory. Reason has again shown us the truth. By confounding common sense in this way, Zeno was able to make even the simplest apparent "facts" of the world seem complicated, befuddling, and ultimately impossible.

Another of Parmenides' followers was Melissus of Samos. He was by no means solely a philosopher. Under his command the Samian fleet delivered a shocking defeat to the Athenian navy around 440 BC. This is the only date of his life that is known with any certainty, however. His main philosophical contribution was to extend Parmenides' basic argument to the conclusion that not only is everything one and eternal, but it must be infinitely extended in space as well.

THE FIRST GREAT PHILOSOPHICAL DEBATE

Three Replies to the Eleatic Challenge

Parmenides and his students changed the whole course of Greek philosophy. Whereas before the Eleatics most philosophers speculated on the nature of the physical world, afterward questions of ontology and epistemology became paramount. In a sense this is a development that is to be expected.

After a century of people making a wide variety of claims about the basic materials and structures of the cosmos, it is only natural that we attempt to sort out the various competing claims by trying to be explicit about what sort of arguments and evidence are to be given credence in support of such claims. Because this turns out to be anything but an easy question to answer satisfactorily in itself, the focus of attention shifts from attempts to answer the first-order scientific questions to second-order questions about the scientific enterprise itself. This is not to say that the Greeks after Parmenides stopped dead the attempt to articulate a theory of the cosmos, but one does notice a marked jump in their attempts to formulate a theory of knowledge as well.

In the short term, there were three main lines of attack against the Parmenides challenge. One came from Empedocles of Acragas, in Sicily. Another came from the atomists, Leucippus (whose town of origin is not known) and Democritus of Abdera, in Thrace, on the northern coast of the Aegean. The third came from Anaxagoras, who was from Clazomenae in Ionia but made his career in Athens, to which the center of the Greek philosophical universe was rapidly moving. Each attempted to address the main claim of Parmenides—that change is impossible—and then to carry out a philosophy of nature on pretty much the same model as people had before. These would prove inadequate, however, and philosophers of the next generation—namely, the Sophists, Socrates, and Plato, who are discussed in the next chapter—were forced to grapple with questions of truth and knowledge more directly. The first generation of responses to Parmenides, however, begins with Empedocles, discussed next.

Empedocles of Acragas

The first major response to the challenge posed by Parmenides came from his fellow Italian philosopher Empedocles (ca. 492–432 BC), who lived and worked in the Sicilian town of Acragas. He was a generation younger than Parmenides, a contemporary of Zeno and Melissus. According to Diogenes Laertius, he heard the philosophy of Anaxagoras early in his career, but his philosophy was decidedly closer to that of Pythagoras, and many ancient sources called Empedocles a Pythagorean, although there is little evidence of his membership in the sect. Apparently somewhat of a showman, he is said to have traveled wearing a purple robe (a very costly item in the ancient world) and a golden crown of laurel leaves, proclaiming himself a god. Traditionally, he was considered a magician and a healer as well as a writer. We are told that he wrote tragedies as well as a hymn to Apollo, although none of these writings have survived. His philosophy was contained in one great poem for which two titles survive: *On Nature* and *Purifications*. Some classicists have argued that actually these titles are of two separate works, one dealing with his cosmology and the other with his mysticism, although this view has come increasingly under attack (see McKirahan, 1994, for a more complete discussion).

Empedocles is also often credited with being the first of the pre-Socratic philosophers to include in his writings all four of the ancient elements—earth, air, fire, and water—and indeed to accord them equal status as the fundamental building blocks of the cosmos. Perhaps based upon Pythagoras' view of ratios as fundamental to everything, Empedocles asserted that all objects of the universe are composed of the four elements mixed in the proper proportion. This mixture is accomplished by a universal force of Love, conceived as a force of attraction between all matter in the cosmos. Empedocles proposed another force, Strife, which was said to oppose the attraction of Love and break down assembled pieces of matter into their constituent elements and thus helped ensure the continued heterogeneity of the cosmos. Thus, his response to Parmenides was that although it is true that nothing that exists can cease to exist and vice versa, the objects we commonly conceive of as material are actually conglomerates of more basic elements that are themselves unchanging but may be mixed with or divided from other elements by Love and Strife; further, that his is the reason that change is manifest in the cosmos:

> When these [elements] have been mingled in the form of a man, or some kind of wild animal or plant or bird, men call this "coming into being"; and when they separate men call it "evil destiny" [passing away]. This is established usage, and I myself assent to the custom. (DK31 B9)[10]

According to Empedocles time is cyclic. At the start of each cycle Love reigns supreme and all the elements that exist come together by this force of attraction, eventually forming a single homogenous sphere. Strife arises and shatters the sphere into pieces and proceeds to battle the resilient force of Love during a long period of cosmology, which we would recognize as our current universe, elements mingling and breaking apart, to form all the objects we routinely experience. Eventually Strife wins out, and all the elements of the universe are scattered. Its work accomplished, however, Strife too becomes dormant, leaving Love to bring the elements back together into the cosmic sphere, and the whole cycle of the universe begins again.

During each cycle the elements are brought together by Love, but it is chance that determines which combinations will occur. This feature of Empedocles' thinking greatly bothered many later writers, most notably Aristotle. If the elements are brought together in chance pairings, what causes the orderly cosmos we see, particularly in such complex arrangements of matter as living things? According to Empedocles, initially all manner of diverse life forms were created, but only a few survived—namely, those with characteristics conducive to success in their environment. Thus Empedocles seems to have had at least a glimmer of what would, in more than two millennia, become Darwin's theory of natural selection.

Like Pythagoras, Empedocles had much to say about the *psychê*. First, he also maintained that the *psychê* is immortal and that metempsychosis is possible. It is worth noting that the doctrine of personal survival is every bit as incompatible with Empedocles' universe of proportioned matter as it is with Pythagoras' universe of pure mathematical ratios. Jonathan Barnes (1982) has suggested one possible compromise solution based upon Empedocles' view of time as cyclic. If the universe is fated to cohere and dissipate in an endless repetition, then perhaps personal immortality can be understood to mean that each time the cycle runs, there will be the correct proportionate mixture of elements to create each individual anew. Thus my *psychê* is immortal and transmigrates following my death in the sense that at some time in the future, though not in the future of *this* universe, I will once again be constituted by the same proportions of elements. Although such a solution does resolve some of the logical inconsistencies in Empedocles' views, it must be stressed that there is nothing in the surviving fragments of his writing to suggest that he held such a compromise position. As with Pythagoras, it seems equally likely that he simply failed to notice, or chose to ignore, this inconsistency in his beliefs.

More intriguing than his views on the immortality of *psychês*, particularly for modern readers of the history of psychology, are his theories of sensation and perception. According to Empedocles every object gives off *effluences* from its surface. These effluences are described as thin membranes of matter that resemble in their proportion and organization of elements the objects that give rise to them. When such effluences enter our sensory organs, by means of channels designed to admit each element, we tally the resulting proportion and perceive the object by resemblance, "[f]or by earth we see earth, by water, water, by air, bright air, and by fire, brilliant fire, yearning [Love] by yearning and Strife by mournful Strife" (DK31 B109).

This resemblance theory of sensation is extended to perception and cognition. According to Empedocles, the blood around the heart, which is the most refined mixture of elements, is the location of thought. Sensation becomes perception because the effluences taken in through the sense organs are able to impress themselves upon the heart's blood, causing a reaction whereby this sensitive mixture of the elements takes on the proportions of the object perceived. Ideas, for Empedocles, are nothing other than mixtures of heart's blood in proportions akin to the proportions of material objects if such objects were present. He states, "For from these [the four elements] all things are joined and compounded and by these they think and feel pleasure and pain" (DK31 B107). In order for such mixtures to be possible, however, it is necessary that prior experience of the imagined object have taken place. In this Empedocles is unabashedly empiricist, stating in a passage quoted by Aristotle in his *De Anima* (427a, 21–23), "Wisdom grows in humans in relation to what is present."

The Atomists: Leucippus and Democritus

Perhaps the most thorough response to the Eleatic challenge came from the fifth-century philosophical movement called Atomism. This response is said to have been formulated first by Leucippus (fl. ca. 435 BC), who is reported variously to have been born in Miletus, Elea, or Abdera. Doubtless the truth was uncertain even in antiquity, and so his biographers simply assigned him appropriate birthplaces on the basis of his naturalism, his response to Parmenides, or his follower Democritus (see McKirahan, 1994, p. 303). Although Democritus and later writers ascribed priority to Leucippus, we have only one surviving fragment of his, "No thing happens at random but all things as a result of a reason and by necessity" (Leucippus, DK67 B2).[11] This passage, though not dealing specifically with any of the major tenets of Atomism, at least reveals something of the determinism that underlay the Atomists' conception of the universe.

We know more about Leucippus' most famous protégé, Democritus (b. ca. 460 BC). We are told that he was young while Anaxagoras was teaching, and thus we can infer his early birth date. Several ancient sources ascribe him a quite long life, one hundred years or greater, although they disagree on the details and there is little corroborating information. He may well have been considered long lived because he was so prolific. We possess the titles of some seventy books he authored on such wide-ranging topics as ethics, medicine, natural philosophy, aesthetics, and military strategy. Unfortunately, most of these writings have not been preserved, and most significantly none of his writings on atomic theory remain for us to study. Instead, we have the later testimony, and usually hostile criticism, of Aristotle, as well as the writings of the later Atomist Epicurus, to guide us to an understanding of the response to Parmenides made by the Atomists.

The defense of plurality, change, and motion was made by asserting that existence is not equal to extended matter, as the Eleatics had suggested. Rather, there exist atoms, moving eternally, in the void.

The atoms are separate from one another in the unlimited void and differ in shape and size and in position and arrangement. They move in the void, and when they overtake one another they collide. Some rebound in one direction or another, but some become entangled with each other in virtue of the relation of their shapes, sizes, positions, and arrangements and so stay together. This is how compounds are produced.

All three points of this cosmology—the atoms, the void, and atomic motion—require elaboration as all of them come to bear on the psychology of the Atomists. The word "atom" comes from the phrase *a tomi,* which means "uncut" or "indivisible." As Simplicius reports in his commentary on Aristotle's *On the Heavens:*

> These men [Leucippus and Democritus] said that the principles are unlimited in multitude, and they believed them to be atoms and indivisible and incapable of being acted upon because they are compact and have no share of void. (For they claimed that division occurs where there is void in bodies.) (DK67 A14)

In short, the Atomists agreed with the Eleatics that whatever existed in material form must be indivisible, unchanging, and eternal; they merely argued that what we perceive as material reality is in fact an illusion. The world we see is in reality composed of countless tiny Eleatic substances. Atoms are distinguished from one another by shape and size, and they come together to form compounds, which are the physical materials we commonly encounter. Thus differences in material substance are the result of differences in their atomic constituents, differences in shape, arrangement, and position. Aristotle gives an appropriate example: "A differs from N in shape, AN from NA in arrangement, and Z from N in position" (*Metaphysics,* 985b, 4–19).

Second, in order to account for the plurality of existence, which Parmenides had rejected on the basis that it would necessitate the existence of "nothing" between the bits of "thing," the Atomists simply asserted the void. There is no argument given to support the existence of nothingness, other than the rather weak "there is no more reason for the thing to be than the nothing" (Democritus, DK68 B156). This assertion of the reality of the void—an area of space without substance—undercuts the second premise of Parmenides' argument, that "Everything that does not exist, does not exist," and thus allows the separation of objects, change, and motion to take place. It is worth noting that although this assertion denies force to the Eleatic argument without actually proving it false, it would not have been possible without the Eleatic philosophers' assertion that the reality of the universe was different from its appearance.

Third, there is the concept of atomic motion. At first atomic motion seems paradoxical because Democritus asserts that the atoms are in continual motion and that all motion is the result of the collision of atoms with one another. This can be resolved if one remembers that between atoms is nothing but void, and thus there is no potential friction to slow or halt the motion of an atom once it has begun. Accordingly, atoms will behave deterministically, moving only in response to their most recent collision, but they will also remain in motion, on the same path, until deflected by another collision. Thus the Atomists seemed to have a theory similar to the idea of inertia usually said to have been first developed by Galileo Galilei (1564–1642) and incorporated into a general physics by Isaac Newton (1642–1727). These collisions are not always elastic; that is, they do not always result in both atoms being deflected into new paths. Sometimes they result in the atoms becoming entangled with one another by virtue of their shapes; they never actually merge, and there is always the possibility of their dividing again because a small "amount" of void remains between the two atoms. When the atoms become so entangled, they form a compound. All the perceptible objects of the physical world were said to be compounds of atoms.

In terms of psychology, Democritus is the first philosopher to have asserted that the human body is a microcosm (a small cosmos or universe). In other words, human life and psychology can be understood in terms of the same physical principles as those governing the universe. The *psychê* is composed of numerous tiny atoms, just as the body is. These psychic atoms are the smallest and smoothest of the atoms, which the Atomists felt explained the speed with which human thought and sensation proceed. It also allows for the interaction of mind and body through atomic collisions, but without risk of psychic atoms becoming entangled in physical compounds. These small atoms of *psychê* are found scattered throughout the body while it is alive, and they disperse gradually from the body when it dies. Although this theory at least recognizes what will later come to be called "the mind-body problem," the solution offered seems inadequate. For example, if psychic atoms are the same physical entities as other atoms, differing only by their small size and smooth shape, how is it that often the movements of our bodies seem attributable to acts of will? Indeed, in what way can this physical theory account for any of the mental qualities of mental phenomena? Finally, how is it that a distributed population of psychic atoms gives rise to our sense of ourselves as unified psychological selves? Note that these objections do not apply uniquely to the Atomists but have, to the present day, plagued all attempts at purely material reduction in psychology.

Perception was said to occur because physical objects give off effluences (as with Empedocles), which for the atomists were thin films of atomic compounds. These films were said to interact with effluences from our sensory organs, producing physical changes that ultimately have an impact on our psychic atoms.

> The visual impression does not come to be in the pupil right away, but the air between the eye and the object is contracted and stamped by the object and by the seeing thing. For there is a continual effluence from everything. Then this [air], which is solid and changed in color, forms an impression in the eyes which are moist. (DK68 A135)

This analysis applies to sensation in all sensory modalities, and thus our perceptions are reduced to physical interactions between our atoms and those of the environment. The fact that we often agree on the objects of perception is simply a function of culture. We label our experiences "by convention, sweet; by convention, bitter; by convention, hot; by convention, color; but in reality, atoms and void" (DK68 B9).

Thoughts are the physical interaction of atoms within our bodies. But of course these atomic motions must have their sources in other physical interactions. Therefore, although acknowledging that the senses often deceive us (Democritus refers to perceptual judgments as "bastards" in contrast with the "legitimate" judgments of cognition), for Democritus there can ultimately be no source of knowledge other than sensation. Stating this in a series of fragments on the relationship between sensations and the contents of mind:

1. "A person must know by this rule [measuring stick] that he is separated from reality" (DK68 B9).
2. "In fact it will be unclear that to know in reality what each thing is like is a matter of perplexity" (DK68 B8).
3. "In reality we know nothing about anything, but for each person opinion is a reshaping [of the psychic atoms by atoms entering from without]" (DK68 B7).
4. "It is because these thinkers suppose knowledge to be sensation, and this to be a physical alteration, that they say that what appears to our senses must be true" (DK68 A112).
5. "Wretched mind, after taking your evidence from us do you throw us down? Throwing us down is a fall for you!" (DK68 B125).

These fragments reveal an incipient, though uneasy empiricism. Democritus recognized that the senses are unreliable, but atomic interactions were simply the only possible source in his cosmology for thought to act on. He was therefore committed to the belief that all knowledge derives from sensory experience.

Anaxagoras of Clazomenae

Anaxagoras (ca. 500–428 BC) was born in Ionia and is said to have been a follower of Anaximenes.[12] He spent most of his adult life in Athens, befriending that city's leading citizens: the politician-general Pericles and the tragic playwright Euripides. He was forced to leave Athens around 430 under a cloud of scandal (more of which in the next chapter) and retired to Lampascus, on the northwest coast of present-day Turkey, where he died soon thereafter.

Anaxagoras developed the last of the three immediate responses to the Eleatic challenge. Let us review the debate so far. Parmenides and his followers had argued that change is impossible because it implies that things pass out of, and into, nonexistence. Because nonexistence does not exist, so the argument ran, this is impossible. Empedocles' response was that change involves not the passing in and out of nonexistence but, rather, the rearrangement of bits of earth, water, air, and fire. This rearrangement was said to be caused by two opposing forces: Love and Strife. The Atomists, by contrast, simply asserted the existence of the void that the Eleatics abhorred. Within this void there existed basic, indivisible particles, the atoms, but these were not limited to just earth, water, air, and fire. No mysterious force caused the motion of the atoms, according to the Atomists; their motion was said to be continuous. They believed the apparent passing into and out of existence of the various things of the world to be a function of particular configurations of atoms temporarily coming together and later breaking apart.

Anaxagoras' position differed from those of Empedocles and the Atomists in several important ways, but he was nonetheless drawn to respond to the Eleatic challenge to the possibility of change. He did not believe in the Atomists' void, nor did he believe that there are indivisible particles of things. Instead he argued that "of the small there is no smallest, but always a smaller (for what is cannot, through cutting, [come to] not be)" (DK59 B3).[13] That is to say, he believed that matter is a continuum rather than made of discrete parts.

Although Anaxagoras did not believe the world to be made of atoms, he did believe that there are many different kinds of basic things in the world—hair, flesh, stone, air, water, and the like. Unlike Empedocles, he did not believe that these could all be reduced to only four basic constituents. Moreover, he believed that everything has portions, however small, of everything else contained within. In a lump of gold, for instance, there is some small portion of blood, of wood, of water, and so on. A lump of gold is, of course, mostly gold, which is why we see it as such. As he put it, "It is necessary to suppose that in all things that are being mixed together there are many things of all kinds, and seeds of all things, having all kinds of shapes and colors and flavors" (DK59 B4). One of the implications of this belief is that nothing is truly pure—there can be no such thing as pure iron or pure milk. Pure substances are just ideals that are never achieved in practice. This explains, in Anaxagoras' view, how things can appear to change. As the proportions in a given thing change, so does its appearance. As dead bodies rot, they change from mostly flesh to mostly earth. This also explains how food can be nourishing, for food carries within it the basic constituents of the body—some bone, some blood, some flesh, some hair, and so on. These are then used to build the body up, and the portions that are not usable are excreted. Thus, meat, which contains more of these things, would be a better food than, say, vegetables, which contain less of them.

So how are the indefinitely many substances of the world thought to rearrange themselves? Not, as Empedocles had claimed, by way of Love and Strife. Instead, Anaxagoras claimed, events are directed by the one thing that remains pure and unmixed with anything else: *Nous*. *Nous* is often translated as "mind" or "intellect," but it is not, for Anaxagoras, the human mind; not the mind studied by psychology. Rather, it is the principle of the organization of the universe. In this sense it is more akin to the mind of God than the mind of a human being. But this too carries with it contemporary religious connotations that are not appropriate. According to Anaxagoras, *Nous* "set in order all things, whatever kinds of things were to be—whatever were and all that are now and whatever will be" (DK59 B12). In this, Anaxagoras' *Nous* is related to Heraclitus' *logos;* it is an explanation of why the cosmos (a word, it will be recalled, that originally meant "order") is not just a chaotic "soup" of change and difference.

Nous is the founding principle of Anaxagoras' cosmology, which is related to Anaximander's. It is said to have caused the circular motion of the universe. This motion led to the various classes of things—to earth, water, air, and so on—being separated from one another. The difference with Anaxagoras, as mentioned above, is that things will never reach the point where they are *completely* separated. In this sense *Nous* is like *psyché:* It is an originator of motion. Anaxagoras also believed that *Nous* has a special connection with living things. In particular, he claimed, "*Nous* rules all things that possess life" (DK59 B12). That is, in some sense that Anaxagoras does not make clear, to be alive is to be specially situated with respect to the thing that orders the universe as a whole.

Up to this time the question of the organization of the universe—the *rationality* of the universe, one might say—had often been conflated with the question of the rationality of human beings themselves. It would be a long time yet until they were disentangled completely, but in Anaxagoras' shift from talking of the *psyché* of both humans and the cosmos to talking about the cosmic *Nous,* we see the beginnings of a distinction that will ultimately allow science to break away from religion. Different principles are at work behind different kinds of order and rationality. What makes the stars and planets move may be different from that which makes a human body move, and their apparently rational orderliness may not be the effect of an explicit plan, such as a person might make before behaving in an orderly fashion.

THE PRE-SOCRATICS: CONCLUSION

We have come a long way from the time of Homer to that of Classical Athens. Homer gave us the first typology, loose as it may have been, of what we would now call "psychological" functions. Of these, only the life principle was attributed to the *psyché.* Other functions were carried out by the *thumos,* the *nous,* the *phrenes, menos,* and *até.* Nothing bound these functions together but for their coexistence in a single person. With the lyric poets we began to see the individual take increasing possession of, and responsibility for, his or her thoughts and emotions. No longer were they considered, in the main, gifts or curses from the gods, as they often had been in Homer.

Beginning with the Milesian philosophers—Thales, Anaximander, and Anaximenes—Greeks began to speculate on the material of which the *psychê* is made. Each of the various elements, but for earth, was considered in turn. The *psychê* was conceived of primarily as being responsible for movement; the other psychological "organs" were given little serious attention. The Pythagoreans seem to have been the first explicitly to consider the *psychê* as a cognitive principle, of a sort, in addition to being a life force. They also believed the *psychê* to be immortal and to transmigrate from body to body. At least one group of Pythagoreans also rejected the search for the basic material of the *psychê*, instead arguing that it is a particular ratio or harmony among the material elements. Heraclitus, although he maintained the Ionian tradition of claiming the *psychê* to be a single element (probably fire), also explicitly linked it with knowledge (in the form of the *logos*). He also developed the idea of there being a structural unity amidst material change that would be so influential on philosophers and scientists of the future, up to the present day.

Parmenides initiated the first major revolution in philosophy with his claim of having proven that all change, including all motion, is impossible, a mere illusion. Although he said little or nothing specifically about the *psychê*, the fallout from his metaphysical argument would have to be grappled with by the philosophers of the *psychê* that came after him. We looked at three major lines of reply to Parmenides. The first, from Empedocles, argued that change is the result of two forces, Love and Strife, that cyclically create and destroy combinations of the four elements. Thus, there is no "something is created from nothing," as Parmenides worried. Rather, what exists is continually mixed around. As for psychological concerns, Empedocles thought that perception and cognition is the action of particularly rich blood near the heart, which is able to detect the effluences of things in the world. The Atomists—Leucippus and Democritus—believed also that change results from the recombination of things existing, not the new creation of matter. In contrast to Empedocles, however, they believed there to be countless elements each of which can be broken down into irreducible atoms of varying shape. These atoms were said to float through the very void that Parmenides believed to be impossible. The *psychê*, they argued, must consist of small round atoms if one is to be able to account for its rapid mobility throughout the body. The third response to Parmenides was from Anaxagoras, who denied both the Atomists' void and their irreducible atoms. He argued that matter is continuous (rather than discrete, like atoms) and that a little bit of every kind of thing is mixed in with every other. Although he said little about the *psychê* proper, he believed the cosmos to be controlled by an overarching intelligence, the *Nous*, which is responsible for all motion and, in particular, life itself.

We are now brought to the brink of another philosophical revolution: that of Socrates and his prolific student, Plato. Plato's work would set much of the philosophical agenda of the Western world for the next millennium. We thus devote to it, and the context in which it arose, the next chapter.

NOTES

1. A hypothesized fifth element, thought by some to permeate the region beyond the sphere of fire.

2. Mary Baker Eddy founded the Church of Jesus Christ, Scientist, commonly called Christian Science.

3. All citations of pre-Socratic fragments that begin with DK are references to the cataloging scheme of Diels and Kranz (1951). Each pre-Socratic philosopher is assigned a number (Pythagoras is 58, for example. Heraclitus is 22). The letter following is a code: A is an original fragment, B is a later reproduction of a fragment (as in Aristotle, etc.), and C is imitations. Readers are cautioned that B and C fragments are therefore of questionable authenticity. This is especially the case for Pythagoras. The final number indexes the specific fragment cited. Translations for Pythagoras fragments are taken from Barnes (1982), McKirahan (1994), and J. M. Robinson (1968), sometimes with slight modifications.

4. Barnes (1982) argues that the mathematical branch of Pythagoreanism was invented wholly after Pythagoras' death. "Pythagoras the *mathematicus*," he says bluntly, "is a fiction" (p. 102). McKirahan (1994) is more inclined to believe that both traditions found their origins in the teachings of Pythagoras.

5. According to Barnes (1982), the crucial fragment is in the *Phaedrus* 245C–246A, where Plato seems to be adopting a form of psychic immortality similar to other fragments of Alcmeon's we possess (see Aristotle's *De Anima* [405a], Eusebius' *Preparatio Evangelica* [XI, 28.9], Diogenes Laertius' *Lives of the Philosophers* [VIII, 83], and Aëtius' *Opinions of the Natural Philosophers* [A 12]). It should be noted that the passage in Plato is much more extensive than any of the others and thus it is impossible to say how much Plato is merely reporting the theory of Alcmeon and how much he has embellished it.

6. The translations of Heraclitus' aphorisms are variously taken, sometimes slightly modified, from Barnes (1982, 1987); Kirk, Raven, and Schofield (1983); J. M. Robinson (1968); and T. M. Robinson (1987).

7. See note 3 for an explanation of the DK system.

8. See, in particular, Marcus Aurelius' *Meditations*, IV, 46.

9. There has been some debate over how to translate this. Aristotle assumed it meant "anger," as it did in his time. Burnet (1892/1930, p. 140, n. 2), however, believed this to be a mistake; Heraclitus' understanding was closer to Homer's, he thought, and thus we should translate it as "one's heart's desire," which makes more sense.

10. See note 3 for an explanation of the DK system. Translations of the Empedocles fragments are taken from McKirahan (1994), J. M. Robinson (1968), or Barnes (1982), sometimes with slight modifications.

11. See note 3 for an explanation of the DK system. Note that the number 67 is reserved for the single fragment of Leucippus we have in the original, as well as all later commentaries on the Atomists that mention both Leucippus and Democritus, whereas 68 is used for those mentioning Democritus only.

12. First recorded in Diogenes Laertius, cited in Barnes (1987, pp. 226, 236). The exact meaning of this claim is unclear. He could not have been a student of Anaximenes, who died decades before Anaxagoras' birth. There may have still been Anaximenian teachers in Ionia as Anaxagoras grew up, however. In any case, as Barnes (1987, p. 226) claims, "there can be little doubt that he was attempting to revive, in the post-Parmenidean period, the enterprise which the Milesians had carried out in the age of intellectual innocence."

13. See note 3 for an explanation of the DK system. Translations of the Anaxagoras fragments are taken from McKirahan (1994).

Chapter 3

The Classical Greek Philosophy of Mind and Soul

As stressed in the introduction, there is no way of really understanding the intellectual history of a given period without also knowing something about its general political and social history as well. Consequently, in this chapter we begin with an overview of the political and social events that led to the rise of Athens to prominence in the Greek world and that not long after led to its catastrophic downfall. It would not be much of an exaggeration to say that far from being irrelevant to the philosophical and psychological history of the period, these events drove the intellectual currents of the time; they lent urgency to particular philosophical issues at the expense of others that had traditionally enjoyed more prominence.

After looking briefly at Athenian history, we examine the most prominent intellectuals of the time. The first of these are the Sophists, a diverse group of itinerant teachers who earned their fortunes and reputations—both good and bad—by teaching the youth of Athens how to be politically successful. The second is Socrates, often mistaken for a Sophist by the people of his own time, but in fact a man who bore a message quite different from those of the Sophists. Finally we come to the main figure of this chapter, Plato, whose philosophical works would not only change the Greek world but also set the stage for European thought up to the present day. Because his work is so diverse and so influential, this account of it is broken up into sections corresponding to the early, middle, and late periods of his intellectual life.

THE RISE AND FALL OF ATHENS

Ancient Greece was not a unified state as we now think of it. It was, rather, divided into dozens of autonomous city-states. Groups of these cities would occasionally band together in order to advance a variety of economic, political, and military causes. Some of these alliances would be freely negotiated among cities with common interests. Others were more or less imposed upon weaker cities by stronger regional powers. The most wealthy cities were able to establish colony cities. Many of these were on the many islands that dot the Aegean or along its northern and eastern shores. More still were established to the west, in southern Italy and Sicily. The leading power in Greece in the seventh and sixth centuries BC was the city of Sparta. It won, or imposed, its hegemony over the whole region of the Peloponnese in southern Greece.

The Spartan form of government was a unique and moderate form of aristocracy (rule by traditional noble, usually wealthy, families), led by two constitutionally constrained kings. Sparta strongly opposed government by *tyrannis,* in which a single powerful individual rules. Leaders of such governments in Ancient Greece were not necessarily, or even usually, particularly oppressive in their rule. Contrary to the negative connotations of the English cognate, "tyrant," *tyrannis* referred to any strong form of "kingship." The main objection to tyranny, which was widespread in early Ancient Greece, was not so much moral as pragmatic: Tyranny was almost inherently unstable in the long run. Usually inherited by a son upon the death of the tyrant, tyrannies tended to last only a generation or two, leading to regular periods of civil strife—a poor pattern of events on anyone's accounting. Yet, Sparta also opposed a newly emerging form of government that included those people known in Greek as the *demos*—the farmers, tradespeople, artisans, soldiers, and others who were neither noble nor necessarily wealthy. Before the fifth century, this form of government was called not "democracy" (power of the *demos*) but, rather, "*isonomia*" (the rule of equals).

Some small cities ran on democratic principles as early as the sixth century. Athens, which would eventually become the most powerful democracy, was not originally among these. Nor did Athens rank very highly among the important city-states at this time. Successive legal and political reforms by a series of great leaders in the seventh and sixth centuries BC, however, led to Athens' emergence in the fifth century BC as both a major power and the leading democracy. The first of these leaders was Dracon (or Draco), whose legal code of around 624 BC (Ehrenberg, 1968, p. 55) was the first to distinguish between murder and manslaughter. This may have been the first time an essentially *psychological* distinction—namely, that between *intending* to kill a person and killing a person without intending to do so—was incorporated into law. The next great Athenian leader was Solon (ca. 640–ca. 560 BC), whose reform of property law made it illegal to sell people into slavery for unpaid debt. Later still came Peisistratus (d. ca. 527 BC), Athens' only tyrant, who forged strong alliances with other Greek states and established colonies around the Aegean, thereby making land, and the wealth that comes with it, available to many otherwise poor Athenians. With the assassination of one of Peisistratus' sons and the exile of the other, Cleisthenes rose to power (ca. 508 BC). His most important reforms are quite technical from a legal standpoint and need not detain us here. Suffice it to say that he enfranchised segments of the population that had never before seen political power, and he arranged the representational structure in the Athenian assembly such that traditional factions were broken up and thereby forced to negotiate and compromise with their traditional opponents. It was these reforms that established the stable democracy for which Athens became famous in the fifth century.

Although the Greeks controlled the territory of present-day Greece and some colonies on the coast of present-day Turkey, they were hardly the major power in their part of the world. The Greeks long felt the threat—sometimes real, sometimes imagined—of Persia, centered in the distant capital Susa, in the southern part of present-day Iran. By any standard the Persian Empire was vast. By the last quarter of the sixth century BC, it extended from the Aegean in the west (including the formerly Greek colonies of Ionia) to present-day Afghanistan in the east; from present-day Kazakhstan in the north to Egypt in the south. Its Great King, Darius, who ascended the throne in 624 BC, was easily the most powerful man in the world and, more importantly, commanded the most powerful army and navy.

In the first decade of the fifth century BC, however, the Ionian colonies revolted, attempting to throw off the yoke of Persian domination. The response of the Persian army, then busy consolidating gains in Macedon and Thrace, far to the north, was slow. The Ionians quickly asked for military support from the Greek mainland, knowing they would be crushed immediately upon the arrival of the Persian forces. Sparta, which traditionally tended toward isolationism, refused to become involved. Athens, by contrast, was always eager to increase its growing influence abroad and was convinced to send soldiers in support of the revolt against the Persians. The Athenians withdrew soon after the Persians had returned to reclaim Ionia—it was about this time that people like Xenophanes and Pythagoras left Ionia for Magna Graecia—but the brief show of force had been enough to raise the ire of Darius, who dispatched a naval force to "punish" Athens for its impudence. Under the leadership of Miltiades, against all apparent odds, the Athenians defeated the Persians at Marathon in 490 BC. The Spartans, who had been reluctant to send support from the beginning, are reported to have arrived two days *after* the battle.

Darius' determination to include Greece under the Persian cloak was passed on to his son, Xerxes, who came to power in 486 BC. After quelling revolts in other parts of the empire, he launched a massive land and sea expedition into Greece in 480. In a state of panic about the alleged size of the Persian force, the Greeks banded together under the leadership of the Spartans to make a stand at Thermopylae, in the northern extreme of Boetia. Defeated by cunning tactics on the part of the Persian land commander, the Greeks retreated to Attica. The Persian army marched to Athens, most Greek cities along the way surrendering without a fight as it passed through. Athens, however, which had been evacuated in advance, was sacked. Then Xerxes turned to eradicating the Greek navy, which seemed trapped in the straits between the island of Salamis and the Attic mainland. The Greeks, led by Themistocles, were ready, however, forcing the huge Persian navy to fight in the narrow straits a few at a time, leading ultimately to a Greek victory. The following year the Persians attempted another land attack against Greece, but they were defeated at Plataea and withdrew from Europe for good.

Athens' leadership in the Persian wars allowed it to challenge Sparta for supremacy among the Greek states. Although Sparta still had the more powerful land force, Athens' navy was supreme. What is more, its willingness to trade with and colonize the Aegean islands and coastal regions gave it economic and political hegemony as well. With its many maritime allies, Athens founded the Delian League, initially headquartered on the island of Delos, as a common defense force against future Persian incursions. Naturally, members of the old Peloponnesian League, headed by Sparta, immediately became suspicious of ulterior motives on the part of Athens. It was in this atmosphere that Pericles (ca. 490–429 BC) rose to power in Athens in the 450s (see Kagan, 1991, for an excellent primer of Pericles' life). While maintaining the strong military, economic, and foreign policies that had led to Athens' initial success, Pericles encouraged, with public money, the development of theater, architecture, sculpture, and philosophy, transforming what had begun as an economic empire into a cultural one as well. This was the age of the great tragedians—Aeschylus (525–456 BC), Sophocles (ca. 496–406 BC), and Euripides (ca. 480–406 BC)—as well as the construction of the great buildings of the Acropolis, including the Parthenon, under the direction of the great architect, Pheidias (ca. 490–ca. 415 BC).

Pericles' consolidated power in 443, when his main political opponent, Thucydides, son of Melisius (not to be confused with the author of the history of the Peloponnesian wars of the same name), was ostracized. Pericles was still required to defend himself against public attacks, however. In 438 his friend Pheidias was tried for impiety and exiled. This was immediately followed by a charge against Pericles' companion, Aspasia of Miletus, which did not succeed. Next, a bill against those who "teach doctrines about the heavens" was passed by the assembly and used to bring a charge against his teacher and advisor, Anaxagoras (whose philosophy was discussed at the end of the last chapter). The trial was never heard; Anaxagoras left the city before it could take place. Finally Pericles himself was brought up on charges concerning his handling of public finances (see Kagan, 1974, p. 90, n. 60, about the confusion over this point). He was not convicted, but the four incidents in such rapid succession damaged his public reputation.

The threat to Pericles' Athens, however, was not all internal by any means. The great Greek historian Thucydides is well known for having claimed that war between Athens and Sparta was, in the end, inevitable primarily because Sparta feared and envied Athens' growing economic and political power. Many have concurred with this conclusion over the last 2,400 years (see Kagan,

1969, however, for an alternative interpretation). Whatever the cause, Athens spent most of the last third of the fifth century BC at war with Sparta and its many allies, finally emerging broken and defeated. It has traditionally been argued that Pericles' initial strategy—namely, that the Athenians wait behind their walls, collecting tribute from their empire, until the Spartans and their allies became exhausted and sued for peace—may well have worked, but that his death in the plague of 429 BC, only the second year of the war, left Athens in the hands of far less capable leaders, such as Cleon, and ultimately led to its destruction. Kagan (1974) claims, however, that the Periclean policy was, in fact, continued under the leaders who succeeded Pericles and was abandoned for a more aggressive policy only gradually and only when it was clearly no longer tenable if Sparta was ever to be convinced to end the war. A truce was established in 421, but it was unacceptable to Sparta's allies, who were to force a resumption of hostilities in 415. Although Sparta ultimately won the war, its victory turned out to be almost as hollow as Athens' defeat. As the saying goes, Sparta won the war but lost the peace. Its victory did not return it to its former position of hegemony in the Greek world, and with Athens neutralized, a power vacuum left Greece without effective economic or political leadership. The age of imperial Greece, brief as it had been, had ended. Although the greatest of the Greek philosophers were yet to come, the political and economic influence of Greece would never again be what it had already been. Soon it would be incorporated into the "Hellenistic" (i.e., Greek-*ish*) empire of Alexander the Great of Macedon; later, after even its status as the main cultural center of the Mediterranean had been lost to Alexandria in Egypt, it would become a province of the Roman Empire.

THE FIRST PHILOSOPHERS OF ATHENS

The Sophists

Democracy made classical Athens the main philosophical center in the Greek world. Parmenides is said to have visited there around 450 with his student Zeno. Anaxagoras moved to Athens, becoming teacher, advisor, and friend to Pericles. It was also at about this time that a whole new class of philosopher—the Sophists—came into being to teach young Athenians (for a fee, of course) the things they would have to know if they were to become wise citizens. They would deliver public speeches in the *agora* (i.e., the marketplace) on prepared topics or sometimes would ask the audience to give them topics on which to speak, as demonstrations of their skills. These performances would also serve to recruit new students from among the audience members or their children. In other cities widespread teaching of oratorical skills was not necessary because of the fairly narrow range of political roles. In democratic Athens, however, almost everyone played a political role—most citizens even held some sort of political office at one time or another—and so the teaching of such skills was in very high demand.

The Sophists as a group did not represent any single coherent school of thought. They are identified more by the way they delivered their messages than by the content of the messages themselves. Some, such as Hippias of Elis (fl. late 5th c. BC), were polymaths, teaching science, mathematics, literature, trades, and whatever else their clients asked of them. Others, such as Protagoras of Abdera (ca. 485–ca. 415 BC)—a friend and advisor to Pericles himself—inveighed against polymathy, focusing his own efforts on the teaching of ethics and politics (Ehrenberg, 1962, p. 331). This must be kept firmly in mind when interpreting his single most famous claim: that of all things, man is the measure. Many have criticized (or embraced) Protagoras for having been a thoroughgoing relativist on the basis of this remark, but it is not at all clear that by "things" Protagoras meant to include the things of the *physis,* the natural world. Instead, he seems to have been referring mainly to what the Greeks called the *nomos:* those laws and customs that allow an otherwise "barbarian" group of people to found and run a *polis,* a city, a society.[1]

Gorgias of Leontini (ca. 490–ca. 390 BC), different again, focused his attention on the teaching of rhetoric, or the art of speaking convincingly in public. Apparently he cared little for the idea of discovering truth, developing instead the methods of successful oratory itself, regardless of the content. He seems to have been first to admit that the tools of rhetoric are double-edged, as it were; they can be used in support of good or of evil. This last trend rapidly descended into the development of skills for swaying public opinion in the service of the highest bidder, rather than in the service of personal conviction about what is the right course of action— "sophistry" in the modern sense of the word. This movement also led to a precipitous decline in the prestige once enjoyed by the Sophists. Finally, public and philosophical ire turned against them. Aristophanes' savagely critical comic play the *Clouds* reflects just how low respect for the Sophists had sunk by 423, when it was first produced.[2]

Although there were some individual exceptions, the Sophists are widely regarded as having represented a major change in philosophical focus away from the speculative science and metaphysics of most of their Ionian and Italian predecessors toward the more day-to-day concerns of politics, ethics, and the problems of human conduct. This shift is not surprising when it is recalled that they reached the height of their influence just when Athens was fighting a series of wars with other Greeks, a time when political decisions about the continued conduct of the war carried with them life-and-death consequences. Achieving and holding political power at this time became more critical than ever before for a number of conflicting groups in the sometimes unstable Athenian assembly, and oratorical skill often made the difference.

Thus, the Sophists mark a change in emphasis from the problems of natural science to the problems of what is sometimes called human science: How is a society to be structured? What is the best form of government? How should I act toward my fellow citizens and toward citizens from other cities? Some Sophists explicitly claimed to teach *aretê*—usually translated as "virtue," but perhaps better rendered as "betterment" or even "perfection." "If you associate with me," Protagoras is said to have claimed, "the result will be that on the very day you begin, you will return home a better person, and the same will happen on the next day too. Each day you will make constant progress towards being better" (Plato, *Protagoras,* 318a). The truth of this claim was doubted by many, however, especially when the sophistic extremes of men like Gorgias came into view.

Socrates (ca. 470–399 BC)

Another philosopher of the time—the first one of significance to be a native of Athens[3]—was Socrates. Like the Sophists, he spent time in the *agora,* talking on a wide variety of topics to whoever would listen. Unlike them, however, he did not charge for his time, and he did not claim to teach *aretê*. In fact, he is said to have doubted that virtue could be taught at all. He is even reported to have denied that he himself knew anything he could teach. The Athenians of the time probably did not distinguish him from the Sophists, but his opinions differed strongly from theirs, inasmuch as there was a coherent body of Sophistic teaching at all. In the conversations he is reported to have had with Sophists, he questioned their ability to really teach anything. He was by no means a skeptic about the possibility of knowledge, however. Through questioning and debate he believed that one could set oneself on the path toward truth and toward *aretê*. What he doubted was that this knowledge could simply be transferred from one person to another.

Relatively little is known of Socrates' life. His father was a stonemason and his mother a midwife. He fought, apparently with distinction, in the earlier part of the Peloponnesian War. He married a woman named Xanthippe, of somewhat higher station than he, fairly late in life. In 406, during the last phase of the Peloponnesian War, he chaired a council that condemned six generals after a disastrous defeat at sea that had been complicated by an unexpected storm. He is said to have been the only member of the council to vote against condemnation. In 404 he publicly opposed an order of the Thirty Tyrants who ruled Athens for a short period after the Peloponnesian War, a very dangerous act considering that the Thirty were said by Xenophon to have killed more Athenians in eight months than the Spartans had in the previous ten years of war (cited in Ehrenberg, 1968, p. 346). In 399 he was charged with teaching new gods and corrupting the youth. We know of no gods that Socrates taught about. As for corrupting youth, Socrates' teachings may have offended the ears of conservatives who were trying in vain to reestablish the traditional ways of Athens' glory years. It is said that he was expected to leave the city rather than to face trial, as had Anaxagoras before him, but he refused to leave, stood trial, and was condemned to death. Instead of leaving at that point, as he might have done, he accepted the verdict, drank the cup of hemlock given him, and is reported to have died discussing philosophy with his friends.

He gathered about him a circle of young, mostly wealthy men, several of whom were destined to become members of the political, military, and philosophical elite of the next generation. These included Alcibiades (ca. 450–404 BC), who was warded by Pericles himself and led the Athenians into the second part of the Peloponneisan War. He defected to Sparta after being (apparently falsely) condemned for heresy, and he later attempted to involve the Persians in a coup attempt against Athens. When he finally returned to the side of the Athenians, he was assassinated by the Thirty Tyrants, who (probably wisely) mistrusted him. Another of Socrates' followers was Xenophon (ca. 428 BC–ca. 354 BC), who opposed the unstable democracy of Athens at the end of the war and fought as a Greek mercenary in the service of Cyrus, a pretender to the throne of Persia. When Cyrus was killed in battle, Xenophon took command of the 10,000 Greek troops and, according to his own story, marched them back home. A third follower of Socrates was Euclid of Megara (ca. 430 BC–ca 360 BC) (not to be confused with the famed geometer Euclid of Alexandria, fl. ca. 300 BC) who became a leading philosopher of the fourth century. His teachings gave rise, on the one hand, to important developments in early formal logic and, on the other hand, to the school of thought known as Stoicism, formally founded later by Zeno of Citium (ca. 334–262 BC). Stoicism would eventually come to deeply influence, and even dominate, Roman philosophical thinking centuries later (see Sanford, 1989, pp. 13–14). The most important of all Socrates' students, however, was Plato, to whom we now turn.

Plato (ca. 428–ca. 348 BC)

Plato's work is too often presented as a static block of arbitrary-sounding claims—"Plato believed this," "Plato claimed that." When seen this way, his work seems more akin to dogma than to philosophy or science. Nothing could be further from the truth. Plato was a brilliant thinker—perhaps the most brilliant—who continuously struggled to make his arguments *convincing*. He seems to have considered opposing arguments carefully, and if he ultimately seemed to win quite often, it was through the incisiveness of his mind, not just the sheer force of his presence. In his time, of course, he was just one of dozens of philosophers working in Athens. In order to maintain independence from the local political authorities, he set up a permanent school, the Academy, outside the city walls in about 385 BC. It was the first of its kind and the forerunner of the modern university. The Academy continued to operate for centuries after Plato's death. Although the exact lineage is difficult to trace, a school of pagan neo-Platonists calling itself the

Academy, claiming direct descent from Plato's school, was shut down by Christian authorities in AD 529, almost a millennium after Plato's death.

In actual fact, we know very little about Plato's life. Simon (1978) tells us the following:

> [I]t is generally accepted that his father died sometime in his youth, that his mother then married her mother's brother, and that from that union came a younger half-brother, Antiphon. Plato's step-father, Pyrilampus, had an older son by a previous marriage. Plato's own parents had three other children: two sons, Glaucon and Adeimantus [both of whom appear as characters in Plato's *Republic*], and a daughter; the birth order of the children is not known. (p. 210)

It is also believed that Plato visited Archytas, the Pythagorean ruler of Tarentum, in Italy (McKirahan, 1994, p. 80), possibly the year just before he opened the Academy in Athens (Lee, 1974, p. 17). Judging by his own work, he must have been deeply impressed by Pythagorean cosmology. The Academy is said to have had a sign above its door admonishing those who entered to know geometry.

Distinguishing Plato's views from Socrates' is a difficult task. All of our most reliable information about Socrates comes from Plato's works (collectively "dialogues" because they are written in the form of conversations between two or more people). There are some works by Xenophon as well, but he seems not to have been as close to Socrates as he would have us believe (he was not at the execution, for instance), nor does he seem to have been in possession of a particularly philosophical turn of mind. It has become conventional to refer to Plato's earliest dialogues as "Socratic" because they are thought to give the most accurate portrayal of the historical Socrates.[4] The Middle and Late Period dialogues[5] continue to use a character named Socrates, but the views expressed in them seem to have been Plato's *development* of Socrates' thought—and quite a development it was—rather than straight reports of conversations he actually had. Nevertheless, Plato insisted that "there is not and never will be a work of Plato. The works which go by that name belong to Socrates, embellished and rejuvenated."[6]

Dialogues of the Early Period

In any case, that Socrates was responsible for a major innovation in the meaning of the term *psyché* seems clear enough. This innovation is reflected in a comment Socrates is reported to have made at his trial: "Are you not ashamed of caring so much for the making of money and for fame and prestige, when you think nor care about wisdom and truth and *the improvement of your psyché?*" (*Apology*, 29, italics added[7]). Up to this time, as we have seen, the *psyché* was mainly considered to be that which keeps bodies alive—a life force, so to speak. Some philosophers hinted that it might serve a cognitive function as well, but there was never any indication that it is something that can be improved through effort or that it has qualities that can be subject to improvement at all. To the Homerics, one either had a *psyché* and was thereby alive, or had lost it and was in all probability dead. To the Pythagoreans, perhaps, one had a *psyché* and thereby could reason, or one did not and could not. But to Socrates, attending to the improvement of the *psyché* was a matter of importance above and beyond even wealth and fame. It seems that something drastic had changed with respect to the term, but exactly what had changed Socrates does not say in the *Apology* (but for a passing association with wisdom and truth). For the details we must look to Plato's other early dialogues.[8]

In the *Crito*, the *psyché* seems to be taken to be the basis of human morality: "What about the part of us," Socrates asks about the *psyché*, "which is mutilated by wrong actions and benefited by right ones? Is life worth living if this part is ruined?" (47E). In the *Euthydemus* (295E, 4), the *psyché* is described as that by which we are able to know things; that is, it serves a cognitive function. In the *Alcibiades I* the *psyché* is given primacy over the body, and said to "use" and "rule" it.[9] Far from being the anonymous life principle of Homer, the *psyché* seems to have expanded, in the thought of Socrates and his followers, to the whole of what we might call the person's *self*. The question then turns to whether Socrates thought the *psyché* to be an entity distinct from the body, or if he conceived of it as the whole living person, including the body. The passage from *Alcibiades I*, cited above, seems to indicate the former, but there are passages in the *Charmides* that suggest the latter. T. M. Robinson (1995, p. 8) suggests that the *psyché* and the body were not merely thought to be added together but, in fact, "entail" each other; that to speak of one without the other is incoherent. This makes better sense once it is understood that the Greeks of this time had different words for living (*soma*) and dead (*nekros*) bodies,[10] so speaking of a dead body implied there being no *psyché*; to speak of a live one, however, implied its integration with a *psyché*.

In any case, in the *Protagoras* and the *Gorgias* the split between the *psyché* and the body seems to have been made definitive. In the former the *psyché* is called "something which you value more highly than your body [*soma*]" (313B), and in the latter, body and *psyché* are referred to as a "pair," and the *psyché* is "in command" of the body [*soma*] (465C). Also in the *Gorgias* (493A), we learn that the *psyché* itself is not a single thing, but is composed of at least two parts. One of these is the seat of reason, but the other is the source of impulse and desire. This conflicts with some other works, particularly the *Phaedo*, in which (irrational) desires were said to emanate from the body and were to be held in check by the (rational) *psyché*. Here, however, both are attributed to the *psyché*, allowing for the possibility of *intrapsychic* conflict,[11] rather than a simple tussle between the wants of the body and the reasons of the *psyché*. This account also presages the more elaborate and influential account that is found later in the *Republic*.

In the *Meno* Socrates asserts that the *psychê* is the seat of all knowledge. What is more, he claims to show that knowledge is not learned through experience, but is instead innate. Experience only brings this innate knowledge to consciousness through a process of recollection (*anamnesis,* or unforgetting). Socrates demonstrates the truth of his claim by showing that one of Meno's slaves, who has no education, can be brought to prove a version of the Pythagorean theorem by simply being asked a series of questions. If this knowledge did not come from the instructor, Socrates asks, then where did it come from? His answer is that the knowledge must have been latent in the boy all the while, and that the questions only assisted him in recalling what he already knew, though unconsciously. When asked how knowledge came to be in the *psychê* in the first place, Socrates concludes that the *psychê* must exist before birth; that it, indeed, must be immortal and inhabit many bodies successively throughout time. He does not argue very strongly for this conclusion here, however. That does not come until the *Phaedo.*

Dialogues of the Middle Period

The *Phaedo* is considered a Middle Period work by Vlastos (1991), and it seems to contain arguments and conclusions that go beyond those likely to have been produced by Socrates the man. It is about here that the "historical" Socrates begins to be overtaken by what is sometimes called the "Platonic" Socrates—the character of the middle and late dialogues who puts forward Plato's own philosophy (built, no doubt, on a Socratic foundation). The *Phaedo* is set in the prison cell in which Socrates awaits the cup of hemlock, the manner of his execution. Many of his friends have come to console him, but Socrates professes to be unconcerned, indeed glad, about his impending doom, for he is convinced that the *psychê* is immortal and his bodily death will, in fact, constitute a freeing of his *psychê* to be one with the eternal verities—called "Ideas" or "Forms" by Plato—he has only been able to glimpse, through philosophy, while his *psychê* has been trapped in his body. Because the body is so liable to being distracted by lights and sounds and pleasures and pains, according to Plato, it is very difficult for the *psychê* to achieve the concentration required to acquire certain knowledge through the use of reason. Once freed of its constant struggle with the body, the *psychê* is enabled to know the Ideas directly.

The details of the argument for immortality need not concern us here, but its centrality to Platonic philosophy can hardly be overstated. F. M. Cornford (1941, p. xxvii) once called the doctrine of immortality of the *psychê* one of the "twin pillars" of Platonic philosophy.[12] (The second "pillar" was said to be the theory of Ideas, alluded to earlier and discussed further later.) What is key about the view presented in the *Phaedo,* for present purposes, is that the *psychê* is explicitly described as being *both* the life force *and* the cognitive principle (that by which reason and knowledge are made possible). Until this time these seem to have been regarded as two separate issues requiring different solutions (though the Pythagoreans had hinted at a unification of the two). There is no compelling a priori reason why whatever it is that keeps us alive should be the same as that which makes us rational. Homer, for instance, seems to have kept the two issues quite distinct. Plato, through the voice of Socrates, was among the first to unite these two functions in one and the same entity—the *psyché*.

This means that contrary to most previous thought, when one dies and one's *psyché* leaves one's body, it takes the cognitive functions—in particular, one's personal memories—along with it. Thus, they can continue to "live" apart from the body after death, and personal immortality, in a much fuller sense than was granted by Homer, here becomes a serious conceptual possibility. The *psyché* is now the true self; the body, just an instrument. This is a defining moment in the history of Western philosophical thought. From Plato the doctrine of the immortality of what might be called the "personal *psyché*" was carried forward through various schools of thought, to the Romans, then to the early Christians and passed on to the European Middle Ages.

The image of the *psyché* presented in the *Republic* is far and away the best known. It also represents a significant change from Plato's earlier accounts. The aim of the *Republic* is to develop an account of the perfect state, the most just and most excellent form of government. Early in the work Plato considers the question of just what constitutes excellence. He concludes that a thing is said to be excellent when it optimally fulfills its proper function— for example, a knife when it cuts well or an eye when it sees well. Then he comes to consider the *psyché*: What makes for an excellent *psyché*? He identifies the functions the *psyché* must perform as, on the one hand, "management, rule, deliberation, and the like" and, on the other hand, "living." At first glance, this seems to simply recapitulate the two functions—cognitive and biological—given in the *Phaedo*. Soon after, however, he adds in moral properties (i.e., being just) as part of the function of the *psyché* as well. The moral principle was attributed to the *psyché* in the *Crito*, but in other dialogues it seemed to take a back seat to cognition. T. M. Robinson (1995, p. 36) suggests that Plato equivocated on the phrase "live well" in order to add the moral principle to the cognitive and biological ones already said to be characteristic of the *psyché*. On the one hand, to "live well" can mean to be healthy and vigorous. On the other, it can be taken to mean to live according to high principles. Whether Robinson is right in this criticism or not (and it seems that he may be), it is clear that by the time Plato wrote the *Republic,* he believed that a single entity, the *psyché,* was responsible for the biological, cognitive, and moral character of the person. Homer's *psyché, thumos,* and *nous* had effectively all been rolled into one. Combined with its alleged immortality, which Plato reaffirmed in the *Republic,* the Greek *psychê* was by this point beginning to look something like the Christian soul, to which it would give way in a few centuries' time.

With all these functions to perform, the *psychê* must have some internal structure. Plato argued that it is much like the political state: There must be (1) wise rulers to develop sound plans for the future, (2) strong and willing soldiers to carry out the decisions of the rulers, and (3) a profit-oriented class of businesspeople and traders to generate wealth. Success at each of these functions demands different psychological characteristics. The rulers, if they are to be wise, must be ruled by reason, for any irrationality will lead them to endorse foolish decisions. The soldiers must be "spirited" and ruled by courage, for any cowardice will result in the rulers' decisions, wise as they might be, coming to nothing. Finally, the business and working classes, if they are to be profitable, must be driven by a desire for money and the things that money can buy. Plato concludes from his analogy to the state that the *psychê*—everyone's *psychê*—contains parts corresponding to each of these three functions. The reasoning part was called the *logistikon* (literally, the apprehender of the *logos*), the "spirited" part the *thumos* (or sometimes *thumoeides*), and the seat of appetites and desires the *epithumetikon* (literally, near the *thumos*).

These three parts make up what is often called Plato's tripartite (i.e., three-part) theory of the *psychê*. In the best *psychê*, Plato continued, the *logistikon* will rule, balancing or "harmonizing" the needs of the various parts through the use of reason (note: an act of reason that did not allow for the basic needs of the body, base as they might seem, would not be wise at all). In the poor *psychê*, by contrast, some other part will rule. For instance, the *epithumetikon*, might take over, allying itself with the *thumos*, which will then strive to fulfill every desire, no matter how wanton or unreasonable.[13] Although Plato recognized that some people would never be ruled by the *logistikon* and thus should not be rulers, he recognized that they still serve a necessary function in the ideal society, generating wealth, as long as they are ultimately answerable to the laws of the rulers.

Although the distinction between reason and desire is well understood, much ink has been spilt trying to make sense of the *thumos*. It has been argued by some that it is derived solely from the analogy to the state, rather than from anything crucial to an adequate psychological account. In at least some instances, however, it seems to map reasonably well on to what would later be called the will. It is the "action" part of the *psychê*, the part that turns plans into results. It is obvious to anyone who has tried to control a bad habit—smoking, drinking, eating too much, and so on—that the best plans in the world can come to nothing if one is unable to carry them out. Plato may have been trying to reflect this very basic psychological fact: Intentions do not inevitably lead to actions. The *thumos* was also said to be responsible for anger and indignation. It is this last function that Plato used to distinguish it from the appetites of the *epithumetikon:* Whereas simple desires are not directed against oneself, indignation can be. Disgust with oneself—for example, for lack of will or courage—is the action of the *thumos* (see, e.g., the story of Leontius in the *Republic,* 439e ff.).

In the *Republic* Plato seems to have returned to an idea that appeared in the *Gorgias* but was absent in the *Phaedo:* the possibility of intrapsychic conflict. It will be recalled that in the *Phaedo* the main challenge to the *psychê* was the body, over which it was supposed to rule. In the *Gorgias,* however, reason and impulse were both psychological functions; the body was only an instrument of these. In the *Republic,* again, desires and impulses are recognized as psychological functions to which the body is subject. Although the *epithumetikon* may be somehow "closer" to the body than the *logistikon* and *thumos,* in the sense that it expresses, among other things, bodily desires, it is still a part, or function, of the *psychê.* The body itself plays little direct role in the conflict.

It is important to note that Plato's development of the theory of the *psychê* was in marked contrast to what had gone before. Until this time the main questions concerned what *substance* the *psychê* is made of—air, fire, number? Plato's main concern, by contrast, was with the *functions* of the *psychê.* The question of its actual physical composition, if indeed he believed it to be physical at all, hardly arises.

The theory of Ideas (or Forms), briefly mentioned above, is laid out in the *Republic* as well.[14] Although it does not bear directly on the theory of the *psychê,* it is central to Platonic philosophy and has many implications for his theory of the *psychê.* The best way to approach this complex topic is probably to follow the narration set out by Plato himself.

In Book V (475–476) of the *Republic* Socrates and his interlocutor, Glaucon, are attempting to arrive at an explicit understanding of what it is to be a philosopher. Socrates suggests that "the man who is ready to taste every branch of learning, is glad to learn and never satisfied—he's the man who deserves to be called a philosopher, isn't he?" Glaucon is dubious. He responds that

> those who love looking and listening [to dramatic plays and musical concerts] enjoy learning about things, and so fall under your description; but they're a peculiar lot to class as philosophers because nothing would induce them to spend time on any kind of serious argument.

Socrates concedes the point and tries again: Philosophers are "those who love to see the truth." Glaucon agrees, but he rightly wonders exactly what this means; what is "truth"? Socrates makes an attempt to answer:

> Those who love looking and listening are delighted by beautiful sounds and colours and shapes, and the works of art which make use of them, but their

minds are incapable of seeing and delighting in the *essential nature of beauty itself.* [italics added]

Here we discover the core of Plato's theory of knowledge: Real knowledge of beauty does not come of simply discovering particular examples of it in artworks and the like. Rather, it comes of understanding its essential nature—the *Idea of Beauty* in which individual things must share if they are to be beautiful. This, Plato argues, is not to be gained by running around looking at beautiful objects. These are merely "pale reflections" of beauty *itself.* The understanding is to be gained, rather, by contemplating what it is for anything to be beautiful. It is this contemplation, rather than mere sensation, that Plato believes separates the philosopher from the mere aesthete. Philosophical reflection can lead one to the "essential nature" of beauty mentioned in the quotation above, the pure Idea (or Form) of Beauty.[15]

Plato then goes on, through the character of Socrates, to extend his argument to all the major issues that concern him. The good, for instance, cannot be understood simply by observing and compiling a list of good acts. To begin with, how would one know which acts were good unless one first had an idea of what good is?[16] One must reflect on what it is for something to be good, and when one finally succeeds at this task, one knows the universal Idea of the Good (rather than just a few particular good things). The same goes for the just (and the Just).

In short, Plato believed that truth is to be gained not through sensation (or, as we might say, observation) but through reason. Knowledge, he argued, can only be of the eternal and unchanging. The world of observation, however, changes continuously. (The strong influence of Parmenides on Plato is nowhere more obvious than here.) Thus, although we might develop true *beliefs* (*doxa*, in Greek) about the world as we see it, because of its continuously changing nature, it is simply not the sort of thing we can ever have real *knowledge* about. Plato at one point compares people looking around the world to prisoners chained inside a cave such that they can see only the cave wall but never out the cave's entrance (514 ff.). The "real" world is outside the entrance, but the prisoners can see only shadows of the outside realities projected against the inner walls of the cave. Philosophical reflection was said to be like breaking free of the chains and catching a glimpse of the "real" world, which for Plato was the world of Ideas.

But why, you might ask, was reflection thought able to bring people in contact with the eternal Ideas any better than sensation? Because, as was discussed above, Plato believed the *psychê* to be immortal. Thus, it was thought to have something crucial in common with the eternal truths. Since Plato accepted the Empedoclean principle that "like knows like," he believed that the *psychê* (at least the *logistikon*) is able to apprehend the Ideas. Such work—the acquisition of knowledge through reflection—Plato believed to be the main work of the philosopher. Because the proper running of the state relies on knowledge as well, Plato believed philosophical reflection to be the work of the wise political leader too. Plato reasoned, therefore, that "there will be no end to the troubles of states [e.g., wars] or indeed . . . of humanity itself, till philosophers become kings in this world, or till those we now call kings and rulers really and truly become philosophers" (473d). It is the proposal and defense of this idea—namely, that "Philosopher-Kings" would run the best possible form of government—that is the main burden of Plato's *Republic*.

Dialogues of the Late Period

The *Timaeus*[17] is primarily a story of cosmogony—the origin of the cosmos. As it happens, for Plato this project entailed quite a lot of discussion about the nature of *psyché*. A great deal of detail is given about the cosmos's *psyché*—Plato gives an exact recipe, as a matter of fact—but because the human *psyché* was said to come from the same pot, so to speak, we can glean quite a lot about his theory of it as well.

Plato's story of the origin of the universe is divided into three sections: the work of reason, the work of necessity, and that of reason and necessity working together. In the first section Plato's character, Timaeus, tells us that the cosmos is a living creature, organized (though not created *ex nihilo*) by a "craftsman" whom he calls the "Demiurge."[18] The relationship of the Demiurge to Anaxagoras' *Nous* is an interesting one. The Demiurge is the source of reason in the universe. The Demiurge is said to have made the *psyché* of the cosmos (often translated as "World Soul") by combining a number of elements together. Unlike pre-Socratic speculation on the composition of *psyché*, which centered on which of the four material elements it is made, Timaeus' story involves six Ideal elements: two kinds of Being (divisible and indivisible), two kinds of Sameness (divisible and indivisible), and two kinds of Difference (divisible and indivisible).[19] If this seems difficult to make sense of, it is little wonder. Even Cornford (Plato, 1937, p. 5) once described this passage as "one of the most obscure in the whole dialogue." In the *Sophist*, however, Being, Sameness, and Difference were three of what Plato described as the five "most important kinds" (see note 15). Desmond Lee gives us another clue in the commentary to his translation of the *Timaeus*,[20] however, when he writes that the Greeks "held that reasoning consisted essentially of judgments of sameness (affirmation) and difference (negation)." Since one of the primary functions of the *psyché* was thought to be reasoning, it would have to be in possession of the Ideas of Sameness and Difference in order to carry this function out. Since Being is the basis of existence itself, the *psyché* would have to have this Idea as well in order to know anything. Having both divisible and indivisible kinds of these Ideas allows the *psyché* to have knowledge of the material world of sensation (inasmuch as knowledge of it is possible at all) and the Ideal world of thought, respectively.

The Demiurge is then said to have reduced the chaos of the universe to order (the original meaning of the word "cosmos," recall) by infusing it with the *psyché* he had made. The "fabric" of the *psyché* is cut into strips that are, in turn, made into rings. Each ring is set in circular motion—one for the sphere of stars, others for the sun and for each of the planets. Finally, the Demiurge gave the stars the job of creating four kinds of living things: the gods (of Greek myth), the birds, the water animals, and the land animals. Humans are, of course, in the last group.

For the humans the Demiurge made up another batch of *psyches*—this one not so pure as the first, Timaeus says—and set one riding upon each star. From this vantage point the second generation of *psychés* was able to apprehend the structure of the whole universe. After its tour of the cosmos, however, each new *psyché* was put into the head of a newly constructed human body, thus bringing that body to life.

The human body, we are told, is built of the four material elements and put together with "rivets too small to be seen" (43). Its function is merely to "act as a convenient vehicle" (44) for the head. Because it is made of material elements, however, it is subject to violent motions in every direction (unlike, say, the stars, which move constantly in a circle). This at first confuses the newly embodied *psyché* just as, we are told, "when a man stands on his head," everything seems reversed (43). This, Timaeus tells us, is why newborn babies seem to act irrationally. Through "education" and "correct nurture" (44), young humans learn to control their motions, and the *psyché* is eventually able to settle down to the process of recalling what it learned of the cosmos when riding on its star before it was put into its body. Those who live good lives are said to return to their stars afterward. Those who do not, Timaeus tells us chauvinistically, are turned into women for a second life. This is quite a change from Plato's comments in the *Republic* to the effect that "the only difference between men and women is one of physical function—one begets, the other bears, children. Apart from that, both can and both should follow the same range of occupations and perform the same functions (though men will, on the whole, perform better)."[21] Finally, if the *psyché* is unable to live a good life as a woman, it is turned into an animal "suitable to its particular kinds of wrongdoing" (42).

Plato paid special attention to the sense organs and their relation to the *psyché*.[22] It is here that Plato first presents his theory of vision. The eyes, he believed, give off a "visual stream" of "pure fire" (45). (It is important to understand that "fire" was a term that referred to any kind of light, and it is unlikely that he meant that the eyes give off a full-blown flame.) Through the character of Timaeus, Plato explains that when daylight and the visual stream combine and fall on an object, the motions caused in the stream by the object "penetrate right through the body and produce in the *psyché* sensation which we call sight" (45). When there is no daylight, however, "the visual stream is cut off; for what it encounters is unlike itself" (45). This is another expression of the Empedoclean belief that like recognizes only like. Although the senses are "completely incapable of reason or intelligence" (46), they are described as the "organs of the *psychê*'s forethought" (45). What is more, they are said to play a role in the development of our understanding of the cosmos. We are told that "the sight of day and night, the months and the returning years, the equinoxes and solstices, has caused the invention of number, given us the notion of time, and made us inquire into the nature of the universe; thence we have derived philosophy" (47).

In the second section of the *Timaeus* we are told of the constraints of necessity under which the Demiurge was forced to work. By this Plato meant those aspects of physical reality not subject to change, even by the powerful Demiurge. In the beginning Plato presents his strongly Pythagorean views of physics. According to Plato, a vague substance—"invisible, characterless, all-receiving"—is the basis of all forms of matter. This substance is given no specific name, although it is compared at one point to a receptacle, at another to space itself. When this "stuff" is formed into different shapes, it takes on the characteristics of one of the four elements: earth if it is formed into a cube, fire if a tetrahedron (i.e., a triangular pyramid), air if an octahedron, or water if an icosahedron (twenty-sided figure). These are four of the five so-called Platonic solids. They are all built up from triangles, the basic figure of Pythagorean geometry. (The fifth Platonic solid—the twelve-sided dodecahedron—is said to represent the whole cosmos.) Thus, what distinguishes the four elements from each other is, not the stuff of which they are made, but the particular shape into which that stuff is formed.

From here Plato moves on to a more detailed account of sensation. Heat comes about because the tetrahedron of which fire is formed is small and fast and has sharp points and edges so that it can "cut into anything it encounters" (62). Hard things, by contrast, resist our push because they have wide bases, like the cube of which earth is formed. Another sensation, heaviness, is said to be the result of our moving masses of elements that tend toward the center of the cosmos—namely, earth and water—into the regions appropriate to air. Air, by contrast, seems light only because it rises to its proper place when put under water, where it does not belong.

Pleasure and pain are dealt with quickly as well: "Any sudden violent disturbance of our normal state is painful, and a sudden return to it is pleasurable" (64). Tastes are the result of the effects of substances on the tongue. If a substance is dry and rough, it is perceived as sour. If corrosive, it is perceived as bitter. If it absorbs the warmth of the mouth, it is pungent. If a substance is effervescent and tends to cause movement of the tissues of the mouth and throat, the resulting taste is acidic. If smooth and "relaxing" it tastes sweet (65–66). Smell is quickly dismissed as having "no definite pattern." Sound is described as "an impulse given by the air through the ears to the brain and blood and passed on to the *psychê*." Plato's account of different qualities of sound, apparently drawn from his Pythagorean training, is much like the current one: Fast movements give rise to high-pitched sounds; regular movements give rise to smooth sounds; large movements give rise to loud sounds (67).

He also gives an account of color. If the particles of the things looked at are larger than those that make up the visual stream and consequently compress it, one sees black. If they are smaller than those of the visual stream and penetrate it, one sees white. A second kind of "fire," with particles that are faster than those of the visual stream, gives rise to the experience of "brightness." He then goes on to say that there is "a [third] variety of fire intermediate between these [white and bright]" that produces the perception of red. Once he has set up the three basic kinds of visual "fire," he starts to color-mix: bright, red, and white make orange; red, black and white [*sic*] give purple or deep blue; and so on (68). Plato's ideas about color clearly have little to do with our current understanding of the topic (although it is, perhaps, interesting that he also chose three primary colors to mix).

The third and final section of the *Timaeus* mainly contains Plato's speculations on human anatomy and physiology. Still, we learn some interesting things about his view of the *psyché*. Until now in the *Timaeus* the tripartite *psyché* described in the *Republic* is nowhere to be found. In the last section, however, we discover that the *psyché* Plato has been discussing up to this point is only the rational part—the *logistikon*. The parts responsible for the passions and the appetites—the *thumos* and the *epithumetikon*, respectively—are said to be the work of necessity, not of reason. They are, in effect, just the necessary result of making a human body out of matter. Only the rational part has been made by the Demiurge, and only that part is immortal and will return to its star after a good life.

It has often been argued that Plato's commitment to the straightforward tripartition of the *psyché* wavered after the *Republic*. Although all three parts appear in the *Timaeus*, T. M. Robinson (1995, pp. 119–125) argues, the main division is between the mortal and immortal parts of the *psyché*, the former being further subdivided into passions and appetites. In the *Phaedrus*, written early in the Late Period, a famous metaphor for the *psyché* is presented: that of a man driving a chariot pulled by two horses, one well behaved and one wild. It is conventionally assumed that the man is the *logistikon*, the *thumos* is the good horse, and the *epithumetikon* is the wild horse. At first glance this seems to be a strong assertion of tripartition, but notice that the main division is between the man and the horses, between master and beasts. Only then do we recognize the lesser division between the tame and wild horses. By the very late dialogues, there is no mention of tripartition at all. Thus it seems that there was always a tension in Plato's thought between the doctrine of tripartition and the more traditional, more theoretically stable dualism of intellect and desire.

Returning to the *Timaeus*, we now learn that just as the *logistikon* is in the head, the *thumos* is located in the chest, and the *epithumetikon* in the abdomen. They seem to be located not in the main cavities of the body but, rather, in the marrow of the bones that support those regions. Marrow is held in very high regard, described at one point as "a kind of universal seed for mortal creatures of every kind" (73). This leads one to believe that *psychê* of some sort is in every living thing, and this is exactly what Plato affirms. Even plants have an *epithumetikon*, a *psychê* that "is without belief or reason or understanding but has appetite and a sense of pleasure and pain" (77).

Plato then identifies three principal causes of disease. The first is an imbalance among the four material elements of which the body is made. Fevers, for instance, are said to be caused by too much fire in the body. The second cause of disease is the deterioration of the "secondary formations" of the body—marrow, bone, flesh, sinew, and blood. When they revert to the elements of which they are made, "the worst disorders" result. The third cause of disease is an imbalance or dislocation of breath, phlegm, or bile. This foreshadows, to some degree, the humoral theory of Hippocrates (discussed in chapter 6), which later comes to dominate Western medical thought.

Diseases of the *psychê* are also discussed. These are said to come in two kinds: madness and stupidity. Plato says that "it is unjust to blame over-indulgence in pleasure as if wrongdoing were voluntary; no one wishes to be bad, but a bad man is bad because of some flaw in his physical make-up and failure in his education, neither of which he chooses" (86). Here he mentions a number of biological and social factors that lead to disordered *psychês*. Plato is not completely deterministic about mental diseases, however, as some have argued.[23] "Man can train himself," says Plato, "and by that training be enabled to lead a rational life" (89). So although there is a certain amount of luck involved in living a good life and in avoiding stupidity and madness, one can improve oneself through an application of will in the service of reason.

By this time the mature Platonic account of the individual *psychê* is complete. In later dialogues—the *Phaedrus, Politicus,* and *Philebus*—he amplifies and fine-tunes the approach outlined in earlier works, but there are few dramatic shifts in view. Increasingly he seems more concerned with *psychê* as a cosmic motive force than with the details of the *psychês* of individuals. He experiments with the idea of a "bad" *psychê* in the *Laws,* but he pulls up short of hypothesizing an evil god opposed to the Demiurge. Plato's latest works, in general, seem more theological in nature than political or psychological. Divine revelation plays a greater role than before. Concern with the rational structure of the cosmos is the guiding interest. One particularly interesting development is that all talk of tripartition of the *psychê* is absent from the *Laws.* Plato never explicitly repudiates the idea, but it never appears in his very late works. A kind of dualism seems to be assumed.

One interest of modern psychologists that Plato comments on relatively extensively throughout his writings is childrearing. Plato is commonly said to have been strictly deterministic about human development. Indeed, Plato does seem to have believed that some people are innately better suited than others to particular functions. Some are just better suited to clear reasoning than others. Some are able follow the reasoning of others but are not suited to reason on their own. Still others can neither reason clearly nor even reliably follow reasoned argument. In the *Republic* he speaks of these as being "men of gold," "men of silver," and "men of bronze and iron." In general, he believes that the first will make better rulers, the second better soldiers, and the last two better merchants and laborers. But the belief that he is a strict biological determinist hardly squares with his frequent attention to education. Correct training is crucially important in Plato's eyes. Without it even the best people can slip into a dissolute lifestyle. As well, people strongly motivated to be good can sometimes overcome their "natural" deficits. Although he expects children of the "golden" people to have the best minds, on average, his political system allows anyone who shows promise to rise to the top. In the final analysis, then, Plato takes a balanced approach to the question of development. There are inborn traits and dispositions, to be sure, but these can be molded, and sometimes even overcome, through proper training and experience.

Plato: Conclusion

It would be difficult to overestimate Plato's importance in the history of Western psychological thought. Lovibond (1991) has said, "It would hardly be an exaggeration to say that Plato *invented* the idea of 'mind' with which modern European languages operate, and that it is his writings which have made this idea available to the Western philosophical tradition" (p. 35). Plato seems to have taken the best of the thought of those who went before him and combined it with important and valuable contributions of his own. The most prominent and influential of his opponents came immediately after him and had in fact once been a student at his Academy: Aristotle, whose contributions to psychological thought we will examine in the next chapter.

First, however, it behooves us to reflect on Plato's spectacular accomplishment once again. When we read Plato's words, particularly those of the Middle Period dialogues, we are, says Lovibond (1991), "witnessing the *début* of a world-historic idea: that of the *centered*, or *integrated*, *subject*. This is the idea that every constituent of our subjectivity should be supervised and, as far as possible, controlled" (p. 50). Impossible as that might seem for any individual person to have achieved—and bearing in mind that its success had as much to do with historical circumstances in the centuries after Plato as with his own personal brilliance—it may simply be true nevertheless.

NOTES

1. We would like to thank Charles Tolman of the University of Victoria (Canada) for his discussions with us about Protagoras.

2. Ehrenberg, (1968, pp. 278–279) notes, however, that the original production of the play was a failure with the public and that its script satirized Sophists

more generally than the later, extant one that singles out Socrates in particular. Socrates did not consider himself to be a Sophist and is not now considered to have been one. His arguments seem to have been of a quite different sort, but it also seems that the Athenians of his day were convinced neither by his denials nor by the disputes he is reported to have had with the leading Sophists of his time.

3. Arcelaus (not to be confused with the Macedonian king who reigned at about the same time), who is said to have been a student of Anaxagoras and a teacher of Socrates, was a native of Athens, as was Critias, about whom Plato wrote a dialogue, but their significance derives more from these connections than from anything they are thought to have written or said.

4. The ordering and dating of Plato's dialogues is by no means certain, but it is widely held (see, e.g., Vlastos, 1991) that the Early Period included, among others, *Apology, Charmides, Crito, Euthyphro, Protagoras, Gorgias,* and *Meno* (transitional). Traditional dating uses features such as back-referencing and the sophistication of argument and prose structure to establish temporal relationships. For early attempts at computer dating of Plato's works, see Cox & Brandwood (1959) and Wishhart & Leach (1970). For more recent such efforts see Ledger (1989) and Brandwood (1990). For critiques of these see T. M. Robinson (1992) and Young (1994).

5. According to Vlastos (1991), the Middle Period dialogues are *Cratylus, Parmenides, Phaedo, Phaedrus, Republic, Symposium,* and *Theaetetus.* (Ledger, 1989, and Brandwood, 1990, believe that *Phaedo* is early or transitional.) The Late Period works include *Critias, Laws, Philebus, Politicus* (or *Statesman*), *Sophist, Timaeus,* and the Epistles, although there is some dispute about the *Timaeus* (see below).

6. Epistle II (which D. N. Robinson, 1986, p. 47, notes is of questionable validity), but see also Epistle VII, sec. 341, for a similar remark.

7. It is conventional to cite quotations from Plato's works by giving page numbers of the Stephanus edition (1578). These are given (usually in the margins) of any good translation and make it possible to find the correct passage regardless of which particular edition is being used. When doing this, we will delete the usual "p." to distinguish Stephanus page numbers from the pagination of particular editions.

8. Much of this account of the development of Plato's theory of the *psychê* follows from T. M. Robinson (1995).

9. The authenticity of *Alcibiades I* is questionable, although Ledger's (1989) computer analysis indicates that it is indeed a true Platonic work.

10. Recall the Homeric Greeks seem to have had no word at all for living bodies; both terms referred to dead ones.

11. An idea that will ultimately culminate in the work of Freud, who was no stranger to Plato's dialogues (see Tourney, 1965).

12. Miscited in T. M. Robinson (1995, p. 21) as being on p. xxv.

13. Here we see a structure quite similar, in some ways, to Freud's, proposed more than 2,000 years later. The precise mapping of *logistikon, thumos,* and *epithumetikon* on to ego, superego, and id, however, turns out to be a fair bit more difficult than some writers have been led to believe. In particular, the *thumos* and superego are quite different concepts.

14. There is some discussion of it in the *Phaedo* as well, but the fuller account is in the *Republic.*

15. Plato used the Greek terms *idea* and *eidos,* which are typically translated sometimes as Idea and Form, respectively. The capitalization of these terms is used to

distinguish them from their more conventional usages. Beautiful, Just, and Good are capitalized to indicate the Ideas of Beauty, Justice, and Goodness. This convention distinguishes them from their simple occurrences in some particular thing (e.g., This is a good knife. It must therefore share in the Good). There is a great deal of controversy over whether Plato continued to believe in the theory of Forms until the end of his life or whether he abandoned it in the *Parmenides*. Because Forms appear rarely and indistinctly in the late dialogues, some argue that he became disenchanted with the theory (see Owen [1953] and Cherniss [1957] for the classic statements of the debate). In the *Sophist* Plato discusses the "most important kinds"—being, change, rest, sameness, and difference (254d ff.). It is a matter of some dispute whether these are to be regarded the highest Forms or whether this was Plato beginning to develop a new theory after having lost faith in the Forms.

16. This paradox—namely, that one cannot discover a thing unless one knows what to look for, but if one knew what to look for, then there would be no need to seek it out in order to know it—actually appears in the *Meno*, not in the *Republic*. It is given here for reasons of ease of presentation.

17. The dating of the *Timaeus* is fraught with controversy. It has traditionally been thought to have been written by Plato very late in his life. Some recent scholars (Owen, 1953; Brandwood, 1990; T. M. Robinson, 1995) have argued that it was, in fact, written at the end of the Middle Period or early in the Late Period—fairly soon after the *Republic*, in any case. The details of this argument need not concern us here. We will proceed as if the latter group were correct.

18. "Demiurge" is a term that derives from the Greek word for craftsman or mason. After Plato, however, it came to have strongly divine, and sometimes evil, connotations.

19. An interesting shift in Plato's theory of Ideas had occurred by the time of the writing of the *Timaeus*. Whereas in the *Republic* the Ideas were said to *cause* things to be what they are (e.g., the Idea of Horse is what makes certain animals horses rather than, say, cows), in the *Timaeus* they serve as examples, or paradigms, from which the Demiurge makes copies (see T. M. Robinson, 1995, pp. 67, 136). In making *psyché*, however, the Demiurge seems to use Ideas themselves. Thus the Demiurge becomes the wellspring of causation. More detail about the Demiurge, which is not further discussed in this chapter, can be found in *Politicus* (or *Statesman*). Plato would become increasingly tentative about his theory of Ideas, going so far as to put into Socrates' mouth the words, "[W]hen I have taken up [the theory of Ideas], I run away, because I am afraid that I may fall into a bottomless pit of nonsense and perish" (*Parmenides*, 130). It is notable, however, that Parmenides reassures him that he has not so fallen.

20. Penguin, 1971, p. 47.

21. The words, again, are Desmond Lee's, from the commentary to his translation of the *Republic* (Penguin, 1974, p. 225).

22. It is important to keep in mind here that although perception is a psychological issue for us, it was not for Plato. The senses were considered to be mere conduits whereby the motions of the material world were transmitted to the *psyché*. They were not regarded as parts of the *psyché* proper.

23. T. M. Robinson (1995, p. 107), e.g., cites, in particular, Taylor (1928, pp. 613–614).

Chapter 4

Aristotle's Account of the *Psychê*

Aristotle (384–322 BC) was born into a world still in flux in the wake of the collapse of the Athenian empire. He was lucky enough, however, to be born within the territory of what would be the next major imperial power in the region—Macedon. Under Macedonian hegemony, Aristotle was able to live out most of his mature life in a relatively stable political environment.

As before, we look to general historical events before narrowing our focus to the intellectual. First we take a brief look at Macedon's rise to power. Then we provide a basic outline of Aristotle's personal life, showing how he was positioned, almost from birth, to play a major role in the intellectual sphere of the time. We then move on to a more detailed examination of Aristotle's philosophical work in logic, metaphysics, and physics, and his psychological thought. Finally, we discuss some of the controversy that his theory of the *psychê* provokes even today.

HISTORICAL BACKGROUND AND THE LIFE OF ARISTOTLE

The Rise of the Macedonian Empire

Within a quarter-century of Athens' fall to the Spartans, the perceived threat of Spartan aggression had once again driven many cities around the Agean to ally themselves with Athens. This "Second Athenian League," as it is commonly known, was founded in 378 BC. Although it never achieved the might of its predecessor, the Delian League, it was able to ward off Sparta's imperialist tendencies, defeating them at Leuctra, in Boetia, in 371. Trouble was in the offing, however. Thebes and all the cities of the island of Euboea left the League in the 360s. Civil war led other cities to leave in the 350s. By the 340s, however, a new threat from the north—the growing kingdom of Macedon—drove many cities back into league with Athens once again. Nevertheless, in 338, Macedonian armies under the command of King Philip II (ruled 359–336 BC) and his eighteen-year-old son, Alexander, were able to defeat a combined force of Athenians and Boeotians, bringing all of Greece under their influence, if not explicitly under their sovereignty, and marking the end of the Second Athenian League.

Philip's ultimate intent was never to crush Greece, however. He considered himself to be a Hellene, and his kingdom a culturally Hellenistic one. His main aim was, rather, to lead a unified Greek army against the Persians, ending once and for all Persia's continuing menace to the Greek states. Although he was assassinated in 336 BC, his dream of spreading Greek civilization across the known world did not die. It was carried on by Alexander (only much later to be called "The Great"), who realized it beyond what must have been even Philip's wildest expectations.

Beginning in 334 from Pella, the capital of Macedon, Alexander captured all of Asia Minor (present-day Turkey) from the Persians, once again led by a king named Darius (III), in 333. These victories were followed by successes in the Levant (present-day Syria, Lebanon, and Israel) and Egypt in 332. It was in Egypt, on the marshy Nile Delta, that Alexander established the city that would later become the intellectual capital of the world and bear his name into the future: Alexandria. In 331 he pushed into the heart of Persia, across the Euphrates and Tigris Rivers (in present-day Iraq), capturing the city of Babylon and the capital, Susa. In 330 his gains were assured by the murder of Darius at the hands of one of his own satraps and a pretender to the throne of Persia, Bessus of Bactria. Still Alexander moved forward, capturing Ariaspai (in the southeastern region of present-day Iran) in 330 and making it beyond the Indus River (into present-day Pakistan) by 326. The two-year march back through the great Gedrosian Desert, however, proved to be the greatest obstacle he had yet faced. He is said to have lost as much as three-quarters of his army to hunger and thirst (Talbert, 1985, p. 66). Arriving back in Babylon in 324, he began planning a campaign into Arabia but died of disease in 323, at the age of only thirty-two. His body was reportedly taken to Alexandria, Egypt, and buried at the main crossroads, wrapped in gold and placed in a glass coffin (Radice, 1973). Evidence of the truth of this story has never been found, however.

The Life of Aristotle

Having had a quick look at the historical context in which Aristotle lived, we now move on to his basic biographical details. Aristotle was born in 384 BC in the town of Stagira near the eastern coast of the Chalcidice in Macedon.[1] His father was physician to the Macedonian king, Amyntas II, father of Philip II and grandfather to Alexander the Great. In 367 he was sent to Athens to be educated at Plato's Academy, where he spent the next twenty years. In 347, the year of Plato's death and of the installation of Plato's successor, his nephew Speusippus, Aristotle left Athens with a group of Platonists for Assos, a town on the northwest coast of Asia Minor. We can only speculate whether the ascension of Speusippus had something to do with the departure of Aristotle and his associates. In Assos Aristotle took up the study of animals, particularly marine creatures. He also married a woman named Phythias, the daughter of the local ruler, Hermeias of Atarneus. Three years after Aristotle arrived in Assos, Hermeias fell from power and Aristotle moved to Mytilene, on the island Lesbos, where he acquired his most successful student, and lifelong colleague, Theophrastus of Eresus (ca. 371–ca. 286 BC). Whereas Aristotle's primary scientific interest was animal life, Theophrastus' was plant life (see Kerferd, 1967a). Together, the two men produced a formidable body of biological knowledge. Aristotle was called back to the capital of Macdedon in 342, however, to take up the job of teaching the young prince, Alexander, for the next three years. He then returned to his home town of Stagira. There is some evidence that Aristotle was considered to head up the Academy upon the death of Speusippus in 339 (Kidd, 1967), but the post was ultimately given to Xenocrates of Chalcedon (ca. 396–314 BC), who had been among those to leave the Academy with Aristotle in 347 (Kerferd, 1967b, p. 151). Far from Aristotle in his primary interests, Xenocrates had the tendency to further develop the abstract mathematical and quasi-religious trends evident in Plato's later works.

Upon the succession of Alexander to the Macedonian throne in 336, Aristotle returned to Athens, where, rather than returning to the Academy, he set up his own school called the Lyceum. There he taught until 323, when Alexander's death brought an anti-Macedonian party to power in Athens. Aristotle was charged with impiety. To avoid prosecution, he fled to Chalcis on the island of Euboea, leaving Theophrastus in charge of the Lyceum. He died the following year, leaving behind him a daughter by Phythias (also named Phythias) and a younger son, Nicomachus, by a woman named Herpyllis with whom he had lived after Phythias' death.

ARISTOTLE'S WORK

It is sometimes said that Aristotle was the last man to know everything there was to be known in his time. If true, this was in no small measure because Aristotle himself authored much of the learned literature of his time. Just those books of his that we still possess cover an enormously wide array of topics: astronomy, biology, politics, ethics, poetics, rhetoric, logic, metaphysics, physics, and psychology.[2] It is on the last four of these that we concentrate in this chapter. After surveying the relevant aspects of Aristotle's logic, metaphysics, and physics, we go on to examine in some detail the theory of the *psychê* given in his book *De Anima*.

Logic, Metaphysics, and Physics

As implied above, before we can make much sense of Aristotle's views of the *psychê*, we must first cover basic elements of his philosophy and science. This is because terms that play crucial roles in his psychological thought—such as "matter," "form," "substance," "cause," and "category"—are first elucidated in his more fundamental works. Thus, we will discuss such matters here before going on to an examination of his main psychological text, *De Anima*.

The first book, conceptually if not chronologically, of Aristotle's work on logic is called the *Categories*. True to its title, it is an attempt to list the most significant groupings into which objects "naturally" fall. By correctly categorizing an object, Aristotle thought, we can thereby know it fully. The categories Aristotle discussed are ten in number: substance, quantity, quality, relation, place, time, position, state, action, and affection. Perhaps it is best to let Aristotle himself explain what he meant by each of these:

> [E]xamples of **substance** are "man" or "the horse," of **quantity** such terms as "two cubits long" or "three cubits long," of **quality** such attributes as "white," "grammatical." "Double," "half," "greater" fall under the category of **relation**; "in the market," "in the Lyceum," under that of **place**; "yesterday," "last year," under that of **time**. "Lying," "sitting," are terms indicating **position**;[3] "shod," "armed," **state**; "to lance," "to cauterize," **action**; "to be lanced," "to be cauterized," **affection** [as in "to be affected by something"]. (*Categories*, 1b–2a)[4]

The first four of these were considered by far the most important, meriting a chapter each. The remaining six, meanwhile, were dealt with together in a single chapter.

Substance, in particular, was considered crucial, for it seemed to be the subject of which all other properties are attributed. There might be substance without color, for instance, but there cannot be color without a substance to possess it. A substance (*ousia,* in Greek) for Aristotle was not a mass "stuff" like water or stone or bronze, as it is for us, but appears to have paradigmatically referred to medium-sized objects like men and horses and trees (see Barnes, 1995, for further discussion of this point). In the *Metaphysics* Aristotle explored the possibilities here by bidding the reader to imagine stripping a substance of its attributes one by one: its state and position and time, its relations to other things, its color and other qualities. What would be left? His answer was as follows:

> [W]hen everything else is stripped off, evidently nothing remains. For while the rest [of the attributes] are active or passive processes or *capacities* of bodies, length, breadth, and depth are *quantities*. They are not substances, for quantity is not a substance; rather substance is that to which first of all these belong. But when length, breadth, and depth are taken away, we see nothing left,

unless there is something made definite by these. So to those who look at it this way, matter [*hulê*] alone must seem to be substance.

By matter [*hulê*] I mean that which is not in itself said to be a given any-thing, nor of a given quantity, nor characterized by any of the other categories which define being. (*Metaphysics,* 1029a, italics added)[5]

Aristotle was after the basic stuff that underlies all other properties. This was a problem he inherited from Plato, who struggled with the same issue, it will be recalled, in the *Timaeus.* Aristotle gave "man" and "the horse" as examples of substances in the *Categories.* They can be big or small (quantity), brown or white (quality), and so forth. But what happens when you take away even the "manness" of the man or the "horseness" of the horse? You are left with a pure substrate, something that has no properties at all, but that has the potential to be anything depending on what properties you now give it. Aristotle called this pure substrate *hulê,* a Greek word originally meaning "wood," but in Aristotle's time coming to mean the basic matter of the cosmos. Aristotle's basic definition of matter was astoundingly straight-forward and lucid: Matter is simply that which can be moved.

Given that we can now imagine, if not actually have, prime matter, how is it that we can turn it into an actual object? By adding to it the various properties representative of the categories listed above. Collectively, these properties were called by Aristotle *eidos* or *morphê,* usually translated as "form." If I want some matter to become a statue of Pericles, for instance, I must in some sense combine it with the form of Pericles. If I want it to be a car, I must combine it with the form of a car. Somewhat more obscurely (and this is why "form" is not a perfect translation), if I want it to be red, I must give it the "form" of redness. In general, then, matter is closely con-nected to *potential* or *power,* that is, the potential or power to become some particular thing. Only by giving it form can it be made *actual* (i.e., made into an actual object of a particular kind). This portion of Aristotle's meta-physics is called *hylomorphism* because it is the claim that all objects are a combination of matter (*hulê*[6]) and form (*morphê,* although Aristotle him-self usually used the term *eidos*).

Aristotle believed that his hylomorphic theory answered the problem of change posed by Parmenides. Recall that Parmenides believed change to be impossible because it implies that something passes into nothing, and some-thing else passes out of nothing. Since the "nothing" was thought not to exist, Parmenides concluded that all change is impossible. Aristotle's reply is that the basic matter remains the same underneath all change. Only new forms are put in the place of old forms. For example, a block of stone be-comes a statue of Pericles because the block-form is removed and replaced with a Pericles-form by the sculptor.

Just as Aristotle concerned himself with matter stripped of all its forms, so he concerned himself with the question of pure form—form that has not yet been combined with matter. If pure matter is pure potentiality, he reasoned, then pure form must be pure actuality. Also, since matter is defined as that which can be moved, then pure form must be immovable. Further, since movement is a kind of form—namely, a combination of the categories of place and time—pure form must be the source of movement. It must, in Aristotle's words, be an "Unmoved Mover." This sounded to Aristotle's ears very much like a definition of God: pure actuality that turns formless matter into actual objects but never moves or changes itself.

In spite of the theological implications, it is important to understand that Aristotle's "form" is not the same as Plato's "Forms." For Plato, the Forms were substances in their own right. All individuals of a particular kind (e.g., horses) must participate in the Form (e.g., Horse) in order to be what they are. The Form is primary. The individual is secondary, a mere "pale reflection," as he said, of the Form. For Aristotle, things are almost exactly the reverse. The individuals are "primary," he says in the *Categories* (2a–b). The groups to which they belong are "secondary"; this is because they depend on the existence of the individuals. That is, the classes themselves have no independent reality of their own, only that of their individual members. If there were no horses, for instance, there would be no species called "horse." The individuals, however, contrary to Plato, are not similarly dependent for their existences upon the groups to which they belong.

We have looked at some aspects of Aristotle's logic and metaphysics. Now we have only to look at his physics—his famous theory of cause, in particular—before we go on to a consideration of his psychological thought. The nature of causation was a central issue of physics for Aristotle. He argued that there are four types of cause. The word he actually used was *"aitia,"* a term that is broader in its meaning than the modern English word "cause." An *aitia* can be a reason or motive or explanation as well as a cause (as *we* understand that term). Thus, a more felicitous rendering of Aristotle's claim might be that he thought there are four kinds of explanation, rather than cause; but we will use the traditional translation here. The four types of cause Aristotle identified were the material, formal, efficient, and final. Material and formal we have already seen. The material cause of a thing is the matter of which it is made; for example, the material cause of a statue of Pericles is the stone of which it is made. Another way of putting this is that the *material* answer to the question, "Why is it a statue of Pericles?" is that it is made of stone. The formal cause of a thing is its form or organization; in other words, the formal answer to the question, "Why is it a statue of Pericles?" is that it is shaped like Pericles. Efficient cause is somewhat similar, though not identical, to the modern concept of cause; it is the initiator of motion or change. Thus, the efficient cause of the statue of Pericles would be the sculptor's work with the hammer and chisel. Finally we come to final cause, which is the end or goal toward which a thing is aimed, its purpose or function. This idea, often called "teleology," has drawn to Aristotle much criticism from modern philosophers and scientists. "How can a future state cause anything?" so the argument usually goes. To return to our statue of Pericles, the answer seems relatively straightforward: The statue is being carved *in order to* glorify the memory of Pericles. That is, the final cause is the goal in the mind of the sculptor, or at least of the person who commissioned the statue. In the case of animal or plant growth, things are a little more dicey. Is it fair to say that becoming a frog is somehow the *cause* of the tadpole's developing in the way that it does? Does "to become an oak tree" explain the growth of an acorn? To Aristotle it was obvious that this must somehow be the case. After all, a tadpole never becomes an oak tree, nor an acorn a frog. Finally we come to the problem of final cause in the physical sciences. Can a rock or a planet *ever* be said to do something for the sake of some future goal? Certainly *we* would say not. Toulmin and Goodfield (1962), however, make a very interesting point about a key difference between the scientific aims of Aristotle and those of modern scientists.

> Why did Aristotle not draw our modern conclusion—namely, that the chemical processes going on inside animals are essentially similar to those in the inorganic world? This answer is: *he did*—but, having done so, he *interpreted* the conclusion in the reverse direction to ours. Instead of treating inorganic reactions as the fundamental model or "paradigm," and going on to explain physiological processes in terms of these, he took *organic* development as his paradigm for explaining all material change; any parallels between organic and inorganic processes only served to reinforce his initial commitment to the physiological model. (p. 94, original italics)

That he did so is hardly surprising when it is recalled that his primary scientific research area was biology. Moreover, as we have noted repeatedly in the previous two chapters, an "organismic" view of the cosmos was as unexceptionable to the ancient Greeks as the mechanistic one is for us. To overturn this long-standing assumption, assuming that Aristotle could even have seen reason to, would have required far more argumentation, and incurred far more criticism, than to work within the boundaries of what was then considered to be established fact.

Aristotle's Psychological Thought

With this background in hand, we are ready to tackle Aristotle's arguments with respect to the *psychê*. We have thus far refrained from calling his views "Aristotle's psychology" because the issue of the *psychê* was, for Aristotle, primarily a biological one. His primary focus was the question, "How is it that things are alive?" and only afterward did he address the things that *we* would consider matters of psychology per se. Early in his adult life Aristotle seems to have believed, like most thinkers of his time, that the *psychê* is a distinct substance from the body, probably located in or near the heart (see, e.g., the early biological works). When his thought had matured, however, he discovered a way to solve the problem of the *psychê* by using his revolutionary position on metaphysics. These later views are contained in the book called *De Anima*. Although this is the title Aristotle's treatise usually goes by today, it is a Latin title—meaning, roughly "On the Soul" or "About the Soul"—that was given to the book by medieval scholars more than a millennium after Aristotle's death. Aristotle's original title was *Peri Psychês*, or "About the *Psychê*."

Although revolutionary in its outlook, *De Anima* is a book full of small inconsistencies and discontinuities. This may reflect the many times it was copied and rewritten by scholars after Aristotle, or it may be the result of quirks in Aristotle's own thinking. In any case, rather than attempting to smooth things over and present a completely consistent interpretation of *De Anima*, we have chosen to present many of the discrepancies and idiosyncrasies, allowing the reader to get a feel for the quality of the text itself. This discussion is divided into three parts. First we look at Aristotle's attempt to define what life is. This involves four key metaphors (those of the house, wax, axe, and eye) that Aristotle uses to elucidate the relationship between the *psychê* and the body. He then attempts an analysis of life using his hylomorphic metaphysics. Second, we look at Aristotle's discussion of whether the *psychê* is divided into parts and if so, how many parts there are and what they do. Aristotle's general remarks here are inconsistent, but they lead us to the chapters in which the various functions of the *psychê* are analyzed individually. These make up the third part of our discussion of *De Anima*.

Definitions of Life

De Anima is conventionally divided into three books. The first book consists mainly of Aristotle's criticisms of accounts of the *psychê* that had been offered by his predecessors. Although the details of these need not concern us here, it is worth noting that he cites for criticism, in particular, the Pythagoreans, Democritus, Anaxagoras, and the account presented in Plato's *Timaeus*. He reserves his most damning words, however, for the theory of Xenocrates—then head of Plato's Academy—although he never mentions him by name.

The problem of defining life is Aristotle's first concern. Here the problem is as much with how things in general are to be defined (i.e., what counts as a definition?) as it is with the definition of life in particular. As an example, he notes that the natural philosopher and the dialectician would give different definitions of anger. The natural philosopher, he says, would define it as a heating of the blood around the heart. The "dialectician," he says, would define it as the desire for revenge (403a–b). Both of these, he says, are correct. One aim of his own theory of the *psychê* is to show how both approaches can be true at the same time.

Rather than immediately attempting a definition of his own, however, Aristotle presents the first of several metaphors that he believes illuminate the relationship holding between the body and the *psychê* of the living organism. First, he compares it to the relationship of a house to the pile of bricks of which the house is made (403a–b). Later, in Book II, he compares the relationship of the body and *psychê* to that of a lump of wax and a pattern stamped into it. It seems somewhat strange to ask whether the wax and the pattern are two separate things. Similarly, Aristotle says, "we should not then inquire whether the *psychê* and body are one thing, any more than whether the wax and its imprint are" (412b).[7] He immediately moves on to another related metaphor. He says, "[I]f some tool, say an axe, were a natural body, its substance would be *being an axe,* and this would then be its *psychê*" (412b, italics added). Finally Aristotle presents a fourth analogy. He says that "if the eye was an animal, then sight would be its *psychê*" (412b). "So just as pupil and sight *are* the eye," he goes on, "so, in our case, *psychê* and body *are* the animal" (413a).

What was Aristotle trying to get at with these four metaphors? The impression in the wax is a *form* (the pattern) that has been taken on by some *matter* (the wax). Note that this is just an instance of Aristotle's metaphysical theory of hylomorphism: Each thing is just certain matter given a certain form. Aristotle believed it is precisely analogous to the relation of the *psychê* to the body; the *psychê* is the form given to the matter of the body. His argument goes as follows.

(1) Substances are either matter, form, or a combination of matter and form.
(2) Bodies are material substances.
(3) Some bodies have life.
(4) The *psychê,* which endows bodies with life, therefore, could not also be a material body (such as air, fire, etc.) because there would then be two bodies in the same place; a logical absurdity.
(5) Thus, the *psychê* must be a form. Together the body, as matter, and the *psychê,* as form, produce a new substance: the living thing.

What kind of thing would the *psychê* have to be in order to be the form (or "formal cause") of life? Bodies must be organized in particular ways in order to be alive. If the various parts come "unglued," life ends. In addition to a particular anatomical organization, they must continuously operate in certain ways—taking in nourishment, circulating blood, excreting toxins, and so on—fulfilling the needs of the body's various parts. The *psychê* might be thought of, then, as just the living body's organization and operation. Without these a body is just a corpse; it does not have the form necessary for life. The body, being matter, is considered to have the potential or capacity (*dynamis*) for life. The *psychê,* being form, is the "actuality" (*energeia*) of life, in the sense that it makes the body's potential for life actual. Together they make the living thing (414a).

In the other three metaphors Aristotle develops and extends this analysis. A house, for instance, combines the matter of bricks with certain structural principles to ensure that the house is sturdy, weatherproof, and so on. These structural principles serve as the form of the house, to be sure, but note that they are also closely related to the house's *function*—namely, that of being a shelter. A function, such as that of being a shelter, is defined by certain goals or aims, such as keeping one warm and dry. In short, functions are *final causes* in Aristotelian terms. Aristotle believed that formal and final causes are often interrelated in this way. The metaphors of the eye and the axe emphasize the functional aspect. Sight is clearly the function of the eye. "Being an axe" (i.e., having the capacity to chop) is the function of an axe. Note that in both cases the capacity to carry out their functions is also closely related to their forms.

This emphasis on function has led many to declare Aristotle to be the first psychological "functionalist," a term very popular in psychology today. If there is a sense in which this claim is true, however, it is important not to confuse Aristotle's precise formulation of functionalism with either that of the early-twentieth-century American psychologists like John Dewey, James Rowland Angell, Harvey A. Carr, and Edward Lee Thorndike, who focused on the *evolutionary* function of psychological processes, or with the *computational* functionalism of contemporary artificial intelligence researchers and allied philosophical psychologists (but see Shields, 1990).

Exactly how we are to understand the claim that the *psychê* is the final cause of life is not entirely clear. Aristotle attempts to elucidate it with his concept of "*entelecheia*," which denotes an end-state of completion or perfection. The *psychê*, he says, is "the first *entelecheia* of a natural body that potentially has life" (412a). In an attempt to elucidate this idea further, he later says that "the *entelecheia* of each thing is naturally inherent in its potentiality, that is in its own matter" (414a). Aristotle seems to be saying that in causing (broadly speaking) a body to live, the *psychê* actualizes and completes the potential that the body possesses, namely, that of being a living thing. It makes actual the body's "purpose" or "goal" (*telos*) of being alive, and thus it operates as the final cause of life.

Does the Psychê Have Parts?

This general analysis of life is important for understanding Aristotle's approach to the topic, but it fails to tell us very much about specific living things. For instance, it does not tell us what distinguishes the life of, say, a plant from that of a lizard or of a person. Aristotle provides a number of more concrete definitions of life. At one point he defines life as "self-nourishment, growth, and decay" (412a). He later gives an expanded definition: "We say that a thing is alive if, for instance, there is intellect or perception or spatial movement and rest or indeed movement connected with nourishment and growth and decay" (413a). Each of these are presumably different functions of the *psychê,* so the key question in giving a concrete account of life is that of giving an account of the various functions of the *psychê* itself. Aristotle says, "[T]he *psychê* comprises cognition, perception and the belief-states. It also comprises appetite, wishing and the desire-states in general. It is the source of locomotion for animals, as also of growth, flourishing, and decay" (411a). But a question immediately arises:

> Is each of these the business *of the whole psychê?* Is it with the whole *psychê* that we think and perceive and are moved and perform and are affected by each of the others? Or do we do different things with different parts? . . . But, if it does have parts, what then can it be that holds it together at any time. (411b)

If there were parts to the *psychê,* and if these parts were located in different parts of the body, then it might be possible to cut living things apart, leaving some functions in one part and other functions in other parts. He notes, however, that when plants and some insects are cut into pieces, the pieces continue to live as before, with the same array of faculties as the single life-form from which they arose. (It is probable that Aristotle was thinking of certain worms here, rather than insects in the strict contemporary sense of the word.) In the case of insects, he notes that "each of the parts has perception and spatial movement." Thus, it seemed to Aristotle that although the parts of the *psychê* are *functionally* discrete, they are not (at least not always) *spatially* so.

Aristotle's answer to this dilemma is to say that the functions of the *psychê* form a hierarchy of functionally distinct "faculties" of the *psychê.* The *psychês* of simple life-forms have only the most basic faculties. Those of more complex life-forms have more sophisticated faculties in addition to the basic ones. Plants, for instance, "go on living as long as they are able to take nourishment. This *faculty* can be separated from the others but the others cannot be separated from this in mortal things" (413a). That is, all living things have this nutritive faculty; what is more, although many have the nutritive faculty without having perception and the rest, none have perception without having the nutritive faculty. Nutrition is basic to life. It is the only faculty plants have.

In order to be an animal, Aristotle continues, a living thing must have perception as well. This is the second rung on Aristotle's hierarchy of faculties. Within the perceptive faculty, Aristotle then begins to build a subordinate hierarchy of the various senses. Touch, he says, is the most basic. All animals have the sense of touch, and no other senses are possible without it. Taste, he later says, is second because of its relation to nutrition (414b). The rest are not spelled out at this point in the text.

In general, he says, the *psychê* is defined by "the nutritive, perceptive, and intellective faculties and movement" (413b). It is not clear here if movement is to be considered a separate faculty, nor what the order of intellect and movement in the hierarchy is to be. Notice, however, that Aristotle's inclusion of growth and movement among the faculties of the *psychê* means that the *psychê* serves as a third of Aristotle's four causes of life. Above we saw that it is both a formal and final cause. As the cause of growth and movement, it is also the efficient cause. The body, as mentioned before, is the material cause, so according to Aristotle's own epistemology we now know essentially what life is. Still, there are many details to work out.

For one, the exact mix of elements to be included in the hierarchy is not stable. Above we saw that they were said to include nutrition, perception, intellect, and possibly movement. In discussing perception, however, Aristotle, makes a side comment on the relation of perception to other apparent functions of the *psychê* not yet discussed: "[I]f perception then also imagination and desire. (For where there is perception there is also pleasure and pain, and where there are these, of necessity also appetite)" (413b). Clearly, he thinks of pleasure and pain as being sensations of the same order as, or perhaps as a part of, touch and taste. How imagination works into this equation is not spelled out at all.

In the next chapter (II, 3), he says plainly that the *psychê* has *five* faculties: nutritive, perceptive, disderative (i.e., that of desire), locomotive, and intellective. This seems to be his definitive analysis of the situation, although it is often said that Aristotle postulated only three. He also says, however, that "the situation with imagination is unclear and must be discussed later on" (414b). Locomotion is the next highest rung on the ladder, above nutrition and perception. Interestingly, Aristotle only attributes it to "some animals." Finally, other animals are said to have, in addition, "the thinking faculty and intellect, such as man and any other creature there may be like him or superior to him." The exact structure of the hierarchy remains unclear, but in the chapters that follow these general comments, Aristotle details the operation, as he sees it, of each faculty. So let us now turn to them.

The Faculties of the Psychê

1. Nutrition.   Chapter 4 of Book II details the nutritive faculty. First Aristotle points out that it is responsible not only for the nourishment of the body but also for reproduction, of which he says, "[A]ll creatures desire this and for the sake of this do whatever they do in accordance with their nature" (415b). It seems here that he is attributing this primitive desire to all creatures, even plants, because he then uses the fact of a reproductive "drive" to bolster his claim that the *psychê* is the final, as well as the formal and efficient, cause of life. Since reproduction is that for the sake of which everything else is done, and since the *psychê* enables a body to do this, the *psychê* is itself the final cause—the reason for life itself, so to speak. Aristotle then embarks on a critique of the Empedoclean view of nutrition—does like nourish like, or do opposites nourish each other? He concludes that both views are partially true, but the details need not detain us here. At the end of the chapter, however, he makes the claim that digestion is the result of heat, "for which reason all ensouled [i.e., living] things have heat" (416b). This is hard to square with the fact, which must have been apparent even to Aristotle, that fish and plants do not have heat (although the formal distinction between cold-blooded and warm-blooded animals was not formalized until two millennia later). Aristotle never explains this apparent discrepancy, although he makes mention of a now-lost treatise on nutrition in which these things are explained.

2. Perception. The final eight chapters of Book II contain accounts of various aspects of sense perception. Chapters 5 and 6 serve primarily to make preliminary terminological distinctions. When we say that a person is a "perceiver," we can mean two distinct things. We can mean that this person has the *capacity* to perceive (i.e., has the right sensory equipment in working order), or we can mean that this person is *actually* perceiving right now. This first is only a "potentiality," to use Aristotle's term, the second an "actuality." To perceive is to be affected in a certain way by objects in the world, but the right potential must exist for perception to become an actuality. Specifically, Aristotle argues that the perceiving sense organ becomes "like" the thing it perceives; for example, to see green is for the eye, in some sense, to become green (418a).

Another distinction Aristotle makes is between those "sense-objects" (or "properties") that are special to particular senses and those that are common to all. Color, for instance, is special to sight, sound to hearing. "Movement, rest, number, shape, and size," he says, are "not special to any one sense but common to all." That is, one can *see* that something is big and moving toward one, and one could also *hear* or *feel* the same thing. He also mentions there being a third kind of sense-objects—those that are "incidental." The example he gives is of "the white thing's being the son of Diares" (418a). This is incidental because its being the son of Diares is incidental to its being white. That is, its being the son of Diares is really not part of perception proper at all.

Each of the next five chapters (7–11) covers one of the five senses. The beginning of the chapter on sight concentrates on the conditions necessary for vision. Color is said to be the main sense-object of sight, but there must be light for the color to be visible. Light poses a problem for Aristotle. Air and water, he notes, are transparent, but "it is not *as* water and air that these things are transparent but in that there is within them a nature that is the same in both these and the upper body [aether]. And light is the activity of this thing, of the transparent as transparent" (418b). Thus, he concludes, light is neither fire nor effluences, for these would imply that it is a kind of matter, but "the presence of fire or something like it in the transparent" (418b).

All this technical apparatus was put in place to help explain what Aristotle saw as a major problem with sight: It operates at a distance. Touch and taste require direct contact between the sense-object and the sense organ, but sight, as well as sound and smell, can detect things not in contact with the sense organs. The solution was to discover a *medium* of sight, something that reaches from the object sensed to the sense-organ and can transmit alterations from one to the other. Aristotle thought the medium of vision to be light (though understood as the activation of "the transparent" in air or water by fire): The object seen alters the light, the altered light alters something in the eye, and vision results. In a void, he argues, there could be no vision because there would be no transparent medium to actualize the light. "The same account can be given in the case of sound and smell," Aristotle claimed. The medium of sound was correctly said to be air. The medium of smell, however, Aristotle said, "has no name. For there is a common affection in air and water which relates to smell, just as the transparent relates to color, and this is present in both of them" (419a). Aristotle is not being entirely arbitrary here. He believed sea animals to have a sense of smell, so he reasoned that air, per se, could not be the medium of smell. The proposal of this nameless medium, present in both air and water, explained how it was that both air- and water-borne creatures could have a sense of smell. (See chapter 2 of Johansen, 1998, for an excellent discussion of the perceptual medium.)

In chapter 8, on hearing, Aristotle says that sound results from "a striking of solid bodies together and against the air" (419b). Echo, he says, is the result of air "bouncing back like a ball." He spends quite a bit of time explaining the action of the human voice. He argues that it must be the result of air being struck by the *psyche* itself, for "voice is a kind of sound *with meaning,* and not, like a cough, just of the inhaled air" (420b).

Aristotle has little to say about smell, in chapter 9. He notes that humans don't have a particularly good sense of smell compared to many animals. He also says that there is an analogy between taste and smell, but that taste "is more exact through its being a kind of touch" (421a). He then breaks into a defense of touch as being more accurate in humans than in any other creature, going so far as to link tactile sensitivity to intelligence itself. This explains, he says, why "those with hard skin are intellectually poor natured, those with soft skin the opposite" (421a). He then returns to smell, naming the primary smells as "acrid, bitter, sharp, and greasy" (421a). Although inhalation is required for humans to sense things by smell, this is a peculiarity of man alone. "This is clear," he says, "to those who make the experiment," which presumably he had done. "The bloodless animals, . . . [who] do not have respiration . . . do perceive smell. . . . It is necessary then that they smell but without breathing in" (421b). Chapter 10, on taste, is briefer still. Because taste is a contact sense, it is said to need no medium. But Aristotle then says that "nothing produces the sensation of flavor without moisture" (422a). This is in contrast to smell, which he says is "of the dry" (422a).

Finally we come to the sense that Aristotle regards as the most basic: touch. Aristotle first notes that touch is not really a single sense but many senses (contact, texture, temperature, etc.). If this is so, he reasons, then there must be more than one sense organ. Thus, flesh must not be the organ of touch, for it is too homogeneous. Flesh must, rather, be the *medium* of touch; the actual different sense organs lie within, and we perceive touch *through* the flesh rather than *with* it. Recall that the original justification for talk about media of perception was that some of them operate at a distance. Contact senses, such as touch and taste, seemed to be excluded. In the taste chapter, however, Aristotle said that moisture is necessary for taste, although he seemed to deny that moisture was the medium of taste. In the touch chapter, however, he says categorically, "[W]e indeed perceive everything through some intermediary, but in the case of the contact senses we fail to notice this" (423b). He finally clarifies the issue when he argues that just as the flesh is the medium of touch, not the organ, so the *tongue* is just the medium of taste, not the organ.

In the final chapter of Book II, having discussed each sense separately, Aristotle gives his general theory of perception. In essence, it is that *perception is the reception of the form of an object, without its matter.* He again explicitly invokes the analogy of the wax impression: The wax takes the shape of the thing pressed into it, but not the thing itself. Similarly, sight is the taking of the visible form of an object without taking the object itself. Analogous descriptions with respect to the other senses can be imagined as well.

Book III opens with two additional chapters on perception.[8] These deal with some general problems of perception. In the first chapter, Aristotle attempts to prove that the five senses we in fact have are all the senses that are possible. His proof may not be very convincing to modern readers, but future refinements of it would give rise to a theory about the relationship between senses and the material elements that dominated psychological thought into the eighteenth century—namely, that each sense is sensitive to one and only one of the elements. Aristotle couched his argument in terms of the various *media* of perception, outlined in the chapters of Book II. Later philosophers would reduce his argument to the idea that touch is sensitive to earth, taste to water, hearing to "thin" air, smell to "heavy" air (i.e., smoke), and sight to fire.[9] He then returns to the problem (from II, 6) of how "common" sense-objects are perceived, since they are not "special" to any one sense. He proposes that in addition to the five senses, there is a "common sense" that combines the things "incidentally" perceived by the five main senses. That is, although color is the special province of sight, information about size is "incidentally" picked up as well. This is passed on to the "common sense," where, in combination with the "incidental" perceptions of the other senses, size is perceived. Chapter 2 is occupied with the questions of how it is we can perceive *that* we are perceiving and how we know with which sense we are perceiving. Aristotle argues that there cannot be another sense-organ to perceive that we are perceiving because this would lead to an infinite regress of sense-organs (i.e., one to perceive that we perceive that we are perceiving, and so on). Consequently, sense organs must do double duty, so to speak—perceiving their special sense-objects *and* perceiving that they are perceiving as well.

3. Imagination.   One might expect chapter 3 to be about the next faculty in the hierarchy: movement. Instead, however, we move on to the issue that was strangely clouded at the beginning of Book II: the imagination. Aristotle begins by noting that most people of his time believed thinking to be a kind of perception. He argues that this is not so, however, because "while all animals have a share of [perception], only a few have a share of [thinking]" (427b). He also says that thinking is "enjoyed by no animal that does not also have rationality" (427b). He tries to show thought to be different from perception by arguing that thought can be either correct (as in "understanding, knowledge, and true opinion," he says) or incorrect (as in "their opposites"). Perception, by contrast, is almost always true. (He briefly mentions perceptual illusions, specifically that of the sun appearing to be smaller than the earth, but seems not to think that they refute his general claim.) Having made his distinction between perception and thinking, he goes on to claim that thought admits of two kinds: supposition and imagination. (It would now seem that the "understanding, knowledge, and true opinion," mentioned above, are all to be considered as species of "supposition.") He gives a number of arguments to show that imagination is different from perception. The most convincing is that one can imagine visual scenes when one's eyes are shut and no visual perception can take place. By the same token, imagination is not the same as knowledge or belief either. It is not the same as knowledge because knowledge is always true, and imagination need not be. It is not the same as belief because although belief can be false, it is accompanied by a sense of conviction, whereas imagination is not. Believing that a terrifying thing is nearby will be accompanied by terror; merely imagining that the same terrifying thing is nearby will not have the same emotional effect. Aristotle notes, "[I]t lies within our power to be affected by imagination whenever we wish . . . while holding beliefs is not up to us" (427b). If you doubt this, try believing—really believing, not just imagining—that you are a bird. If you think you are convinced that you are a bird, examine your behavior. Consider all the things you would do differently (e.g., jump off high window ledges expecting to fly) if you really believed yourself to be a bird.

Having carved out a place for imagination, Aristotle then goes on to say just what imagination is. Imagination, he says, seems to be a kind of movement in the sense-organs. Perception itself was thought to be such a movement, but one caused by things outside the organism. Imagination, by contrast, is a voluntary movement of the sense organs, causing them to respond *as though* they are perceiving. Because it is under voluntary control, however, the pseudo-perceptual results are not believed.

Aristotle does not discuss the issue of memory in *De Anima*, but this is an opportune place to bring it up. He presents his theory of memory in a small treatise called *On Memory and Recollection*. There, he says, "it is obvious that memory belongs to that part of the *psychê* to which imagination belongs" (450a).[10] It will be recalled, however, that imagination is the voluntary activation of one or more of the senses. Since memory necessarily involves the apprehension of time (namely, that whatever is being remembered occurred in the past), which sense is it that is activated? Because time is incidental to the five main senses, Aristotle argued, memory must involve activation of the common sense, for it can only be from here, he thought, that we derive our perception of time (450a).

4. Intellect. Chapters 4–6 of Book III are concerned with the intellect, which he calls *nous*. In apparent contrast to what he has already said on the topic, he begins by arguing that thinking is analogous to perceiving in that "it will either be some kind of affection [i.e., the intellect will be affected] by the thought-object or some such thing" (429a). He rapidly moves on to a major *dis*analogy, however. Unlike the sense organs, which are fully bodily and material, "that part of the *psychê* then that is called the intellect . . . is[,] before it thinks[,] in actuality *none of the things that exist* [italics added]. This makes it unreasonable that it be mixed with [i.e., be a part of] the body— for, if so, it would have to have some quality, being hot or cold, or indeed having some organ like the perceptive faculty, whereas it in fact has none" (429a). To repeat the point in, perhaps, simpler words, Aristotle is claiming that in order to have the capacity (or potential) to understand everything, the intellectual faculty must have no material (or actual) properties of its own, for these would interfere with its ability to know. He later explains this with a metaphor that has become, perhaps, the best known in all of psychology: "[T]he intellect is in a way potentially the objects of thought, but nothing in actuality before it thinks, and the potentiality is like that of the *tablet on which there is nothing actually written*" (429b–430a, italics added). This is the famed *tabula rasa,* or "blank slate," metaphor of the mind. It must have nothing on it, so the analogy goes, for knowledge to be written on to it freely. Contrary to the interpretation often given to this phrase, Aristotle was really not a radical empiricist; that is, he did not believe that everything in the mind is the result of sense perception. It is anything but clear, for instance, that the "thought-objects" referred to here are strictly the result of observation, as the strict empiricist would claim. The result of contemplation— the proof of the Pythagorean theorem, for instance—can serve as a thought-object as well.

Aristotle concludes the chapter with a telling comment about the "thought-objects." He says, "[E]ach of the objects of thought is potentially present in the things that have matter [namely, their forms], so that while they will not have intellect, which is a capacity for being such things without matter, the intellect will have within it the object of thought" (430a). That is, although material objects themselves potentially contain their own thought-objects, they are not able to think of themselves precisely because they are material. Only the intellect can use the thought-objects to think because it is without matter of any kind. This is as striking a defense of the immateriality of the mind as had ever been presented and would make Aristotle the most important of the Ancient scholars for both Muslim intellectuals and for the leaders of the Christian Church (after they had recovered his works from the Muslims around AD 1200).

In the next chapter (III, 5), Aristotle distinguishes between what he calls "active" and "passive" parts of the intellectual faculty. This distinction has caused no end of scholarly debate in the intervening two millennia. Aristotle gives the active intellect no specific function, other than to say that it is superior to the passive intellect because of its activity. He also says that it is the only part of the *psyché* that is "immortal and eternal" (430a).[11]

This is difficult to square with a comment early in Book II (contra the then-popular Pythagorean and Platonic beliefs about the *psyché*) that "it is quite clear then that the *psyché* is not separable from the animal" (413a). Indeed, given Aristotle's metaphysics, how could a form be separated from its matter and still continue to exist? Does the form of, say, a table exist after the table has been destroyed? Nevertheless, Aristotle immediately retreats somewhat from the position to which he seems to have committed himself, saying of the *psyché* that only "some parts of it are not [separable from the body], if it is its nature to have parts" (413a). He then declares that the intellect "alone admits of being separated, as that which is eternal from that which is perishable" (413b). Interestingly, it will be recalled, this was Plato's claim as well. Only the *logistikon* was said to be immortal. The *thumos* and *epthumetikon* were said to die with the body in the *Timaeus*.

Here (in III, 5), however, Aristotle restricts the immortal part to the *active* intellect only. It is difficult to know precisely what he means here, but he may have intended to say that the *capacity* to engage in intellectual activity is eternal, but that the result of this activity—the actual knowledge we gain during bodily life—is lost when our bodies die. The capacity itself is somehow divine, however, and lives on. This interpretation of this point would become crucial to both Muslims and Christians in the Middle Ages.

Theophrastus, Aristotle's primary student, connected the "active" intellect with the "unmoved mover" of Aristotle's metaphysics (see above), but Aristotle himself did not. Lawson-Tancred suggests that the inclusion of the distinction between the passive and active intellects here may have been "an afterthought, or even a later interpolation designed to bring the doctrine of *De Anima* in line with *Metaphysics* (Book Lambda)" (p. 204).[12] In chapter 6 Aristotle only repeats the point, found in his presumably earlier *De*

Interpretatione, that the "indivisible thoughts" (i.e., concepts) manipulated by the mind cannot themselves be true or false. Only combinations of them (i.e., propositions) have this property.

Chapter 7 serves as an appendix to the previous ones on the intellect. It is fragmentary, but its main claim seems to be that thinking always occurs in the form of images. Chapter 8 summarizes the section on the intellect. In it Aristotle argues that the *psychê* is like a hand. Because the hand is what allows one to use tools, it might be thought of as the "tool of tools." Similarly, the *psychê* is what allows one to use forms to think. It is, therefore, he says, the "form of forms" (432a). He also makes the remark that "if one perceived nothing one would learn and understand nothing." This shows just how far Aristotle had moved away from the position of his one-time teacher, Plato. For Plato, perception was considered a source of confusion. For Aristotle, it was the source (but, note, not the full actualization) of knowledge.

5. Movement. In chapter 10 Aristotle returns to the issue of bodily movement. Here, the issue is more confused than it seemed at the beginning of Book II, when the hierarchy of faculties was first proposed. Since then, we have been told that some movement—namely, growth and reproduction— is handled by the nutritive *psychê.* Imagination, too, we have been told is a kind of voluntary movement of the sense organs. Aristotle first redivides his faculties according to two superordinate capacities: that of discernment, into which he places perception and intellect, and that of locomotion, which he proposes to discuss here. Desire, he says, seems to be the initiator of movement, but he criticizes Plato's tripartite division of the *psychê,* as well as the more traditional division into rational and irrational parts, for implying that desire must then be divided among the various parts (the desire for nutrition, for perception, for movement, etc.). He argues that the division of desire among various parts of the *psychê* would be a "patent absurdity" (432b). Desire must be its own faculty. He then reminds us that he had proposed a separate desiderative faculty (in chapter 3) as a subordinate part of the perceptive *psychê.*

Movement, he says, "invariably has a purpose and is accompanied by imagination and desire" (432b). He goes on to argue that it must be a separate faculty because none of the other faculties discussed have the power, of themselves, to initiate purposive bodily movement.[13] Nevertheless, in the opening of chapter 10 he says that the two producers of movement are desire and intellect ("if we take the imagination as a kind of thinking," he now explains). It is a particular intellect at work here, however, directed at a particular end and distinct from pure contemplation. He then comments, "[A]ll desire is also purpose-directed. The object of desire is the point of departure for action," and thus, he concludes, "there is only one thing that really produces movement, the faculty of desire" (433a). So the faculties of desire and movement are one and the same part of the *psychê* (433b). The production of the object of desire, however, he leaves to the intellect and imagination. That is, an animal can move, per se, solely in virtue of its faculty of desire, but it cannot formulate desires (i.e., to give its movements an aim) without the faculty of intellect or that of what he now calls "perceptive imagination." It is not until the next chapter (III, 11), however, that he divides imagination into perceptive and deliberative kinds. Although the former, he argues, "is enjoyed no less by the other animals than by man" (433b), the latter is said to exist only in those with reason, in which it is used to make choices among imagined alternatives.

In the final two chapters Aristotle briefly summarizes his work and returns to the issue of perception. (These chapters appear to have originally been from somewhere in the middle of the book and mispositioned by later interpreters.) He again lays strong emphasis on the crucial importance of the sense of touch for all animals. Without it, he says, they would not be able to nourish themselves, and they would die.

If this account of Aristotle's psychological thought seems somewhat disjointed, it is because we have tried to stay as close to the text as possible, for the reader's benefit, rather than imposing on it a single consistent interpretation, as many other accounts do. *De Anima*'s inconsistencies and occasional downright obscurity allow for a wide array of interpretations. Evidence of this can be found in the huge philosophical literature that it has generated through the ages since. Through it all, however, one can see a brilliant mind of a single individual grappling with many of the problems of mind that continue to vex us and have served as the starting points of many modern attempts to solve them.

CONTEMPORARY DEBATE ABOUT ARISTOTLE'S THEORY OF THE *PSYCHÊ*

More so than any thinker thus far surveyed, Aristotle continues to provoke controversy. His theory of *psychê* is able to stir debate among philosophers of mind even today. We close this chapter with a discussion of only one of the more active of these debates. It has to do with just what sort of theory, in modern philosophical terms, Aristotle's is; that is, is Aristotle a materialist? a dualist? a functionalist? An important part of this debate concerns whether Aristotle had a concept of consciousness similar to our own, and if so, what part it may have played in his theory of the *psychê*.

What Sort of a Theory Is It?

Perhaps not surprisingly, the debate about what sort of theory Aristotle proposed has pretty well tracked the debate about what sort of a theory of mind is actually true. This is by no means a phenomenon unique to our own age; the complaint that Aristotle seems to be recruited to support whatever position a particular writer seems to hold dates back to the early Middle Ages, at least. The sixth-century Alexandrian Neoplatonist John Philoponus once noted that "commentators on Aristotle are inclined to try to attribute to him doctrines which they themselves think sound" (ca. 550/1991, p. 12).[14] Philoponus' assessment continues to ring true, and so we briefly explore its contemporary manifestations here.

First, however, let us review historically more significant options with respect to "the mind-body problem." Dualism is a position advanced by René Descartes (1596–1650) in the seventeenth century. It holds that there are separate "substances" corresponding to the body (namely, matter) and the mind. Descartes called this mental substance the *"res cogitans."* Descartes' position came under attack almost immediately. The most telling criticism had to do with how an immaterial substance, such as the mind was supposed to be, could cause a material substance, such as the body, to do anything? Cause, by Descartes' time, was generally thought of as a relationship that holds between to material objects alone. It would appear that Descartes' claim that a causal relationship holds between minds and bodies was metaphorical at best. Very soon people began working to develop monist theories—theories that posit only one kind of basic substance. There are, obviously, two basic monist alternatives: idealism, which posits that there is only mental substance (and that the body, and all other matter, is just a "projection," or some such, of the mind), and materialism, which posits that there is only material substance (and that the mind is somehow material, or it doesn't exist at all). One very well known materialist theory of the mind is behaviorism. Behaviorism holds that all mental talk (e.g., "Horatio *wants* to play baseball") is really just talk about dispositions to behave in certain ways (e.g., "Given appropriate conditions, Horatio is likely to play baseball").[15] Another materialist theory of mind, called physicalism, was also popular in the middle of the twentieth century.[16] Specifically, it holds that "all matter of fact and real existence can be formulated as statements about publicly observable physical objects and activities" (Flew, 1983, p. 267). One very strict form of physicalism holds that anything one says about the mind should, if one wants to be scientific, be redescribed as something about the brain. Put another way, mental events and brain events are *identical* with each other. For this reason this sort of physicalism is sometimes called "central state identity theory" (or just "identity theory" for short). One important implication of physicalism is that consciousness, if it exists at all, is wholly reducible to brain activity. At about the same time as physicalism rose to prominence, it also became popular to claim that Aristotle's theory was of renewed importance precisely because it had been physicalist, although Aristotle, or course, never said so specifically; he never seemed to say anything very specific about consciousness in *De Anima* or his other works. Many believe that this is so because the very concept of consciousness was not developed until well after Aristotle's time.

Jonathan Barnes (1979/1971–1972) countered that the argument for Aristotle's theory of the *psyché* having been physicalist is erroneous (p. 32). Although he conceded that Aristotle never proposed a mental substance, as had Descartes, this does not commit him to physicalism (p. 34). Instead, Barnes claimed, Aristotle's theory is both non-substantialist (i.e., there is no mental substance) *and* non-physicalist (i.e., the *psyché* is not completely redescribable in purely physical terms). For Barnes, the question, then, was to articulate a theory that is still materialist without being strictly physicalist. What he ultimately argued is that Aristotle's theory holds that the *psyché* is only an attribute or property of the matter of which the body is composed (in the sense that a functioning body can be said to have the property of being alive, but there is no particular material part that can be credited with giving life to the body). This position is sometimes called "property dualism" because although it denies that there is a mental *substance* of the sort that Descartes proposed, it accepts that there may be mental *properties* (such as consciousness) that are somehow products of the activity of the material body, especially the brain. Although Barnes denied believing that Aristotle's theory is correct, he said that it seems "at least as good a buy as anything else currently on the philosophical market. Philosophy of mind has for centuries been whirled between a Cartesian Charybdis and a scientific Scylla: Aristotle has the look of an Odysseus" (p. 41).[17]

Richard Sorabji (1974) has argued against both the traditional physicalist view of Aristotle's theory and Barnes' "attribute theory," as well as against the view, still held by some, that Aristotle was, in fact, a dualist of the Cartesian sort.[18] Instead, he claimed, "Aristotle's view is something *sui generis*. It is not to be identified with the positions of more recent philosophers" (p. 64). Sorabji was most impressed with Aristotle's comparison of the relation of the *psyché* and the body to that holding between a house and the bricks that make it up. These cannot be identical, as physicalism argues, because as Sorabji points out, the "bricks can outlast the house" (p. 78). Aristotle's view was not Cartesian either, however, because he believed the *psyché* to be dependent for its existence on the body in a way that Descartes did not (just as a house is dependent upon the bricks out of which it is made for its existence). Descartes believed the mind to be separable from the body, at least in principle. Aristotle states several times, however, that it is not (the problem of the "active intellect" notwithstanding). Thus, Sorabji claims, "Aristotle improves on some present-day materialists, and on Descartes" (p. 78). Sorabji's ultimate interpretation of Aristotle's theory is somewhat difficult to paraphrase briefly. He focuses on Aristotle's claim (in *On the Motion of Animals*) that desire is just a heating of the blood around the heart. This heating is said to cause an expansion that, in turn, moves the body. Given this account, Sorabji argues, the fact "that desire should cause movement is no more (and no less) puzzling that that heating around the heart would cause expansion. But if desires lead to movement, then there is a sense in which the *capacity for* desire is responsible for movement" (p. 86). The capacity itself is not material, although it is dependent upon being composed of particular materials, just as the house is dependent on being made of certain materials in order to satisfy its function of being a shelter (consider, for instance, a house made of tissues). Since Aristotle says repeatedly that the *psychê* is a set of functions or capacities (for nutrition, perception, etc.), Sorabji concludes that "this in turn means that the *soul* [*psychê*] is responsible for movement" (p. 86).

Even though Sorabji claimed not to want to assimilate Aristotle's theory to any modern one, H. M. Robinson (1978) argued that Sorabji's interpretation is very close to being "functionalist." Functionalism is a view of mind that rose to ascendancy when physicalism and behaviorism began to fall out of favor in the 1960s and 1970s.[19] Recall that behaviorism said that mental talk is just talk about dispositions to behave in certain ways. Functionalism is, in part, the claim that this is not good enough. A cone, for instance, might be said to have a "disposition" to fall over when set upon its point, but this does not justify mentalist descriptions of its behavior (*e.g.*, that it *wants* to fall). Thus, according to functionalists, the disposition must be accompanied by an "internal state" that can be said to tend to cause the behavior. That is, the *function* of the internal state is said to be to bring about the behavior of interest.[20] Psychology, then, is the study of the structure of these internal states, not just the identification of the dispositions for which they are responsible. In the 1970s the structures of these internal states began to be explored by attempts to simulate them with computer programs. The claim that the states must operate in the same way as computer programs is called "computational functionalism" and is the ground of much of the research done in contemporary cognitive science.[21]

H. M. Robinson (p. 115) argued that Aristotle's theory was not functionalist because Aristotle was crucially concerned with the issue of "awareness" (or consciousness) of sensations, something that functionalism denies or, at best, ignores. Notice that this view is exactly the opposite of that which led physicalists to show renewed interest in Aristotle's theory earlier in the century. In a later article H. M. Robinson (1983) argued that Aristotle's theory is, contrary to most late-twentieth-century interpretations, dualist after all. The primary piece of evidence for this view is Aristotle's account of the intellect, which is plainly said to be immaterial and (at the least the active intellect) separable from the body. So how could twentieth-century interpreters of Aristotle ever have thought him a materialist in the first place? Robinson (p. 124) said that they typically tried to dismiss the active intellect as the "unfortunate" effect of Aristotle's overall metaphysical position and as not central to his psychological theory in any case. Robinson (p. 127) went on that this was, in fact, *necessary* if Aristotle was to have an account of how people can think about abstract properties (such as a thing's being a triangle). Robinson did not believe Aristotle's dualism to have been equivalent to Descartes', however. It was, he said, "more sophisticated" (p. 132) than Descartes' because of the hylomorphic (i.e., matter and form) relationship posited between body and mind (rather than the simply coexisting mental and material substances of Descartes). Specifically, he said (pp. 141–142), for Aristotle the conscious subject is the *compound* of mind and body, rather than, as for Descartes, the mental substance alone, "trapped" somehow in the body. Thus, Aristotle's theory goes some way toward explaining why consciousness cannot exist (in any nontrivial sense) apart from a body (for it requires bodily sense organs in order to get thought-objects to be conscious of), whereas Descartes' theory implies that it could.

At least one recent philosopher disagrees with Robinson utterly. Christopher Shields (1990) argues, "Aristotle and contemporary functionalists share deep theoretical commitments. So deep are these commitments that it is fair to regard Aristotle as the first functionalist" (p. 19). In particular, Shields (p. 20) believes that Aristotle's theory was a response to theoretical pressures analogous to those that gave rise to contemporary functionalism— namely, to the need to remain within the confines of materialism and the recognition that physicalist versions of materialism are too constraining to be plausible. His response to H. M. Robinson's caution that Aristotle was committed to conscious phenomena that have no place in strict functionalism is that "weak" functionalism need not restrict the use of "mentalist vocabulary," as he puts it. In any case, he continues, because Aristotle sometimes presented definitions of mental states that do not include such vocabulary (such as anger being a heating of the blood around the heart), "there is reason to suppose that Aristotle accepts strong functionalism" (p. 28).

This battle continues. What we have presented here is only a taste of a debate that continues to be engaged on many sides (see, e.g., Durrant, 1993; Everson, 1995; Green, 1998; Irwin, 1991; Lawson-Tancred, 1986; Nussbaum & Rorty, 1992; Ostenfeld, 1987; D. N. Robinson, 1989). As can be seen, philosophers of mind of almost every stripe seem to continue to be eager to enlist Aristotle's theory on their side. The reasons for this are not entirely clear. To understand Aristotle is a laudable goal, but it is not likely to be much advanced by attempts to bring him "to heel" in contemporary debates about the mind. It seems dangerous to assume that a man who lived over 2,000 years ago, working in a very different language and culture, with conceptual schemes rather alien to our own, *could* have framed complex issues such as these in ways appropriate to our own time. The relationship between Aristotle's theory of *psyche* and our own current ones of *mind* (a difference in terms that is frequently forgotten) seems to be one of assimilation more than of similarity.

NOTES

1. Many of the details of Aristotle's life presented here follow from Bambrough (1963). Other sources are cited as necessary.

2. The question of the relative dating of Aristotle's works is considerably more difficult than it is for Plato's, in no small part because he seems to have continuously revised them throughout his life. See Kerferd (1967b) for a good, brief account.

3. For the sake of consistency I have dropped the quotation marks that were put around "position" here.

4. I have used W. D. Ross' (1942) translation (London: Oxford University Press).

5. Translation is from Sorabji (1988, p. 5).

6. Recall that the Greek letter upsilon can be transliterated as either *u* or *y*.

7. All quotations, with slight modification, are taken from Hugh Lawson-Tancred's translation (Penguin, 1986) unless otherwise specified.

8. The book and chapter divisions in *De Anima* were not the product of Aristotle himself but the additions of later editors. Thus, they may well not reflect the proper "punctuation" of his thought as he saw it.

9. It is most explicit in an illustration in Robert Fludd's *Faculties of the Mind* (1619), reproduced on the cover of D. N. Robinson (1986) and on p. 46 of Roney (1990).

10. Translation is W. S. Hett's (revised, 1957, Loeb Library).

11. He goes on to say, somewhat enigmatically, "though we have no memory." Presumably he means it is immortal and eternal, although we have no memory of anything the active intellect did *before* it came to be in the body. That is, he is claiming immortality of this one part of the *psychê* but rejecting Pythagoras' claim to have remembered past lives.

12. Summary of III, 5, in his translation of *De Anima* (Penguin, 1986).

13. As opposed to mere growth or decay.

14. We would like to thank Simon Kemp for pointing out the passage to us.

15. There are many different specific formulations of behaviorism. The one discussed here is the one entertained by philosophers, particularly Gilbert Ryle (1949), during the middle of the twentieth century. Others, formulated by psychologists such as Watson, Tolman, Hull, and Skinner, differ somewhat.

16. See, in particular, Feigl (1960/1970) and Smart (1959/1970).

17. Scylla and Charybdis were said in Greek myth to be two monsters that guard the Straits of Messina, between Italy and Sicily. The story of Odysseus' navigation past them is told in Book XII of the *Odyssey*.

18. Sorabji (p. 70), in fact, assimilates Barnes' view to that of the Cartesian, arguing that the true materialist (he cites Rorty, 1970) must give up talk of mental properties altogether.

19. Again, this should not be confused with the evolutionary functionalism of Dewey, Angell, and others in the early part of the twentieth century.

20. See, in particular, Armstrong (1968).

21. See, in particular, Putnam (1975) and Fodor (1968, 1975, 1981).

Chapter 5

Hellenistic Philosophy of the Mind and Soul

The vast majority of the works written about the antecedents of psychology in ancient thought have been focused on the best-known philosophers of the classical world, Plato and Aristotle. Relatively little attention is generally paid to the psychology of the later Hellenistic philosophers, the Stoics, Epicureans, and Skeptics, beyond some mention of the ethical systems of Epictetus or Marcus Aurelius, or some mention of a Hellenistic, physicalist reaction to the systems of Plato and Aristotle. Although focusing on the giants of fourth-century philosophy certainly has much to commend it, one should be cognizant of the fact that whereas much of Plato's work became blurred after his death, often inextricably intertwined with the mystical systems of Neoplatonism and early Christianity, and most of Aristotle's work was lost to scholars in the West for centuries following his death, it was Stoicism, Epicureanism, and Skepticism that reigned largely unchallenged during the years of the Pax Romana.

That having been said, recent years have shown a nearly exponential growth of scholarship on the philosophical schools of the Late Hellenistic era, and there has been a concomitant rise in availability of good source materials in translation.

FROM THE DEATH OF ALEXANDER TO THE END OF THE EARLY ROMAN EMPIRE

Alexander's Legacy

Alexander's conquests had taken him to the gates of India and enticed him with rumors of China beyond. However, after battling extensively more than two years' march from home, his army had finally had enough. Forced to return to the Mediterranean world, Alexander and his army limped westward to Babylon. There he died, in his thirty-third year, while contemplating an invasion of the Arabian peninsula before an eventual drive westward to Italy. The exact cause of his death is uncertain, although the most likely explanations are a long-term infection following an arrow wound he is known to have suffered while in the East, malaria contracted on the withdrawal back to Babylon, or syphilis. Regardless of how he died, he did so in sole possession of the largest land empire anyone in the Mediterranean world could envision, and with only one heir, an infant born while Alexander was away in the East. A popular though doubtless apocryphal tale relates that his generals gathered at Alexander's deathbed and asked to whom the empire was to go. He is said to have responded, "To the strongest."

Regardless of the truth or falsity of this story, Alexander's death did result in many years of bitter conflicts among his surviving relatives and his generals. One of these generals, Ptolemy, settled in Egypt and determined to hold its frontiers secure. The dynasty he founded would survive nearly three hundred years. The remainder of Alexander's European and Asian empire was hotly contested by a number of factions during a bloody period known to historians as the wars of the Diadochi, or successors.

The Hellenistic Monarchies

All these developments in the wake of Alexander's remarkable career were to become largely insignificant in light of an advancing power based in the western Mediterranean. The Roman Empire would consume nearly all Alexander's holdings, with the sole exception of the Far Eastern territories, which would form the nucleus of a new Persian Empire. Thus in just three centuries, all the political changes wrought in the eastern Mediterranean by Alexander and his successors would fade, although the legacy of Hellenistic culture would endure.

The most significant bulwark of this culture was the community of scholars that established themselves in Alexandria, the city established by Alexander the Great in the Nile Delta. Under the leadership of the early Ptolemies, Alexandria became the principal site of learning, embracing both scholarly and scientific investigations in the Museum, established for this purpose. The Museum quickly became not only a center of scholarly activity but also a repository of important texts, although the term "library" is somewhat misleadingly applied to this repository. It is at the Museum that Euclidean geometry and Hippocratic medicine reached their zenith. Here that Plato's dialogues, the histories of Herodotus and Thucydides, the works of the great tragedians, but not, alas, any of Aristotle's writings, were preserved. The Museum remained a center of scholarly activity for centuries and was not destroyed, as has often been asserted, by either Julius Caesar's legions or a fanatical Christian mob. Rather, it seems to have fallen into disuse with the general collapse of Mediterranean civilization, with the fall of the Roman

Empire, and to have been eventually destroyed by the Islamic Jihad in the seventh century, although most of the important works in the collection were lost long before this.

Greek was the common tongue of the various Near Eastern kingdoms and would remain the language of the eastern half of the Roman Empire for over 1,000 years. The intellectual traditions of the Eastern peoples were studied, but it was Greek philosophy, medicine, and science that would be the dominant themes in this region. Even Near Eastern religious traditions were absorbed into a Greek philosophical framework. The influence of Stoicism on the Judeo-Christian tradition can be seen in the Hebrew Bible, where the book of Ecclesiastes essentially recasts Judaism into Stoic form, an influence found in rabbinical Judaism to the present day. The influence of Stoicism on the New Testament is nowhere more clearly present than in the cosmological Christ of the Gospel of John, who prior to his incarnation is explicitly identified with the Stoic idea of the *Logos*. The influence of Neoplatonism on these traditions is discussed in chapter 7.

Meanwhile, in the West . . .

The Latin-speaking people of central Italy claimed descent from Prince Aeneas and his band of refugees from the sack of Troy. Recent ethnographic and linguistic analyses suggest, however, that the Roman people originated in the area north of the Danube and west of the Black Sea, among the peoples they would eventually war with, under the name of Dacia.

The traditional date for the founding of the city of Rome is 753 BC, when two brothers, Romulus and Remus, are said to have chosen the site among the rolling hills surrounding the Tiber River, doing so on the basis of an oracle involving sightings of vultures. Details of the early history of Rome are thus sketchy and inextricably entwined with mythology, but a few points can be established for certain. The initial settlement was quite small, occupying just one of the later "seven hills" of Rome. It was ruled by a monarchical dynasty called the Tarquins and stood at the head of a coalition of the Latin-speaking people of the Tiber valley, who were, in turn, surrounded on all sides by large, hostile groups: These included the culturally more advanced Etruscans to the immediate north; the head-hunting Celts to the north and east of them; and various warlike tribes of indigenous Italian peoples, most notably the Samnites in the central mountain range of the peninsula and the Campanii and Brutii in the south.

Rome began its series of wars of expansion and unification under the leadership of the Tarquin monarchy. In 510 BC a coalition of aristocratic families expelled the last of the Tarquins and the Roman Republic was born. Under the leadership of the newly created Senate, the Roman people went on to conquer the rest of the Italian peninsula by a series of wars against the Etruscans (capture of Veii in 396 BC), the survival of an invasion by Celts

(387 BC), the supression of rebellions among her Latin clients (340–338 BC), and three wars against the mountain-dwelling Samites (343 BC, 327–304 BC, and 298–290 BC). From 280 to 272 Rome weathered an invasion from one of Alexander's successor's, Pyrrhus of Epirus, who won most of his battles, but at such great cost that he eventually had to flee Italy. His name is associated with gainless victories to the present day. By this time Rome had subjugated most of Italy and begun colonizing efforts in Sicily and southern France, when she came into direct conflict with the other emerging power of the western Mediterranean: Carthage.

Centered on the Tunisian peninsula in North Africa, Carthage was primarily a maritime power in the process of creating an empire of trading colonies from Spain to Malta. Ethnically, the Carthaginians were Phoenician, leading to the Latinization of their name as Poenii and history's use of the Roman term "Punic Wars" to describe the lengthy series of conflicts between these two nascent giants. Rome fought three wars against Carthage (264–241 BC, 218–201 BC, and 149–146 BC) and experienced many humiliating defeats. Most notable was their humiliation by the Carthaginian general Hannibal, who defeated them at Cannae in 216 BC. Rome endured such setbacks, as well as the fruits of military triumphs and colonial conquest, before finally razing her hated enemy to the ground, salting the earth lest she rise for a fourth time. It was under the tempering of the Punic Wars that Rome acquired much of her distinctive character: escalating militarization, distrust of other nations and cultures, paranoia about invasion and insurrection, and unbridled expansionism.

By the middle of the first century BC, Rome had conquered most of the Mediterranean world, this under the leadership of several charismatic and ambitious generals whose armies owed more loyalty to their personal commanders than to the Roman state. Through a lengthy period of civil war, one of these commanders, Julius Caesar, eventually became the dominant figure in Roman society, a king in all but name. A group of conservative senators, worried by the prospect of a return to monarchy, assassinated Caesar in 44 BC, but it was already too late to save the Republic. Rome had grown too large, too fast, for the old constitution based on the government of a single city to cope. Having made contact with the large Eastern monarchies of Alexander's successors, the Roman people were attracted to their opulence, court life, and efficient bureaucracies. Caesar's nephew Octavian, who would later change his name to Augustus, was proclaimed Princeps (literally "First among equals") by the Senate, a step that heralded the birth of a new institution: the Roman Empire.

During the reign of Augustus and his immediate successors, the empire grew to its greatest expanse and entered a period of relative stability, punctuated only by the occasional war or revolt. Sadly, perhaps inevitably, things could not remain this way, and the Pax Romana eventually gave way under the burden of economic crises and internecine disputes among rival claimants for the imperial title. By the end of the first century AD the once invincible Roman Empire seemed on the verge of collapse, and it is interesting to note that at this dire time we find the imperial mantle resting on a Stoic philosopher, Marcus Aurelius (AD 161–180).

STOICISM

History of the School

The history of Stoicism can be divided into three general phases. In the earliest of these, the Old Stoa, are included the founder of the movement, Zeno of Citium (334–262 BC),[1] his student Cleanthes (331–232 BC), and his student Chrysippus (ca. 280–ca. 206 BC), the most prolific writer of the Old Stoa. None of the writings of these three remains intact with the exception of the philosophically unimportant *Hymn to Zeus* penned by Cleanthes. As a result we must reply upon writers of later periods of Stoic philosophy, particularly of the third or Roman Stoa, and upon general doxographers for information on this period. Of these sources, the most important are Sextus Empiricus, a Skeptical philosopher of the second century; Diogenes Laertius, author of the *Lives of the Philosophers,* in the third century; the Roman physician Galen (ca. AD 130–200); and Aëtius, a supposed biographer of the second century, used by later authors such as Stobaeus and the pseudo-Plutarch. Since these authors bring their own philosophical principles to bear in their descriptions of early Stoic thought, it must be apparent that much of what we believe about the three founders of this movement must be taken with a grain of salt. It seems, however, that it was during the period of the Old Stoa that most of the Stoics' work on physics and logic was completed. Because both logic and physics have an impact on Stoic psychological thought, we examine each in turn.

The second phase of Stoicism, the Middle Stoa, began with Posidonius of Rhodes (ca.135–50 BC) and Panaetius (ca.185–ca.110 BC), both of whom are important chiefly for the influence they had on the writings of Cicero (106–43 BC), who introduced Stoicism to the Roman world, where it would become the nearly unrivaled philosophy of the aristocracy and educated classes for centuries. The Middle Stoa can be characterized as a time of compromise, when Stoic ethics were softened to be more pragmatic, and when Stoicism was made more hospitable to the writings of Plato and Aristotle.

The third phase of Stoic history is known as the Roman Stoa and is best represented in the writings of Seneca the Younger (ca. AD 1–65), Epictetus (ca. AD 55–135) and the emperor Marcus Aurelius (AD 121–180). During this final period Stoic physics and logic were largely forgotten as Stoicism became an increasingly applied discipline whose goal was the perfecting and leading of an ethical life in the presence of difficult circumstances. It thus represents one of the first applied psychological movements in history.

It is important to note that while stressing the changes in emphasis of Stoic philosophy throughout its history, one should not forget that Stoicism, more than most philosophical schools before and since, always attempted to present a total philosophy embracing everything from the rules of cosmology to the rules of personal conduct within a single framework. The dominant theme of this philosophy remained unchanged throughout its history, namely, that the world is orderly. All things operate in accord with a universal reason, or *Logos*. Much of Stoic doctrine is thus presented in the language of reason, and so, accordingly, we turn first in our survey of Stoicism to a description of Stoic logic.

Stoic Logic

Aristotle had developed one of the first fully articulated systems of logical inference. His logic was based on categorical syllogisms—that is, on short formulas for arriving at true conclusions from true premises when arguing about categories of things, about either all or some members of those categories, making either positive or negative assertions about them. For example, one of his most famous syllogistic forms can be rendered:

All A are B.
All B are C.
Therefore all A are C.

Or to make the syllogism concrete:

All Athenians are Greeks.
All Greeks are men.
Therefore all Athenians are men.

Such a system has the advantage of allowing one to draw new valid conclusions on the basis of prior established conclusions without fear of making an erroneous inference. Other examples of syllogism apply to "Some" members of a class, rather than to "All," and premises can be phrased negatively as well as positively. Thus, for example:

All bankers are wealthy.
Some Athenians are not wealthy.
Therefore not all Athenians are bankers.

Discovering which syllogistic forms were valid and how widely they could be applied comprised the study of logic throughout the later Middle Ages. Unfortunately, powerful as it is, Aristotle's system can only be applied to classes of things, not to the individual things themselves or to their properties. Consider the most often quoted example of a syllogism:

All men are mortal.
Socrates is a man.
Therefore Socrates is mortal.

This is not technically a syllogism at all, however, for Socrates is an individual, not a class of individuals.

The Stoics developed a rival system of logic akin to modern propositional calculus. Stoic logic departed from the Aristotelian forms and concentrated on statements about individuals rather than classes. Such statements could be combined using connectives familiar to students of logic to produce valid conclusions when combined according to five forms of argument (see Table 5.1).

What all of the above forms have in common is that they are arguments about the contents of propositions, statements that are either true or false, (e.g., "It is day"). This distinguishes Stoic logic from that of Aristotle, in which the variables represent terms rather than propositions. Also worth noting are the types of connectives used to link these propositions. The first two argument forms use a connective called a conditional, which affirms one proposition on the basis of the truth of another proposition. Such conditional reasoning is quite different from the Aristotelian syllogism and much closer to modern propositional logic.

Table 5.1

Stoic Form	Modern Form	Concrete Example
If the first, then the second.	$p \rightarrow q$	If it is day, then it is light.
The first	p	It is day.
Therefore the second.	q	Therefore it is light.
If the first, then the second.	$p \rightarrow q$	If it is day, then it is light.
Not the second.	$\sim q$	It is not light.
Therefore not the first.	$\sim p$	Therefore it is not day.
Not both the first and the second.	$\sim(p\&q)$	It is not both day and night.
The first	p	It is day.
Therefore not the second.	$\sim q$	Therefore it is not night.
Either the first or the second.	p or* q	Either it is day or night.
The first	p	It is day.
Therefore not the second	$\sim q$	Therefore it is not night.
Either the first or the second.	p or* q	Either it is day or night.
Not the second	$\sim q$	It is not night.
Therefore the first.	p	Therefore it is day.

*It must be noted that the Stoics always used an exclusive disjunction, thus differing from contemporary propositional logic, which employs an inclusive disjunction symbolized by a vel (v).

Stoic Physics

As stated earlier, Stoicism always attempted to be a total system of philosophy. As such, principles from one branch of Stoic thought—logic or physics, for example—should inform scholarship in every other branch of thought. Nowhere is this integrative approach more apparent than in the most fundamental principle of Stoic physics: All things operate in accord with a universal reason, or *Logos*. Accordingly,

> [t]hey believe that there are two principles of the universe, the active and the passive. The passive, then, is unqualified substance i.e., matter, while the active is the rational principle [*logos*] in it, i.e., god. (Diogenes Laertius, *Lives of the Philosophers,* 7.134a, in Inwood & Gerson, 1988, p. 96)

It should be noted that the god referred to above bears no resemblance to the Olympian gods of orthodox Homeric Greek religion or indeed to any personal deity. Rather, as stated, it refers to a rational, organizing principle, one that holds sway above the apparent flux of the universe.

One might well ask how committed physicalists such as the Stoics could envision such a rational principle operating upon the cosmos. The answer is to be found in the Hellenistic doctrine of the *pneuma*. *Pneuma* is first alluded to in the writings of Aristotle, but it is the Stoics who most fully develop this construct. Essentially, it is conceived of as a material substance with properties of both fire and air, and it is thus often translated as warm breath. The *pneuma* permeates everything in the cosmos and brings about orderly organization according to the tension (*tonos*) it exhibits. The Stoics divided up the cosmos according to the degree of organizational tension each part exhibits. All matter, for example, was said to have at minimum the *hexis* level of organization. *Hexis* can be translated as state, and it is the level of *tonos* that gives iron its harness, gold its sheen, chalk its brittleness and whiteness; in short, all purely physical properties of objects are the result of the *hexis* level of *tonos*. Plants also exhibit *hexis,* but in addition they are capable of growth, nourishment, and reproduction and thus are said to exhibit *physis,* a higher level of *tonos*. Animals, capable of perceiving the world and forming impulses to action on the basis of this perception, are said to exhibit *psyche,* a yet higher level of *tonos*. Finally, humans, who are capable of exercising some control over their perceptions and impulses, are said to have *nous,* or reason. It should be noted that although what is being proposed is a single underlying substance under different levels of tension, permeating rocks and rational people alike, it is not tension, simply understood in the sense of physical cohesiveness. Clearly, what differentiates entities at each level of this hierarchy from those at other levels is the complexity of their organization and thus their flexibility of response.

One final point needs to be made about Stoic physical theory prior to discussing functionalism. Although the Stoics were uncompromising about the claim that what exists must exist as a physical body, they were willing to entertain the idea of things that did not exist in the strictest physical sense, but that were nonetheless real in their ontology. For example, Stoics accepted the existence of the void, although they banished this to beyond the fringes of the cosmos:

> [They say] that the cosmos is one, and limited at that, having a spherical shape; for that sort of thing is most fit for movement, as Posidonius, in book five of his *Account of Physics,* and the followers of Antipater, in their treatises on the cosmos, say. Spread around the outside of it is the unlimited void, which is incorporeal. (*Lives of the Philosophers,* 7.140a–b, in Inwood & Gerson, 1988, p. 97)

Likewise, other real things were said to be similarly non-corporeal.

The Stoics, though, thought that time is incorporeal. For they said that of "somethings" some are bodies and some are incorporeals, and they listed four kinds of incorporeals: *lekton* [things said] and void and place and time (Sextus Empiricus, *Adversus Methematicos,* 10.218, in Inwood & Gerson, 1988, p. 120).

Although willing to accept the reality of such non-bodily things, it cannot be stated too strongly that the Stoics were true physicalists, for whom only physical, existent, corporeal things could be involved in causal relationships. "According to them, the incorporeal can neither do anything nor have anything done to it" (*Adversus Methematicos,* 8.263, in Inwood & Gerson, 1988, p. 119).

Stoic Philosophy of Mind

According to Julia Annas, whose work *Hellenistic Philosophy of Mind* (1992) stands as the first serious attempt to discuss the psychological thought of post-Aristotelian antiquity, the Stoics had many similarities to the physicalist leaning of Aristotle's psychology but differed sharply from Aristotle in emphasizing the contents and processes of the mind, rather than its biological substrate. In short, in modern terminology they were more interested in cognitive than physiological psychology. Nonetheless, the Stoics were committed physicalists who attempted to ground their psychological theory in the most recent medical theories of their day. As stated previously, *pneuma* formed an important part of Hellenistic medical theory and was central to Stoic physics. According to the Stoics, at least from the time of Chrysippus on, the *pneuma* is seen as the physiological substrate of the mind. The soul, we are told, is the connate *pneuma* (i.e., the *pneuma* that is part of our body). The Stoics spend a great deal of time attempting to elaborate the way in which the connate *pneuma* is mixed with the other matter of our body. To accomplish this they contrast several possible types of mixture. This connate *pneuma* is said to permeate every part of the body, not in juxtaposition, with each part remaining distinct and separable, such as a mixture of wheat and beans; nor is it fused with the body as, for example, the ingredients flour, oil, and so on, become fused in bread dough, losing their own properties as they merge; rather, it is as a drop of wine diffused through the ocean, so that the whole becomes a blend of wine and salt water. (See Alexander, *On Mixture*, in Long & Sedley, 48C.)[2]

The Stoics introduce this idea of total blending so they might solve the problem of mental causation—that is, to explain how states of mind and states of the body can interact. In fact, their justification for asserting that the soul must be composed of a physical substrate is justified precisely on the ground of mental causation. The arguments of the early Stoic thinkers on this point are preserved in Nemesius when he reports:

> He [Cleanthes] also says: no incorporeal interacts with a body, and no body with an incorporeal, but one body interacts with another body. Now the soul interacts with the body when it is sick and being cut, and the body with the soul; thus when the soul feels shame and fear the body turns red and pale respectively. Therefore the soul is a body. (*De Natura Hominis*, 78, 7–79, 2, in Long & Sedley, 45C)

Again reporting a similar argument, he declares:

> Chrysippus says that death is the separation of soul from body. Now nothing incorporeal is separated from a body. For an incorporeal does not even make contact with a body. But the soul both makes contact with and is separated from the body. Therefore the soul is a body. (*De Natura Hominis*, 81, 6–10, in Long & Sedley, 45D)

Thus the soul is a body, or physical substance, and, recall, the Stoics drew upon contemporary medical theory to postulate the substance of *pneuma* as this physical substance. (More will be said about medical theories of the *pneuma* in chapter 6.) Interesting to note at this juncture is that when it came time to provide a physiological mechanism for the mental operations to be discussed shortly, the Stoic philosophers chose to consult the most recent medical theories. A similar trend can be noted in modern cognitive psychology.

The Stoics further divide the *pneuma* within a person into eight parts. Five of these parts are extensions of this tensed *pneuma* to the five major organs of sense—namely, eyes, ears, nose, tongue, and skin surface. The sixth part of the *pneuma* is an extension to the vocal apparatus, involved in the production of speech. The seventh part of the connate *pneuma* is an extension to the reproductive organs. And the eighth is a central organ of thought, called the leading part of the soul, or *hegemonikon*, said by various authors to reside in the heart (although Strato of Lampsacus, third leader of the

Lyceum, located it in the head). It is within the region of the *hegemonikon* that all thought takes place, with inputs arriving along the tensed extensions of *pneuma* from the senses and flowing outward toward the body along similarly tensed extensions of *pneuma*. The *hegemonikon* is likened to a spider at the center of its web, alert to vibrations of the strands. Diogenes Laertius tells us:

> According to the Stoics, "sense-perception" refers to [a] the *pneuma* which extends from the leading part to the senses and [b] the "grasp" which comes through the senses and [c] the equipment of the sense organs (which some people may be impaired in). And [d] their activation is also called sense-perception. According to them the grasp occurs [a] through sense-perception (in the case of white objects, black objects, rough objects, smooth objects) and [b] through reason (in the case of conclusions drawn through demonstration . . .). (*Lives of the Philosophers,* 7.52, in Inwood & Gerson, 1988, p. 81)[3]

The notion of "grasp" or assent is crucial to Stoic accounts of perception and keeps their theory, which is otherwise unabashedly empiricist, from concluding that humans are merely passive receivers of sensory information and are thus guided by fixed action patterns of stimulus and response. Indeed, the notion of presentations to the sensorium either being grasped or not is essential to save the minimal voluntarism necessary for Stoic ethics.

> The Stoics did not make sense-perception consist in presentation alone, but made its substance depend on assent; for perception is an assent to a perceptual presentation, the assent being voluntary. (Porphyry, *De Anima,* as quoted by Stobaeus, *Anthology,* 1.49.25, vol. 1, p. 349.23–27, in Inwood & Gerson, 1988, p. 91)

The key to understanding how such ardent determinists maintain the notion of voluntary assent to stimulus presentations is to understand what assent implies: Assent for the Stoics is the engagement of the *hegemonikon* in its role of rendering the data from the senses rationally comprehensible. Thus for the Stoics, perception is a two-stage process involving both the mechanics of sensation and the top-down processing of cognition.

Not all creatures capable of sense perception are capable of acting rationally upon the stimuli of sense, and it is this fundamental inseparability of reasoning from perception that is crucial for an appreciation of the functionalist nature of Stoic theory of mind. Diogenes Laertius furnishes us with confirmation of this point when he draws the following distinctions:

> According to them, some presentations are sensible, some are non-sensible. Those received through one or more sense organs are sensible; non-sensible are those which come through the intellect, for example, presentations of incorporeals and the other things grasped by reason. . . . Again, of presentations,

some are rational, some are non-rational. The presentations of rational animals
are rational, those of non-rational animals are non-rational. The rational, then,
are thoughts, and the irrational have no special name. (*Lives of the Philosophers,*
7.51, in Inwood & Gerson, 1988, p. 81)

Remembering that all sense perception, in human and beast alike, is oc-
curring because of physical stimulation of the *pneuma* within the organism
by outside causal agents, what does it mean to divide rational presentations
from irrational? In short, a simple, reflexive mechanist answer may suffice
to explain how sensory perception affects the organism and can thus presumably bring about action and, indeed, presumably does suffice for animals,
who have *pneuma* organized only at the level of *psyche*. What, then, is distinctive about human sensory presentations that necessitates an additional
level of pneumatic tension, the *nous*? The answer is that whereas in animals
sensory presentations leave their mark on the *pneuma*, participating in physical causal chains there, in humans an additional process occurs, one in which
these rational presentations, or thoughts, take on their distinctively mental
character. The process is one of representation in an internal language of
thought, a representation of events as propositions, the incorporeal *lekta*
(plural of *lekton*) mentioned in the earlier discussion on Stoic physics. According to Sextus Empiricus,

> They say that what subsists in accordance with a rational presentation is a thing
> said [*lekton*] and that a rational presentation is one according to which the
> content of a presentation can be made available to reason. (*Adversus Methe-
> maticos,* 8.70, in Inwood & Gerson, p. 122)

To this Diogenes Laertius adds,

> For the presentation is first and then the intellect, which is verbally expressive,
> puts into rational discourse what it experiences because of presentation. (*Lives
> of the Philosophers,* 7.49, in Inwood & Gerson, p. 81)

The *lekta*—from *legein* (like *logos* and "logic") and meaning roughly "the
sayable"—subsist as thoughts in the physical states of the *hegemonikon* and
should not be understood as words per se. Rather, in this context at least,
they are more like the meanings of propositions, for example, one's belief
that "All bankers are wealthy." The Stoics are very careful to distinguish *lekta*
from discourse in natural language, although even in natural language *lekta*
are the conveyors of meaning from speaker to listener. In Stoic theory of
language several important distinctions are made between utterances, speech,
rational discourse, and *lekta*. Again from Diogenes Laertius:

> Utterance and speech differ in that utterance also includes echoes, while only
> what is articulate [counts as] speech. And speech differs from rational discourse
> in that rational discourse is always significant, and speech [can] also [be] mean-

ingless, like the "word" blituri, while rational discourse cannot be. There is a difference between saying and verbalizing. For utterances are verbalized, while what is said are facts (which [is why they] are also "things said" [*lekta*]). (*Lives of the Philosophers*, 7.57, in Inwood & Gerson, p. 82)

The same term, *"lekta,"* is used throughout Stoic accounts of logic, as discussed above, to refer to the propositions. It is to the rules of their propositional logic that the phrase "rational discourse," used in the above selections, alludes. According to Stoic logicians, discourse is rational if it is composed of propositions linked with connectives according to one of the five previously described argument schemes known to preserve truth from some set of propositions, the premises, to a novel proposition, the conclusion. The implication is that internal rational discourse, subsisting in the physical substrate of the *hegemonikon,* proceeds according to these rules as well. Stoic propositional logic thus provides the compositional syntax for the language of thought.

Syntax alone, however, as some contemporary philosophers (e.g., John Searle, 1980) like to point out, is insufficient grounding for a theory of mind. There must be a semantic content to the language of thought. It should be apparent that the Stoic response to this would be that the semantic content of the *lekta* is their grounding in the physical, causal nexus of sensory presentations and impulses to action in the *pneuma,* in which they are said to subsist. All this sounds remarkably like computational functionalism, a modern account of the mind-body relationship.

This brings us to the nature of knowledge itself. As will perhaps not be surprising, according to the Stoics, knowledge is simply accreted with experience, remaining as physical-causal links in our *hegemonikon*. This point is made in a passage from Sextus Empiricus, contrasting truth and the true:

Some, and especially the Stoics, think that truth differs from the true [or what is true] in three ways: in substance, composition and power. In substance, in that truth is corporeal and the true incorporeal. And reasonably so, they say; for the true is a proposition and a proposition is a thing said [*lekton*]; a thing said is incorporeal. And again truth is a body in that it seems to be knowledge which declares all which is true; and all knowledge is the leading part of the soul [*hegemonikon*] in a certain state (as the hand in a certain state is thought of as a fist). (*Adversus Methematicos*, 7.38–39, in Inwood & Gerson, p. 121)

Thus knowledge is the representation of true propositions in the *hegemonikon*. This representation is accomplished by the alteration of the *hegemonikon*'s physical state, an alteration of its *tonos* presumably. Thus the intangible meanings of propositions, the incorporeal *lekta,* are capable of subsisting in the material substrate of the *pneuma* in the *hegemonikon*.

For the Stoics there is no separation of cognition and perception. At birth we have no knowledge, no thought, having had no experience. Aëtius reports that the Stoics likened the newborn soul to a blank sheet of paper, in a manner reminiscent of later empiricists evocation of a tabula rasa (See 11.1–2, Long and Sedley 39E). Single experiences build up in our memory in the form of preconceptions (*prolepsis*), the simple accreted bits of experience, being bound into rational concepts (*ennoiai*) or abstractions from experience according to several rules of association:

> It is by confrontation that we come to think of sense-objects. By similarity, things based on thoughts of something related, like Socrates on the basis of a picture. By analogy, sometimes by magnification, as in the case of Tityos and Cyplopes, sometimes by diminution, as in the case of the Pigmy; also the idea of the center of the earth arose by analogy on the basis of smaller spheres. By transposition, things like eyes on the chest. By combination, Hippocentaur. By opposition, death. Some things are conceived by transition, such as sayables and place. The idea of something just and good is acquired naturally. That of being without hands, for instance, by privation. (Diogenese Laertius, *Lives of the Philosophers,* 7.53, in Long & Sedley, 39D)

These rules of association allow for the production of the complex concepts and wide variety of thoughts that fill our mental life. How, then, did the Stoics address the other half of the problem of mental causation? How are these thoughts to drive out actions? According to the Stoics, our actions are the results of impulses (*horme*). They divide these into nonrational impulses, such as those that guide the actions of non-human animals, and rational impulses that motivate human action. As the names imply, the Stoic position is that action, like perception, is a rational process, best described in the language of reason. Even with the nonrational impulses of animals, Chryssipus cannot resist the temptation to introduce the vocabulary of logic into his description of a dog that "comes to a triple fork in the path, and, after sniffing the two paths which his quarry did not take, sets off at once down the third without even sniffing it. For the ancient philosopher says, the dog is in effect reasoning: 'either my quarry went this way, or this way, or this way. But neither this way, nor this way. Therefore this way'" (from Sextus Empiricus, *Outlines of Pyrrhonism,* 1.69, in Long & Sedley, 36E). It must be noted that although they made the analogy to human rational thought, the Stoics were adamant that animals did not reason in this way. The actions of the dog are to be understood in terms of the mechanical operation of the *pneuma* within it.

If the dog's impulses are to be understood as only like reasoning, what does it mean to say that human impulses are rational? According to the Stoics, impulse to action follows from the rules of logic. To feel an impulse to action is nothing more than to have an incomplete predication in mind. Let us consider, for example, the impulse to bake a loaf of bread. For the Stoics, this impulse takes the form of the incomplete predicate "is baking" within our *hegemonikon*. Such an incomplete predicate arose from the whole physical causal nexus of beliefs and desires instantiated in our connate *pneuma*. The predicate "is baking" cannot stand in isolation, however, and in completing the phrase with a subject, to something like "The bread dough is baking," we have our impulse to action. The motions of the *pneuma* necessary to complete this predication will, under normal circumstances, also lead to the bodily motions necessary to bring about this state of affairs. Should the drive to bake the bread be thwarted, for example, by my being tied up, the process would back up one step with the introduction of new incomplete predicates such as "is untied," which may necessitate "calls for help," and so on.

Impulses, then, are incomplete predicates, and actions are the conditions that bring about their completion. We are routinely presented with the metaphor of action as movement of the soul toward something. As for the locations of these operations, there was some dispute among the early Stoics as to the site of mental causation. We are told by Seneca that there was disagreement between Cleanthes and Chryssipus as to whether the commanding faculty itself or mere *pneuma* extending from it was responsible for the motion of the limbs (See for example *Letters* 113.25 SVF 2.836). For Cleanthes it was important to stress the continuum of action from the deliberations of the *hegemonikon* to the pneumatic tension moving the muscles. For Chrysippus, once the *hegemonikon* has succeeded in predication, the mental aspect of mental causation is essentially done.

The Passions of the Soul

The picture of impulse we have been presenting thus far is one of rational impulse. The Stoics, however, divided impulses into rational and irrational just as they had done with the presentations of perception. Rational impulses are those that follow the above scheme, presenting appropriate solutions to the problems raised by having incomplete predicates, or desires. The irrational impulses are those that provide impulses that are in some way inappropriate. The Stoics called such irrational impulses "passions," and according to Stobaeus they are "excessive and disobedient to the dictates of reason, or a movement of soul which is irrational and contrary to nature" (*Eclogae*, 2.88, in Long & Sedley, 65A). He goes on to explain that by irrational he means, not that they are not lawfully described by the same syntax as the rest of the language of thought, but merely that they are disobedient to reason, liable to overpower a person if left unchecked. In describing them as contrary to nature, he means contrary to reason, for they are excessive in their force and lead to predication that is unwarranted; in other words, passions are of such intensity that they lead to errors of reasoning, such as when one is deceived by one's senses. We are told, for example, that the state of distress is an impulse generated as though one were presented with an aversive stimulus, even when one is not present.

One might be tempted to ask whether there can be such a thing as a good passion according to the Stoics. The answer is that when impulses are under the control of reason and appropriately directed toward the right objects, then feelings can be said to be rational and good. For each species of irrational passion, we are told, there is an equivalent, more emotionally mature good feeling. For example, joy is the rational equivalent of pleasure, and watchfulness is the rational equivalent of fear. Just as the irrational passions have subspecies (e.g., pleasure at another's misfortune, self-gratification, and trickery are all subspecies of pleasure), so too are there subspecies of the good feelings (e.g., delight, sociability, and cheerfulness are all subspecies of joy). (See Stobaeus, *Eclogae,* 2.9, and Diogenes Laertius, *Lives of the Philosophers,* 7.116, for a full discussion.) How, then, does one gain control of one's passions and convert them to appropriate good feelings? The answer to this question is to be found in Stoic ethical philosophy.

Stoic Ethics

Most people who are acquainted with Stoic philosophy are acquainted with Stoic ethics. In fact, two works of later Roman Stoics, the *Handbook* of Epictetus and the *Meditations* of the Roman emperor Marcus Aurelius, have remained classics of Western thought and are still consulted by many as guides to life. Certainly this is a state of affairs that would have pleased both Roman writers, who felt they were producing in their philosophy a remedy for illnesses of the soul, illnesses common to all human experience. This "medical model" of philosophy has been discussed at length by Martha Nussbaum (1994), who refers to the whole spectrum of Hellenistic ethics in the title of her book as *The Therapy of Desire*.

As with the other two branches of Stoic philosophy, logic and physics, ethics proceeds from the assumption of a rational world. The *Logos* governs the world. The ethical life is one that is lived in accordance with the *Logos*. The question raised, then, is how to know what the *Logos* wants. To make sense of this question we must remember that the notion of *Logos* does not imply anything like a personified deity in the Judeo-Christian sense. The *Logos* is the principle of reason at work in the cosmos, just as *nous* is the principle of reason at work in an individual. The way to harmonize oneself with the *Logos,* then, seems clear. One must attempt to keep one's soul operating according to the dictates of one's *nous,* rather than under the sway of one's passions. How is one to cope with the vagaries of life? How is one to come to terms with the fact that bad things happen to good people? The answer is to be found in one's sense of duty and in the proper interpretation of events. Marcus Aurelius tells us that

[i]f the power of thought is universal among mankind, so likewise is the possession of reason, making us rational creatures. It follows, therefore, that this

reason speaks no less universally to us all with its "thou shalt" or "thou shalt not." So then there is a world-law; which in turn means that we are all fellow-citizens and share a common citizenship, and that the world is a single city. (*Meditations,* 4.4)[4]

From this sense of community with our fellow human beings comes the duty to treat all as one would treat kinsmen. Petty arguments over position or power, nationality, or religious creed are contrary to reason. Likewise in our personal lives, we are to perform our roles as members of a given class and occupation with the same sense of duty and responsibility as mandated by reason. What about becoming inflexible and fatalistic with such an outlook, unable to change in response to one's environment? Marcus Aurelius would answer that he never suggested we become thoughtless robots. Rather, by following one's duty in accordance with universal reason, one is freed to make the most of opportunities.

If the inward power that rules us be true to Nature, it will always adjust itself readily to the possibilities and opportunities offered by circumstance. It asks for no predeterminate material; in the pursuance of its aims it is willing to compromise; hindrances to its progress are merely converted into matter for its own use. (*Meditations,* 4.1)

How is such freedom in the face of circumstance possible while adhering to a notion of universal reason? Bear in mind that their are no random events in a world governed by *Logos,* and it will be apparent how attuning oneself to reason would highlight the best course of action under any circumstance. The key is not to judge an event as a surprise but to see it as part of a larger design. Then you will "take no event in hand at haphazard, or without regard to the principles governing its proper execution" (*Meditations,* 4.2).

Such a notion of duty to reason and such an appreciation of the inner logic of even the most arbitrary circumstance seem like at least a partial remedy to the human condition, but what about the fact that many of these arbitrary events will be quite injurious to oneself in a way that seems quite unfair? The key to self-mastery under seemingly arbitrary fortune is to recognize that there are events that are simply beyond one's control. Although one may not have complete sway over the exigencies of life, one can strive for control of one's inner mental life. Epictetus sums up this notion of self-mastery in the face of adversity quite well in the opening passage of his Handbook:

Some things are up to us and some are not up to us. Our opinions are up to us, and our impulses, desires, aversions—in short, whatever is our own doing. Our bodies are not up to us, nor are our possessions, our reputations, or our public offices, or, that is, whatever is not our own doing. The things that are up to us are by nature free, unhindered, and unimpeded; the things that are not up to us are weak, enslaved, hindered, not our own. So remember, if you think that things naturally enslaved are free or that things not your own are your own, you will be thwarted, miserable and upset, and will blame both gods and men. But if you think that only what is yours is yours, and that what is not your own is, just as it is, not your own, then no one will ever coerce you, no one will hinder you, you will blame no one, you will not accuse anyone you will not do a single thing unwillingly, you will have no enemies, and no one will harm you, because you will not be harmed at all. (*Handbook*, 1)[5]

By seeking to take charge, not of the course of events, but of your response to those events, including your perceptions of them and your impulses toward them, you can free yourself from irrational passions and live happily in accordance with reason, whatever may befall you. A similar theory of mental health has been expressed in the twentieth century by the psychologist Albert Ellis in his Rational Emotive Therapy (RET). According to the chief principles of RET, what matters in life are not one's experiences but, rather, one's interpretation of those experiences, something that Epictetus would agree is up to us. It is not surprising to find a connection in the thoughts of two theorists concerned with helping people through the vagaries of life, though separated by nearly 2,000 years. In fact, in this situation the influence of one theory on another is quite direct, for Ellis acknowledges Epictetus as one of the most formative influences on his life and career.

EPICUREANISM

History of the School

Epicureanism takes its name, perhaps not surprisingly, from that of its founder Epicurus (341–270 BC). Originally trained by one of Theophrastus' students in Aristotelian philosophy, he eventually left to pursue higher education with a mentor in Atomist doctrine (see chapter 2). Accordingly, much of Epicurus' writings are dependent upon the philosophy of Democritus as seen through an Aristotelian filter.

Epicurus began teaching in a garden attached to the home he purchased in Athens, and thus the Ancients often referred to his school of thought as the philosophy of The Garden. The school begun by Epicurus was never large. In addition, unlike other philosophical schools of the time, there were no donations or bequests accepted for its upkeep or for the pay of the masters. Rather, each senior philosopher connected with the school was expected to earn his own keep from fees for instruction and from publication of research. The result was a somewhat decentralized institution with none of the perks for central authority, which plagued the Academy and other schools at the time.

Epicureanism was never popular in the Roman world, and there were many writers, such as Cicero, who spent a great deal of ink decrying the school. It is from Roman sources, however, that we have most of our information about this philosophy. First, although contemptuous of the school, Cicero was at least intellectually honest enough to quote directly large sections of Epicurus' writings into his own polemics. Second, and most important, we have the epic poem of one of Epicurus' most ardent disciples, Lucretius (ca.100–ca.55 BC), called *On the Nature of the Universe.* This text contains our fullest account of Epicurean physics (including philosophy of mind) and ethics. Finally we have other testimonia such as poetical fragments from Philodemus and fragments of a wall inscribed with Epicurean maxims apparently commissioned by Diogenes of Oenoanda (not to be confused with the famous Cynic). We also have the usual sources for Hellenistic thought, such as the doxographer Diogenes Laertius, who preserved several complete letters of Epicurus in his *Lives of the Philosophers,* the most important of which is the *Letter to Herodotus,* in which Epicurus presents a summary of his physical and moral philosophy. Much of the material we have concerning Epicurus and his followers has come to us from the ruins of Pompeii and Herculaneum, which were destroyed by the eruption of Mount Vesuvius in 79 AD. There seemed to be a scholarly community of Epicureans present in Pompeii at the time of the catastrophe, and many of the texts we have were recovered from this library.

Epicurean Physics

As stated previously, most of Epicurus' education came from a latter-day follower of Democritus. As might be expected, much of Epicurean physics is taken directly from that of the fifth century Atomist (see chapter 2 for details). This physical system is quite elegantly summarized by Lucretius by his epic *On the Nature of the Universe* (see Books I and II) as a series of fourteen maxims:

1) There is no divine creation, only natural causes bring things about.
2) Nothing is ever truly destroyed, only reduced to constituent atoms.
3) Atoms are too small to be seen, but nonetheless exist.
4) Only physical objects are capable of interacting with one another.
5) The void also exists, but cannot interact with anything.
6) Only physical objects, and the void, exist.
7) Everything physical that exists is a solid atom, or composed of solid atoms.
8) The universe is infinite in scope.
9) There is a fixed, though infinite, quantity of physical matter in the universe.
10) Atoms are in motion.
11) Left to themselves, atoms fall toward the center of the universe (down colloquially), unless they suffer a collision, or swerve unpredictably.
12) There is conservation of both atoms and atomic motion.
13) Atoms vary in shape and size.
14) a) Although atoms themselves have no sensation, beings which experience sensations are nonetheless composed of them.

    b) Life and sensation take place in physical objects composed of atoms in an appropriate way.

    c) There is no external yardstick against which sensation could be measured, so it cannot be challenged. (Adapted from the translations in Gaskin, 1995, esp. p. xxivf)

Many of these maxims will seem familiar from the account of fifth-century Atomism in Chapter 2. Maxim number one is meant to be an affirmation of the system as physicalist—there will be no recourse to nonphysical entities in this cosmology. Numbers two, five, eleven, and thirteen present the reader with the general Atomist ontology of tiny indivisible particles, or atoms, and the empty space, or void, in which they move. The only properties of these particles are size, shape, and motion. All other properties are properly ascribed to compounds of these atoms. Maxims two, seven, and nine embody the general Atomistic response to the Eleatic challenge. Anything that exists must be permanent; change is possible, however, because we live in a macrocosm composed of compounds of changeless physical entities, the atoms. We think we see change, creation, and destruction all the time, but in reality we are witnessing only the recombination of basic particles. There are a few notable differences, however, between Epicurus' cosmos and that of Democritus. Maxims ten and eleven spell out the nature of atomic movement. According to Democritus, atoms move only in response to collisions with other atoms. According to Epicurus, in contrast, atoms are self-propelled according to three principles: Atoms fall down by their own weight. "Down" in this case means toward the center of any world system. Remember, the Epicurean universe is infinite, with infinitely many worlds each based on a vortex like our own (see chapter 2). In addition, atoms can be deflected upwards by collisions with other atoms and thus in principle generally circle the vortex. Finally, atoms can swerve in the downward trajectories at random times and by random amounts. This introduction of random error into atomic motion is an attempt by Epicurus to remove total determinism from his physical system. In so doing, he hoped to open up space for free will. This is crucial to Epicurus' ethical theory. Also added is a principle (number twelve) of conservation of mass and energy. The last three points, each traditionally considered a subpoint of maxim fourteen, have to do with the nature of consciousness in Epicurean Atomism, and so for further consideration of these, we turn to an examination of Epicurean philosophy of mind.

Epicurean Philosophy of Mind

The most important, single principle of Epicurean philosophy of mind is that for Epicurus, as for Democritus before him, the mind is composed of matter. The ontology of Epicurus' cosmos is purely physicalist. He reasons his way to this position from a consideration of mental causation, outlined in maxim four above. Since our minds are influenced by the material world and in turn influence the actions of our bodies, our minds must be bodies. Since all physical things, with distinguishable properties other than size and shape, are composed of compounds of atoms, so too must our mind be a compound. We are told that there are four kinds of atoms involved in the compound of the mind. The first three of these atoms are described by analogy to other physical atoms they are said to resemble. Accordingly, we are told that the mind contains atoms that are fire-like, air-like, and *pneuma*-like. The question remains how a unified mind could arise from such a physical composite, and to serve this integrative function, Epicurus introduces a fourth atom, which he called "nameless." Whereas most theorists, ancient and modern, are understandably resistant to the introduction of theoretical entities that defy description, Annas believes that the introduction of nameless atoms may be more benign than it seems. As a committed empiricist for whom only perceptible features are describable, Epicurus may simply have felt he had to abstain from attempting to describe something that defied perceptual analogy.

The mind is thus composed of these four kinds of atoms. What, then, is the nature of mental operation? Like Democritus, Epicurus believed that mental operations are atomic collisions. Principle among these are the collisions that result from sensory stimulation. And like the fifth-century Atomists, he held that physical objects give off effluences, thin atomic films, which when they strike the atoms making up the sensory organs give rise to sensations. For Epicurus there is nothing like the Stoic *hegemonikon*, however, to which such collisions must ultimately converge. Lucretius tells us that the eyes are not doors, out of which the mind sees (see Book III). Rather, we are told, it is the eyes themselves that see, the foot itself that feels pains.

The Epicureans do, however, make a distinction between the psychic atoms, which are thus operating peripherally, called the irrational soul, and those that operate centrally within us (usually said to be within our chests), called the rational soul. It is within the rational soul that images first perceived at the periphery can be recombined to form novel associations, memories, and dreams. Indeed, novel associations and images, collectively known as *"simulacra,"* can even form out of atomic collisions in thin air. Such images can penetrate to the core of a human mind and there be perceived and considered precisely as if initially presented through the senses. One of the important functions, then, of the rational soul is to make distinctions among those *simulacra* that are genuine and those that are the results of fancy or, indeed, of random atomic motions.

The process, though described as rational, must be understood to be purely mechanical. There is nothing like the Stoic language of thought, expressed in *lekta*. Memories are simply preserved (sometimes distorted) sensory images. It should also be noted that it is only in the rational soul that errors of understanding can occur, for it is only here that there is any recombining or editing of sensory images. The senses, for the Epicureans, can never be deceived; only the mind can be deceived about what the senses have faithfully reported. As Lucretius says:

> And yet do not grant that in this the eyes are a whit deceived. For it is theirs to see in what several spots there is light and shade: but whether it is the same light or not, whether it is the shadow which was here, that now passes there, or whether that rather comes to pass which I said a little before, this the reasoning of the mind alone must needs determine, nor can the eyes know that nature of things. Do not then be prone to impute to the eyes this fault in the mind. (*De Rerum Naturae*, III.379, in Gaskin, p. 167)[6]

Images become expressible in language, thus allowing the application of reason, only through repeated pairings of images with names we have given as labels for those images. Such pairings are known by a word Epicurus coined, which became an important part of Stoic accounts of thought and which we have previously encountered there: *"prolepsis."* This literally means "preconception" and refers to the fact that after repeated pairings of images with labels, the label itself will soon suffice to call up the image and, indeed, to function in cognitive operations (atomic collisions) as the image itself. Such *prolepsis* can arise not only for images derived from sensation but also for those images created by association or analogy within the rational soul. Thus we can have a *prolepsis* for an abstract concept like Truth or Justice, as easily as for Horse or Cart. In many ways these preconceptions fulfill the same role as the Ideas employed the theories of the British empiricist philosophers nearly 2,000 years later.

Action is also the result of the mind operating on images. Lucretius gives us this description of volition, taking as his example the impulse to walk:

> I say that first of all simulacra of walking fall upon our mind, and strike the mind, as we have said before. Then comes the will; for indeed no one begins to do anything, before the mind has seen beforehand what it will do, and inasmuch as it sees this beforehand, and image of the thing is formed. And so, when the mind stirs itself so that it wishes to start and step forward, it straightway strikes the force of the *anima* which is spread abroad in the whole body throughout limbs and frame. And that is easy to do, since it is held in union with it. Then the *anima* goes on and strikes the body and so little by little the whole mass is thrust forward and set in movement. (IV.880–891, in Gaskin, p. 215f.)

Note that the word *"anima"* is used throughout the above translation. This is the word that appears in Lucretius' poem, written in Latin, and which would have expressed the same concept as *psyché*, which would presumably have been used by Epicurus. Two important features are noteworthy here. First, the impulse to action is seen to be a part of the same causal chains governing all thought processes—namely, atomic motions reflecting concepts or ideas in the form of images. Second, there is the introduction of the will into this causal chain. For Epicurus it was crucial that mechanistic explanation not exclude the possibility of free will in making moral (or indeed any) decisions to act. Remember that precisely to avoid the problem of strict determinism Epicurus had introduced the swerve as a third force generating atomic motion. Free will is crucial to an understanding of Epicurean ethics, which we examine next.

Epicurean Ethics

Epicurus provides a brief synopsis of his ethical theory in another of his letters preserved for us by Diogenes Laertius. The *Letter to Menoeceus* is presented in Book 10, sections 121–135, of his *Lives of the Philosophers*. In this letter Epicurus explains that the ultimate goal of life is pleasure. This is not to be understood as wantonness or the pleasure from indulging one's every desire; it is, rather, pleasure that is to be found when one's soul is content. Such contentment comes from lack of desire, which in turn is the result of moderation and self-control.

> And we believe that self-sufficiency is a great good, not in order that we might make do with few things under all circumstances, but so that if we do not have a lot we can make do with few, being genuinely convinced that those who least need extravagance enjoy it most; and that everything natural is easy to obtain and whatever is groundless is hard to obtain; and that simple flavours provide a pleasure equal to that of an extravagant life-style when all pain from want is removed, and barley cakes and water provide the highest pleasure when someone in want takes them. Therefore, becoming accustomed to simple, not extravagant ways of life makes one completely healthy, makes man unhesitant in the fact of life's necessary duties, puts us in a better conditions for the times of extravagance which occasionally come along, and makes us fearless in the face of chance. (10.130–10.131, in Inwood & Gerson, p. 24f.)

Epicurus is aware of the possibility that his exhortations to seek pleasure could be misinterpreted as license. Indeed, many ancient critics charged that hedonism (the belief that pleasure is the ultimate aim) could not form the basis of an ethical system, certainly not for corruptible humans. To this day we use the term "epicure" as a pejorative term for one who is overindulgent in eating, drinking, sexual behaviour, and so on, although as can be seen from an examination of Epicurus' own writings this was not what he had in mind. In fact, the ethical system of the Epicureans leads to behavior not too dissimilar from that of the Stoics. Both seek moderation in lifestyle and a reasoned approach to the decisions of life. The important difference is that for the Stoics the goal was harmony with the universal *Logos,* whereas for the Epicureans, with their cosmos operating according to chance,their ultimate goal was freedom from the distress that accompanies feelings of want and fear.

Epicurean fearlessness is extended even to fear of one's own death. In perhaps one of the most famous passages of Epicurean thought, Epicurus himself argues, in words later echoed by Lucretius, that to fear death is the ultimate folly. Pleasure and pain depend upon sensation, and when dead all sensation ends. Therefore one can either experience both pleasure and pain, and thus be alive, or be dead and experience neither. "So death, the most frightening of bad things, is nothing to us; since when we exist, it is not yet present, and when present, we do not exist" (10.125, in Inwood & Gerson, p. 23).

STOICISM AND EPICUREANISM: A COMPARISON

In the present chapter we have examined two major schools of philosophy that appeared in the flowering of Hellenism following the career of Alexander the Great. Both have a great deal in common, including a desire to provide complete philosophies ranging from theories of the physical universe to what constitutes the ethical life. The following table (5.2) reviews key features distinguishing these two systems.

In addition to Stoicism and Epicureanism, several other philosophical systems came to prominence in the Hellenistic and Roman eras. First there were the schools that actively rejected the possibility of knowledge—the Cynics and the Skeptics—and in response to these came Neoplatonism, embodying the rejuvenated scholarship of Plato's academy, which took its cues from some of his less mainstream works. The first two schools of thought are discussed briefly next; the last, Neoplatonism, is covered in detail in chapter 7.

Table 5.2

	Stoicism	Epicureanism
Basic Physical Substance	*Pneuma* (Fire in some sources)	Atoms & Void
Organization of the Cosmos	*Logos*	Chance
Basic Unit of Thought	*Lekta* (Words)	Images
Primary Source of Knowledge	Reason	Observation
Basic Ethical Goal	Accordance with *Logos*	Pleasure
Basic Ethical Methods	Attention to duty	Moderation of want

THE REJECTION OF KNOWLEDGE

Skeptics

Skepticism in the Hellenistic world can generally be divided into two schools of thought. The first of these, Academic Skepticism, had its origins in the Middle Period of Plato's Academy (hence Academic) and taught that certain knowledge was in principle impossible—a sentiment that would hardly have found much sympathy with the school's founder. Based upon Socrates' assertion that if he was wise, it was only in that he knew he knew nothing, Academic Skepticism was advanced by such Middle Platonists as Arcesilaus (268–241 BC) and Carneades (213–129 BC). It is the writings of Cicero, himself a student at the Academy during this time, that have preserved the most of this tradition.

The second branch of Skepticism, founded by Pyrrho of Elis (360–275 BC) was appropriately enough called Pyrrhonian Skepticism or more often just Pyrrhonism. Pyrrhonism amounts to the claim that there exist inadequate data to judge whether knowledge is possible, and thus for the present we have no choice but to suspend such a judgment. Followers of this branch therefore held that it was wisest to avoid making any determinate claims in any field. This branch has been most thoroughly preserved in the writings of Sextus Empiricus (3rd c. AD), and it is this form of Skepticism that was most influential upon later Skeptical writers in the Renaissance and Enlightenment.

Cynics

The Cynics, like the Academic Skeptics, prided themselves in being followers of the pre-Platonic Socrates. The Cynics traced their lineage to a student of Socrates, Antisthenes (445–360 BC), who lived simply, in accordance with Socratic ideals of self-sufficiency and asceticism. The most famous of their number was Diogenes of Sinope (400–325 BC), who is famous for his outrageous public behavior, including living in the marketplace in a wine tub, eating scraps, urging the defacing of coinage, and wandering the streets in broad daylight bearing a lamp, searching for an honest man. His behavior caused him and his followers to be ascribed the name Cynic, from the Greek *kuon*, "dog." Cynicism made no claims about knowledge, arguing instead that the only goal should be a return to natural virtue, where natural was understood to mean the minimal social conventions necessary to keep people alive.

NOTES

1. Not to be confused with the student of Parmenides and writer of famous paradoxes Zeno of Elea (see chapter 2 for details).

2. Unless otherwise noted, all quotations in this section are taken from the translations by A. A. Long and D. N. Sedley, (1987), *The Hellenistic Philosophers, vol. 1.* References such as 45C are to their numbering scheme, which has the topic section numbered (e.g., 45 is the section on Body) and the selection within each topic identified by a letter.

3. Translation from B. Inwood and L. P. Gerson, (1988), *Hellenistic Philosophy: Introductory Readings,* p. 81.

4. All quotations from the *Meditations* are taken from the translation of Marcus Auerlius, *The Meditations* by Maxwell Staniforth (trans.) (1964), Penguin Classics.

5. All quotations from the *Handbook* are taken from the translation of Epictetus, *The Handbook* by Nicholas P. White (trans.) (1983), Hackett Publishing Co.

6. Translated by John Gaskin (1995) in *The Epicurean Philosophers,* Everyman.

Chapter 6

The Medical Tradition

The first chapters of this book recorded the historical dissociation of two traditions, one of poetry and the other of philosophy, each encompassing various perspectives on the human condition, and those issues that would in our times be collected under the heading of psychology. It is worth noting, however, that these were not the only two traditions of discourse to emerge in the Mediterranean world that dealt with these issues. In particular, a third tradition, that of rational medicine, arose almost in parallel with the development of philosophy, and it is to this development we now turn our focus. It would be impractical, to say the least, to attempt here, in the space of one short chapter in a book on psychology, to give a comprehensive history of medicine in antiquity. Accordingly, no such attempt is made. Rather, what follows is a brief survey of texts illustrating the development of rational medicine, as exemplified in the writings of Hippocrates and Galen, from earlier traditions, and the views of rational medicine on the nature of humanity. In the material that follows there is much that does not bear specifically on psychological issues; however, it is necessary to present enough of the general medical systems in order to make sense of those passages that do deal with issues we would consider psychological.

MEDICAL PRACTICE IN EARLY ANTIQUITY

The practices of the earliest human inhabitants of the Mediterranean basin that could be called medical are shrouded in the fog that encompasses so much of preliterate history. The clues we have to what these people thought about health and disease and how those thoughts connected to their psychological views can be drawn only from a few bits of material evidence, mostly in cave art, and the few primitive tools left us, as well as from the physical remains of these people themselves. The art and artifacts suggest a shamanistic tradition of healing, whereas the physical evidence suggests that somewhat sophisticated techniques of caring for those suffering from trauma must have existed. Skeletal remains have been found with set and healed fractures, but perhaps most intriguing are those remains pointing to an early surgical technique called trepanning (or trephining), which involved drilling or sawing holes into the skull of the patient. Whatever the reasons for this practice—and there is widespread speculation on that score—what remains remarkable is the evidence that at least some patients survived the procedure, for around some of these man-made holes there is evidence of healing and new bone growth (see Janssens, 1970, for a classic description of these finds).

Egypt and the Near East

It was from the earliest civilizations of the Fertile Crescent, from Egypt and Mesopotamia (Sumer and Babylon), that the first records of medical practice emerge. Many of these records retain the presumed shamanistic or at least spiritualistic character of an earlier age. It is clear that in many ways health and disease were considered the domain of the divine. For example, the *Ebers Papyrus* contains the following prayer that a bandaged wound will not become infected:

> O Isis, great in sorcery! Mayest thou loosen me, mayest thou deliver me from everything evil and vicious and red, from the spell of a god or from the spell of a goddess, of a dead man or of a dead woman, of a fiendish man or of a fiendish woman who will be fiendish within me, like thy loosening and thy delivering thy son Horus. (*Ebers Papyrus*, 1. Trans. Majno, 1991/1975, p. 127)

Similarly, in a passage from Mesopotamia we see the use of a clay figurine in Sumerian medicine. By linking the figurine with the disease and then carrying out the figure and destroying it, it was believed the demon responsible for the malady would be removed along with the figurine.

> Go, my son <i.e. Marduk>,
> Pull off a piece of clay from the deep,
> Fashion a figure of his bodily form and
> Place it on the loins of the sick man by night,
> At dawn make the "atonement" for his body,
> Perform the incantation of Eridu,
> Turn his face to the west,
> That the evil plague-demon which hath seized upon him
> May vanish away from him. (Sumerian incantation, Trans. Campbell Thomson, 1903–1904, vol. 2, p. 101)[1]

Table 6.1
Egyptian Medical Papyri*

Papyrus	Approximate Date	Contents
Kahun	1820 BC	Gynaecological
Ramesseum III,IV,V	1700 BC	Gynaecological, opthalmic and paediatric
Edwin Smith	1550 BC	Surgical, mainly trauma
Ebers	1500 BC	General, mainly medical
Hearst	1450 BC	General medical
London	1300 BC	Mainly medical
Carlsberg VIII	1300 BC	Gynaecological
Chester Beatty VI	1200 BC	Rectal diseases
Berlin	1200 BC	General medical
Brooklyn snake	300 BC	Snake bite
Crocodilopolis	AD 150	General
London and Leiden	AD 250	General medical and magical

*Adapted from Nunn, 1996, Table 2.1.

Although these examples stress the link between magical practice and theories of health and disease, it is important to note that it was in Egypt and Mesopotamia that the first seeds of rational medicine, as a separate professional practice and style of discourse, were first sown. We have in our possession many papyri from Egypt that deal with medical themes. These are summarized in the Table 6.1.

These papyri do contain many magical formulas—for example, the quoted passage from the *Ebers Papyrus*—yet they contain as well much that is of a more modern clinical nature. For example, the Kahun papyrus contains much practical lore gathered by its author on pregnancy and childbirth. The most famous of these, the Edwin Smith papyrus, contains quite specific descriptions of medical cases, laying the foundation for later cases books and sources for epidemiology, as well as a list of impressive surgical interventions that might be attempted. Similar documents have been recovered from other cultures in the ancient Near East, most notably Assyria and the Hittite empire, which point to a growing appreciation of the need to keep records of diseases and their progress, as well as of potential therapeutics.

Homeric Medicine

The earliest discussion of health and disease in the Greek world is, perhaps not surprisingly, found in Homer. Here, the themes of the connection between disease and the supernatural are evident. For example, the inciting incident of the *Iliad* is a plague caused by the god Apollo:

The arrows rattled on the shoulders of the angry god when he moved and his coming was like the night. Then he sat down apart from the ships and let fly a shaft. Terrible was the twang of the silver bow. He attacked the mules first and the swift dogs, but then he loosed his piercing shafts upon the men themselves and shot them down and continually the pyres of the dead thickly burned. For nine days the missiles of the god ranged throughout the host. (*Iliad*, 1.46–53, in Longrigg, 1998, p. 8)

In other passages it is made clear that in addition to having the ability to slay with disease, Apollo is also a healer.

So he spoke in prayer and Phoebus Apollo heard him. Straightaway he made his pains cease and staunched the black blood that flowed from his grievous wound and put strength in his heart. Glaucus knew in his mind and rejoiced that the great god had swiftly heard his prayer. (*Iliad*, 16.527–531, in Longrigg, 1998, p. 10)

Asclepius and the Healing Cults

Other examples of pre-rational medicine in Greek society are the numerous healing cults prevalent in Ancient Greece. The most influential of these was the cult of Asclepius, held to have been a human physician taught by the centaur Cheiron and later deified for his efforts on behalf of humankind. Such cults often flourished side by side with the growing practice of lay healer and physicians and were, in fact, often used as a last resort to human medicine:

No longer counting upon mortal skill, I placed all my hope in divinity. I left Athens [and] . . . I came, Asclepius, into your sacred wood and I was cured in three <nights?> of a wound that I had in my head for a year. (*Palatine Anthology*, VI.330, in Longrigg, 1998, p. 13)

In other cases the healing cults were used when a miracle was thought necessary. One tale, for example, tells of the search for a miraculous cure by one visitor to the cult of Asclepius:

A woman had a worm and the cleverest of the physicians despaired of curing her. So she went to Epidaurus and begged the god to free her from the parasite. The god was not there, but the attendants made her lie down where the god was in the habit of healing the suppliants and she lay quiet as she was enjoined. But the servants of the god began to treat her and removed her head from her neck. Then one of them inserted his hand and drew out the worm, a great brute of a beast. But they were no longer able to fit the head in place and restore it to its usual fitting. Then the god arrived and was angry with them for undertaking a task beyond their wisdom and he himself with the irresistible power of a god restored the head to the body and raised up the suppliant. (Aelian, *Nature of Animals* IX.33.1, in Longrigg, 1998, p. 12)

Such tales were commonplace throughout the Hellenic and Hellenistic eras, indicating the continuing popularity of cultic rituals even as the rational medicine of Hippocrates and his followers was becoming ever more prevalent.[2] The evolution of rational medicine from these cultic and poetic beginnings paralleled the dissociation of philosophy from its roots in poetry, and thus it is to the early philosophers that we must turn for the next chapter in this history.

PHILOSOPHY AND THE DEVELOPMENT OF RATIONAL MEDICINE

As mentioned in chapter 2, biographers and fellow philosophers described Empedocles as a physician. It therefore comes as no surprise that it is in the fragments attributed to Empedocles that we find the first clear attempts at medicalization or naturalization of many disorders previously thought to be of supernatural origin. For example, one of the testimonials of Empedocles, a doxographic fragment from Caelius Aurelianus (a later Roman physician) in his *On Chronic Diseases,* shows that this connection was acknowledged even in antiquity.

> Likewise, following Empedocles, they say that one form of madness comes about from the purification of the soul and another from mental aberration arising from a bodily cause or indisposition. It is this latter form of madness that we shall now consider. The Greeks call it *mania,* because it produces great mental anguish (which they name *ania*); or because there is excessive relaxation of the soul or mind. (For they call that which is relaxed or soft *manos.*) (Empedocles, DK31A98, in Longrigg, 1998, p. 27)

Note that the author does not completely discount supernatural causation for some forms of madness but indeed implies that neither did Empedocles. Further, it is worth noting the connection between the notion of madness as the result of relaxation and the Stoic view of *tonos* discussed in chapter 5.

Alcmeon of Croton, discussed earlier as one of the influences on Plato's view of the immortality of the *psychê,* incorporates a theory of health as a unity of opposites, anticipating somewhat the Hippocratic theory:

> Health is the equality of rights of the functions, wet-dry, cold-hot, bitter-sweet and the rest; but single rule among them causes disease; the single rule of either pair is deleterious. Disease occurs sometimes from an internal cause such as excess of heat or cold, sometimes from an external cause such as excess or deficiency of food, sometimes in a certain part, such as blood, marrow or brain; but these

parts also are sometimes affected by external causes, such as certain waters or a particular site or fatigue or constraint or similar reasons. But health is the harmonious mixture of the qualities. (Alcmaeon, DK24 B4, in Freeman, p. 40f)[3]

Returning to Empedocles, we see an early identification of health and human physiology with his four physical elements:

> Empedocles says that flesh originates from the four elements mixed in equal proportions; sinews from fire and earth mixed with double the amount of water; the claws of animals come into being from the sinews in so far as they happen to be chilled by contact with the air; bones from two parts of water and two of earth but four of fire; these parts being mixed with the earth. Sweat and tears come from blood as it dissolves and melts away according to its fluidity. (Empedocles, DK31 A78, in Longrigg 1998, p. 35)[4]

A four-element theory of human nature will be a prominent feature of the most famous writer in the Greek medical tradition, Hippocrates. Accordingly, we now turn to the man later generations would revere as the father of medicine.

HIPPOCRATES OF COS (CA. 460–370 BC)

The Hippocratic Corpus

Although Hippocrates is doubtless the most famous name in any history of medicine, surprisingly little know about him as a person. What we do know about him comes largely from later commentators and historians of medicine, whose testimony is of dubious reliability.

Plato in his dialogue *Protagoras* speaks to an interlocutor also named Hippocrates about his famous namesake. He identifies the famous Hippocrates as being from the island of Cos, an Ascleipiad, and a doctor. We have no way of knowing whether the appellation Ascleipiad (i.e., a follower of Asclepius) is meant here to imply that Hippocrates was a practicing member of that cult or whether Plato is merely speaking metaphorically of his reputation as a healer.

Aristotle also makes reference to Hippocrates, but he gives no biographical details. In the *Politics,* he uses Hippocrates' being noted as a good doctor, rather than as a good man, as an example of functional categorization. Aristotle's pupil Meno was a historian of medicine, and according to him Hippocrates would be an approximate contemporary of Socrates.

An anonymous biography, previously attributed to Soranus of Ephesus but since refuted, refers to Hipporcrates as a patriot who refused to treat the Persian king Artaxerxes. In the same passage he refers to his treatment of King Perdiccas of Macedon as evidence of his eminence.

Finally, the *Decree of the Athenians* extends honorary Athenian citizenship to Hippocrates of Cos and offers perpetual welcome to his descendents and pupils in recognition of his service to all Greeks.

What we do have in our possession is a large number of documents that have come to be known as the Hippocratic Corpus. These diverse treatises, largely composed between 430 and 330 BC, are clearly not the work of one man. There are three primary sources of evidence for this. First, in some cases authorship can be established by independent means; for example, it is generally accepted that Hippocrates' son-in-law, Polybus, was the author of the majority of *The Nature of Man*. Second, the treatises contain many conflicting passages clearly representing in some cases opposing medical theories. Finally, based upon their contents, some of the documents must be considerably later in origin; *The Heart,* for example, could not possibly have been written prior to the anatomical investigations at Alexandria. What in the treatises was genuine to Hippocrates seems to have been a question even in ancient times, for many later commentators, such as Galen, write about it. Then as now, however, the common practice was simply to accept that the writings had no singular author, yet nonetheless to continue to attribute them to Hippocrates (throughout this chapter we maintain this tradition, and henceforth all references to the Corpus identify Hippocrates as author). Whoever may have penned it, doubtless the most famous of the Hippocratic writings is *The Oath:*

I Swear by Apollo the healer, by Asclepius, by Health and all the powers of healing, and call to witness all the gods and goddesses that I may keep this Oath and Promise to the best of my ability and judgment.

I will pay the same respect to my master in the Science as to my parents and share my life with him and pay all my debts to him. I will regard his sons as my brothers and teach them the Science, if they desire to learn it, without fee or contract. I will hand on precepts, lectures and all other learning to my sons, to those of my master and to those pupils duly apprenticed and sworn, and to none other.

I will use my power to help the sick to the best of my ability and judgement; I will abstain form harming or wronging any man by it.

I will not give a fatal draught to anyone if I am asked, nor will I suggest any such thing. Neither will I give a woman means to procure an abortion.

I will be chaste and religious in my life and in my practice.

I will not cut, even for the stone, but I will leave such procedures to the practitioners of that craft.

Whenever I go into a house, I will go to help the sick and never with the intention of doing harm or injury. I will not abuse my position to indulge in sexual contracts with the bodies of women or of men, whether they be freemen or slaves.

Whatever I see or hear, professionally or privately, which ought not to be divulged, I will keep secret and tell no one.

> If, therefore, I observe this Oath and do not violate it, may I prosper both in my life and in my profession, earning good repute among all men for all time. If I transgress and forswear this Oath, may my lot be otherwise. (Hippocrates, *The Oath*, p. 67)[5]

What is important for our purposes is not the oath's general or even specific exhortations to moral behavior for physicians but, rather, the clear tone that medicine was to be seen as a separate branch of knowledge, with its own teachings and traditions, separate not only from earlier therapeutic traditions such as the healing cults but also from sister traditions such as surgery. Hippocrates having made a claim to a unique discipline, the question for us becomes, what sort of discipline will this be? A primary characteristic, distinguishing medicine not only from poetry and superstition but also from philosophy, is its epistemological stance, as presented in the text *The Science of Medicine*.

The Science of Medicine

Epistemology

Despite his clear debt to pre-Socratic philosophy, mentioned above, in the development of rational medicine Hippocrates demonstrates little patience with the philosophical discourse of his day. In fact, in his treatise *Ancient Medicine* he claims that the primary problem with medical traditions older than his was their tendency to proceed from a set of theoretical principles. Hippocrates chooses, instead, to state his position with the blunt empirical outlook common to many modern physicians. On the question of what can be said to exist, for example, he takes the position that only what can be observed is real:

> But may not the truth by something like this: what exists is always visible and recognizable, and what does not exist is neither visible nor recognizable? The activities of the sciences that are taught are things that can be seen and there is none that is not visible in one form or another. (Hippocrates, *The Science of Medicine*, 2, p. 139f.)

He continues this line of reasoning to attack any doctrine such as Plato's theory of Forms, which suggests that the identities of things are somehow timeless and preeminent, instead emphasizing the physical constitution of things as their determinant:

> I at least am of the opinion that it is from the visible forms of things that they take their names. It is absurd to suppose that forms spring from names that were impossible since names are adopted by convention, whereas forms are not invented but are characteristic of those things from which they spring. (*The Science of Medicine*, 2, p. 140)

He does not, however, let his belief in the power of raw empiricism blind him to the fact that very often physicians will have to make inferences about the nature of illnesses confronting them. In fact, one of the principle distinctions he draws in *The Science of Medicine* is between external diseases, which manifest clear visible signs, and internal diseases that must be diagnosed from reported symptoms and not direct observation. For example:

> What escapes our vision we must grasp by mental sight, and the physician, being unable to see the nature of the disease nor to be told of it, must have recourse to reasoning from the symptoms with which he is presented. (*The Science of Medicine*, 11, p. 145)

Regardless of his acknowledgment of the need for reason, Hippocrates remains, first and foremost, a committed empiricist. It must be noted, however, that this empiricism is itself not to be taken as a strongly argued philosophical position. Rather, as suggested by this discussion of epistemology, much of the Hippocratic writing on the nature of medicine is a deliberate attempt to distance the discourse of this field from that of philosophy altogether.

One final point worth noting is that in contrast to many of his contemporary thinkers, with the notable exception of the Atomists, Hippocrates is a thoroughgoing determinist. "Indeed, upon examination, the reality of chance disappears. Every phenomenon will be found to have some cause, and if it has a cause, chance can be no more than an empty name" (*The Science of Medicine*, 6, p. 142). This determinism, coupled with the aforementioned empiricism, permeates the whole of the Hippocratic Corpus.

The Nature of the New Medicine

The treatise entitled *The Science of Medicine* is largely a spirited defense of the medical tradition against charges of chicanery. In the main, it seeks to distance the emerging tradition(s) of rational medicine from other common contemporary healing practices of a more superstitious nature. Hippocrates writes of medicine in tones that are both proud of its accomplishments and mindful of its limitations. For example:

> First of all I would define medicine as the complete removal of the distress of the sick, the alleviation of the more violent diseases and the refusal to undertake to cure cases in which the disease has already won the mastery, knowing that everything is not possible to medicine. (*The Science of Medicine*, 3, p. 140)

Despite that final caveat, Hippocrates holds out great hope for medicine to produce cures in many if not most cases. This leaves him with two specific problems to address. First, if the science of medicine is the way to health once one is ill, why are there some people who seek no medical attention and yet recover? Second, why do some people who are under a physician's care nonetheless fail to recover?

The answer to the first question is that afflicted people may stumble upon remedies by chance, remedies that could have been more expertly and quickly prescribed had they consulted a physician:

> But it seems to me that even those who do not employ a doctor may chance upon some remedy without knowing the right and wrong of it. Should they be successful, it is because they have employed the same remedy as a doctor would use. And this is a considerable demonstration of the reality and the greatness of the science, when it be realized that even those who do not believe in it are nevertheless saved by it. (*The Science of Medicine*, 5, p. 141)

The final point mentioned is somewhat intriguing, for one might well question in what sense those who have never seen a physician can be said to have encountered the science of medicine much less been saved by it. Hippocrates seems to be equivocating on medicine, the discipline, and medicine, the materials employed by those in the discipline. His emphasis on the unimportance of belief is perhaps more interesting and less confusing. It seems to be yet another attempt to distinguish the nature of rational medicine from the modus operandi of healing cults and other similar practices of the day. Turning to the question of why some who seek medical attention nonetheless succumb to their illness, Hippocrates lays most of the blame at the patients' lack of compliance with their physicians' instructions, a lamentation common to even modern doctors:

> As if doctors can prescribe the wrong remedies but patients can never disobey their orders! It is far more likely that the sick are unable to carry out the instructions than that the doctors prescribe the wrong remedies. Physicians come to a case in full health of body and mind. They compare the present symptoms of the patient with similar cases they have seen in the past, so that they can say how cures were effected then. But consider the view of the patients. They do not know what they are suffering from, nor why they are suffering from I, nor what will succeed their present symptoms. Nor have they experienced of the course of similar cases. Their present pains are increased by fears for the future. They are full of disease and starved of nourishment; they prefer an immediate alleviation of pain to a remedy that will return them to health. (*The Science of Medicine*, 7, p. 142)

One might well argue that perhaps some patients do not recover because the doctor has insufficient time to effect a cure; however, Hippocrates specifically denies this claim. According to him, no disease progresses faster than its potential cure. Still, he does allow that certain diseases, particularly internal ones, may be undetected until they are too advanced for any remedy to be effective. In order to more fully appreciate these points, let's consider exactly what in the Hippocratic Corpus constitutes health and disease, and to do that necessitates a look at the Hippocratic text *The Nature of Man*.

The Nature of Man

This work, subtitled "a popular lecture on physiology," starts by reaffirming the Hippocratic desire to avoid philosophical debates. Accordingly, we are told that the study of the nature of man is not a philosophical inquiry but, rather, more profitably approached from the perspective of physiology. The remainder of the work consists of a description of the basic substances that comprise the physiology of human beings.

The first principle to be defended is that multiple elementary substances comprise a human. This view is set in sharp contrast to the efforts of some pre-Socratic philosophers, most notably the Milesians, to simplify cosmology by unifying the elements. The primary argument given for preferring a plurality of substances to a single element is one of analogy to biology and in particular to zoology. According to Hippocrates,

> [i]n the first place, generation cannot arise from a single substance. For how could one thing generate another unless it copulated with some other? Secondly, unless the things which copulated were of the same species and had the same generative capabilities, we should not get these results. Again, generation would be impossible unless the hot stood in a fair and reasonable proportion to the cold, and likewise the dry to the wet; if for instance, one preponderated over the other, one being much stronger and other much weaker. Is it likely, then, that anything should be generated from one thing, seeing that not even a number of things suffice unless they are combined in the right proportions? (*The Nature of Man*, 3, p. 261f.)

The notion of balancing elements—as well as balancing the specific characteristics of heat, cold, wetness, and dryness listed in this passage—forms the core of the Hippocratic understanding of human physiology. As the text progresses, we are told that the basic constituents of the human body are four substances (called humors elsewhere): blood, phlegm, black bile, and yellow bile, which can best be described by their possession of combinations of heat, cold, wetness, and dryness, as seen in Table 6.2.

Table 6.2
The Four Humors

	Hot	Cold
Wet	Blood	Phlegm
Dry	Yellow Bile	Black Bile

Each set of these polar opposites—wetness versus dryness, heat versus cold—is kept in balance within the body, and it is this balance that constitutes life and health. One must not suppose, however, that this balance is static. Rather, as the seasons progress and other environmental forces act upon the body, there are times when one is hotter and times when one is colder, for example, with a concomitant increase and or decrease in the corresponding humors. Thus we are told that in the spring, when it is warm and wet, blood predominates. In summer it is warmer still, but now dry, and thus yellow bile predominates. By autumn it has become colder, although it is still dry, and so the black bile is ascendant. Finally, phlegm dominates the cold, wet months of winter.

Such seasonal fluctuations or more localized ones brought about by more abrupt changes in the weather or by travel to distant locales are to be expected, and in general the body acts to restore equilibrium among the humors. When the balance cannot be restored, illness results.

Two important points must be raised here. First, although these humors, particularly blood, may seem commonplace and familiar to a modern reader, it is important to note that for the author of these treatises they were not. Blood was not simply a fluid that circulated in the body, bearing nourishment to the extremities. For the ancients, blood was the essence of life— not the vehicle for nourishment, but the nourishment itself. Second, Hippocrates is primarily presenting a theory of human physiology, both here and in the treatise *On Humors*; it is later writers, and in particular Galen (see below), who will expand this idea to one of psychological temperament. Thus those individuals in which blood is dominant are warm and cheerful. Those in which phlegm dominates are cold and sluggish. Yellow bile dominates in persons who are hot tempered, whereas black bile dominates in those who are morose or depressed.

The Sacred Disease

Another important treatise of interest to those who wish to construct something of a theory of psychology from the writings of Hippocrates is *The Sacred Disease*. Two important issues are discussed in this treatise: the first is the nature of "the sacred disease" as so named by earlier authors, and the second is the role of the brain in human life and activity.

On the first issue Hippocrates is adamant that the "sacred disease" is not in any way concerned with divine or supernatural influences; it is merely so named by the ignorant, by quacks and charlatans.

> I do not believe that the "Sacred Disease" is any more divine or sacred than any other disease but, on the contrary, has specific characteristics and a definite cause. Nevertheless, because it is completely different from other diseases, it has been regarded as a divine visitation by those who, being only human,

view it with ignorance and astonishment. (Hippocrates, *The Sacred Disease,* 1 p. 237)

The symptoms of this disease certainly sound like a description of many seizure disorders.

This causes loss of voice, choking, foaming at the mouth, clenching of the teeth and convulsive movements of the hands; the eyes are fixed, the patient becomes unconscious and, in some cases, passes a stool. (*The Sacred Disease,* 10, p. 243)

In addition, the author notes many other features that permit us to identify the sacred disease of the ancient writers with any number of seizure disorders, most notably epilepsy. First, there is the fact that infants are more likely to suffer from this disease than adults and that when they do, it is more serious in nature (11, 12). Second, the author notes that the symptoms are not always global; they are occasionally lateralized to one side of the body or the other (13). Finally, there is the recognition that attacks of this disease are frequently preceded by an aura or premonition of the impending incident (15).

The author identifies three classes of causes for the symptoms described: heredity, environment, and metabolism. The latter two are most interesting in that they both make reference to the brain. When the environment is hot, as when the south winds blow, we are told that the brain softens, precipitating an attack (13–16). Metabolically, when too much phlegm is presents, the blood leading to the brain is cooled, again causes symptoms of seizure (8–10).

This discussion of the causes of what is a disorder of consciousness, and the role of the brain in its etiology, leads to a general discussion of the function of the brain. Here the author of the treatise is quite specific, stating in no uncertain terms:

It ought to be generally known that the source of our pleasure, merriment, laughter and amusement, as of our grief, pain, anxiety and tears, is none other than the brain. It is specially the organ which enables us to think, see and hear, and to distinguish the ugly and the beautiful, the bad and the good, pleasant and unpleasant. Sometimes we judge according to convention; at other times according to the perceptions of expediency. (*The Sacred Disease,* 17, p. 248)

Not only normal functioning but also disordered perceptions and other disorders of consciousness have a physical cause in the brain.

It is the brain too which is the seat of madness and delirium, of the fears and frights which assail us, often by night, but sometimes even by day; it is there where lies the cause of insomnia and sleep-walking, of thoughts that will not come, forgotten duties and eccentricities. All such things result from an unhealthy condition of the brain; it may be warmer than it should be, or it may be colder, or moister or drier, or in any other abnormal state. Moistness is the cause of madness for when the brain is abnormally moist it is necessarily agitated and this agitation prevents sight or hearing being steady. Because of this, varying visual and acoustic sensations are produce, while the tongue can only describe things as they appear and sound. So long as the brain is still, a man is in his right mind. (*The Sacred Disease,* 17, p. 248f.)

We are further told that the substance of the brain is susceptible to negative influences by both phlegm and bile (18), that consciousness is caused by the intake of air into the brain (19), and that headaches have their source in the membranes covering the brain (6).

What is interesting is that at least some of these ideas must have been in common circulation at the time. For example, Plato agrees with the author of *The Sacred Disease* that such seizures are the result of humoral imbalances affecting the substance of the brain.

When <white phlegm> is mixed with black bile and is diffused over the most divine circuits in the head and throws them into confusion, the visitation, if it comes during sleep, is comparatively mild, but when it attacks those who are awake it is harder to throw off, As an affliction of the sacred substance <i.e. the brain marrow> it is most justly termed the "sacred disease." (Plato, *Timaeus,* 85A–B, in Longrigg, p. 22)

The connection between consciousness and breath is further emphasized by Hippocrates in his work *On Breaths.* Here he states that

[a]poplexy, too, is caused by breaths. For whenever cold and frequent breaths pass through the flesh and puff it up, those parts of the body lose the power of feeling. If, then, many breaths rush through the whole of the body, the whole patient suffers and apoplectic seizure. (*On Breaths,* 13, in Longrigg, 1998, p. 23)

In contrast, there was a rival medical tradition that would have its greatest impact on the surgeons (to be discussed shortly) and on the writers in the Stoic tradition. Chief among these was another Coan physician, Praxagoras of Cos (fl. ca. 300 BC). In his writings he emphasized the role of pneumatic movement (see chapter 5) and the centrality of the heart. We are told that:

Praxagoras says that epilepsy occurs in the region around the thick artery [aorta] when phlegmatic humors aggregate within it. These being formed into bubbles, block the passage of the psychic *pneuma,* from the heart and thus the *pneuma* makes the body shake and convulse. Again, when the bubbles have been settled, the condition ceases. Diocles also believes that there is an obstruction in the same region and concurs in other respects with Praxagoras. (Anonymous Parisinums 3, Praxagoras, Fragment 70)[6]

Madness and Mental Illness in Hippocratic Thought

Finally, in contrast to the above writings on the centrality of the brain in explanation of normal consciousness and also disorders of consciousness and perception, there is another tradition within the Hippocratic Corpus that identifies delusions, particularly in young girls, with blocked blood flow, and in particular with the flow around the heart. In *Diseases of Young Girls* we are told:

> First of all I shall deal with the so-called "Sacred Disease" and with apoplexy and with terrors which people fear exceedingly—to the extent that they become deranged and imagine that they see hostile demons, sometimes at night, sometimes in the daytime, sometimes both. Because of such visions many already have hanged themselves: more women than men; for the female is more fearful and weaker by nature. Young girls, who remain unmarried when ripe for marriage, suffer this affliction more at the descent of the menses. Before this time they are not much distressed by these matters. For later on, the blood streams into the womb to flow away outside the body. Thus when the orifice of the exit is not open and more blood keeps on flowing in, then, having no outlet, the blood, because of its quantity, wells up into the heart and diaphragm. When these parts were filled, the heart became stupefied. Then, from this sluggishness came numbness and from numbness delirium took hold . . . shivering coupled with fever starts up . . . the patient is driven mad by a violent inflammation; she becomes murderously inclined because of the putrefaction; fears and terrors are aroused by the dark; the compression around the heart causes these girls to hang themselves; their spirit, being distraught and in anguish through the corruption of the blood, brings an evil in its train. (Hippocrates, *Diseases of Young Girls*, 1, in Longrigg, 1998, p. 24ff.)

Praxagoras attributes madness to a similar cardiovascular cause in one fragment, saying:

> The cause of mania. Praxagoras said that mania is engendered by a swelling of the heart, where thinking also takes place, as he believes. But fever does not occur with it, since superficial swelling does not cause fever. (Praxagoras, Fragment 72)

It must be remembered that for Praxagoras, the heart was primarily concerned with the movement of *pneuma* and was the seat of the *hegemonikon* of the soul.

Thus within the Hippocratic Corpus and the medical writings of Cos in general, there were two competing theories of the biological foundation of conscious mental life. In the first, exemplified by the Hippocratic text *The Sacred Disease,* it is the brain that is the seat of consciousness, perception, and mood. In the second tradition, that of the Hippocratic *Diseases of Young Girls* and the writings of Praxagoras, Hippocrates' fellow physician from Cos, the heart is given primacy. Both of these traditions were further augmented later in antiquity by writers from a tradition Hippocrates considers rival to that of medicine, namely, that of surgery, as exemplified by two great anatomists working in the Museum at Alexandria.

THE SURGEONS OF ALEXANDRIA

As already described in chapter 5, the Museum at Alexandria was the premier research institution of the Hellenistic era in a number of diverse fields. The medical tradition recognized the importance of this center primarily for the anatomical investigations of two surgeons who worked there in the third century BC, Herophilus of Chalcedon and Erasistratus of Ceos. Their work was performed upon live criminals, released into their custody by the Ptolemaic rulers. Cornelius Celsus describes the practice of vivisection in Alexandria, saying:

> Moreover, since pains and various kinds of diseases arise in the interior parts, the dogmatists think that no one can apply remedies for them who is ignorant of the parts themselves. Therefore it is necessary to cut into the bodies of the dead and examine their viscera and intestines. They hold that Herophilus and Erasistratus did this in by far the best way when they cut open live criminals they received out of prison from the kings and while breath still remained in these bodies, they inspected those parts which nature had previously kept enclosed. (*On Medicine,* Proem 23–24, in Longrigg, 1998, p. 85)

This practice is significant in two respects. First, there was a universal prohibition against any dissection or other desecration of human remains throughout the Greek world. Second, after the work of Erasistratus, the practice of vivisection was discontinued at Alexandria. Thus it was only during the careers of these two surgeons that any accurate knowledge of human anatomy was recorded. The practice was considered morally reprehensible by various parties, not least of which was the Christian writer Tertullian, who, it must be remembered, was no supporter of secular knowledge to begin with. He describes Herophilus as

> that doctor, or rather butcher, who cut up innumerable human beings so that he could investigate nature and who hated mankind for the sake of knowledge. I do not know whether he investigated clearly all the interior parts of the body, since what was formerly alive is altered by death, not a natural death, but one which itself changes during the performance of the dissection. (*On the Soul,* 10, in Longrigg, 1998, p. 86)

Thus, although it must be acknowledged within any history of psychology that later writers are indebted to these surgeons for their pioneering work in the study of the human central nervous system, their work carried a terrible price. Let's briefly survey their principal investigations as they pertain to the history of neuroscience and psychology.

Herophilus of Chalcedon (fl. ca. 270 BC)

Our evidence for the work of Herophilus is unfortunately quite fragmentary, drawn from later commentators, some admiring, some quite critical. The extant fragments concerning him have recently been collected into a comprehensive volume by von Staden (1989), and it is to that volume that the reader further interested in his work is directed. Herophilus is generally credited with the first documented anatomical investigations of the human brain. Although in earlier traditions there exist many descriptions of brain tissue—and, indeed, those who engaged in the practice of trepanning or mummification must have been exposed to the tissue of the brain—he is the first to describe it in detail. He is credited with the identification of the major features of the human brain, most notably drawing the distinction of cerebellum from cerebrum. Of primary interest to him was the ventricular system, which he claims was the source and distributor of psychic *pneuma* (see chapter 5).

Of all the ventricular chambers in the brain, according to Herophilus, the interior of the cerebellum is the key. Galen tells us:

> Those who have considered this cavity to be a sort of fourth ventricle say that it is the most important of all of the ventricles throughout the whole of the brain. But Herophilus seems to suppose that not this ventricle but the one in the cerebellum is the more important. (Galen, *On the Use of the Parts*, 8.11, in Longrigg, 1998, p. 87)

It should be noted that the fourth ventricle referred to above is probably the cerebral aqueduct; the ventricle of the cerebellum mentioned here would be called by modern anatomists, the fourth ventricle. We are further told that Herophilus considered this region to be the seat of the intellect, in part because the floor of this ventricle was shaped like the nibs cut into reed pens at Alexandria. This connection between a writing instrument and the seat of the intellect is probably yet another example of Stoic doctrine of the importance of *lekta* in Late Hellenistic theory of mind.

Finally, Herophilus is said to have made the first distinction between sensory and motor nerves. We are told by a later commentator that "the excerscensces from the brain he calls sensory and purposive nerves, through which sensory and purposive motion and all bodily action are accomplished" (Herophilus, Fr. 125, in von Staden, 1989).

Erasistratus of Ceos (fl. ca. 260 BC)

Erasistratus is primarily important in that he provides the compromise between the heart-centered pneumatic theory of Praxagoras and the later head-centered nervous theory of Galen. Among his anatomical discoveries, he is credited with distinguishing between the nervous system and the arterial system, a confusion Praxagoras had frequently made. For Praxagoras, the veins carried blood from the heart, whereas the arteries (and nerves) carried *pneuma*. His primary evidence for this had been that the arteries of dead animals are frequently found to be empty of blood (as we now know, because circulation has stopped). Many commentators hostile to Praxagoras take note of the readily observable fact that freshly cut arteries do bleed. Erasistratus defends Praxagoras, however, explaining away this apparent contradiction by stating that escaping *pneuma* creates a vacuum in the arteries that draws in blood from nearby veins.

Although Erasistratus doesn't deny Praxagoras' claim that the arteries carry *pneuma*, he does distinguish between two types of *pneuma*. According to him, arteries carry the vital *pneuma* of the heart, whereas nerves carry the psychic *pneuma* of the brain. Many fragments of his demonstrate that he holds the brain in the highest esteem as the seat of the intellect. As many later and even present-day biologists would do, he argues from comparison with the brains of other species:

> So the observer learns from these that, just as it is in the other animals—deer, hare, and any other that far excels the others in running being well provided with the muscles and sinews useful for this activity—so in man, since he is far superior to the other animals in thinking, this (member) is large and has many folds. (Galen, *On the Doctrines of Hippocrates and Plato*, VII, 3.10, in De Lacy, p. 443)

He goes on to justify the prominence of the brain by noting its proximity to the organs of sense and its centrality in the network of nerves. He observes:

> [T]he outgrowths of the nerves were all from the brain; and by and large the brain appears to be the source of the nerves in the body. For the sensation that comes from the nostrils passed to this member through apertures, and also the sensations that come from the ears. And outgrowths from the brain went also to the tongue and the eyes. (Galen, *On the Doctrines of Hippocrates and Plato*, VII, 3.10–11, 1984, p. 443)

In conclusion, then, the anatomical investigations of Herophilus and Erasistratus are important historically as the first systematic attempt to map the human brain. This work, as well as the medical tradition from the Hippocratic Corpus, will in turn become part of the theories of human nature and the relationship between psychology and the brain in the writings of the Roman physician Galen.

GALEN (ca. AD 130–200)

Turning to the career of Galen, a man referred to by the scholars of the Middle Ages and Renaissance simply as "the physician," we are at last fortunate to have a large body of work authored by a single individual. Galen writes on all aspects of medicine, surgery, anatomy, and indeed philosophy with a clear systematic style from a vantage point some five centuries later than Hippocrates.

Early Life and Education

Galen was born some time around the year AD 129 in the prosperous and cultured city of Pergamum, a protectorate of the Roman Empire in western Asia Minor. His father was an architect, and we are told by Galen that he was the chief influence on his son's professional path. At first Galen tells us he was schooled at home, as "[m]y father was himself competent in the fields of mathematics, arithmetic and grammar, and reared me in these as well as in the other subjects necessary for the training of the young" (Galen, *The Order of My Own Books*, 4.59, p. 27).[7]

Galan's basic education attended to, his father took him to each of the major philosophical schools in Pergamum in turn in order to ensure his son of the broadest possible education. Galen lists his philosophical tutors with some sense of pride, telling the readers of his work on *The Affections and Errors of the Soul* that

> on completion of my fourteenth year, I began to attend the lectures of philosophers of my home city—mostly those of a Stoic, a pupil of Philopator, but also for a short time those of a Platonist pupil of Gaius, . . . Then there was another fellow citizen, too, who had returned from a long trip abroad—a pupil of Apasius the Perpatetic; and after him another from Athens, an Epicurean. (*The Affections and Errors of the Soul*, I, 8.41–42, p. 119)

We are told that Galen's father selected these men after a careful examination of their credentials and characters. From this experience of higher education, Galen seems to have developed a lifelong passion for reading the classics, and perhaps more important, for reading all sources critically. It is no small irony that a scholar charged with the imposition of dogma, retarding serious inquiry for centuries, was himself so keenly aware of the dangers of blind adherence to any teaching. In fact, he identifies as one of the principal precepts he took from his father and from this period of his life to "not declare allegiance to any sect, rather subjecting them all to a thorough examination" (*The Affections and Errors of the Soul,* I, 8.43, p. 120), a sentiment we will see displayed again and again when we turn to our discussion of his methodology.

At some time into Galen's young adulthood, his father had a divine vision involving Asclepius the healer, who had a larger temple complex in Pergamum; Galen was subsequently dispatched for medical training under the finest anatomists in Corinth and Alexandria. Upon completion of this training, he returned home to serve a term there as the surgeon to the gladiatorial school. But it was in Rome that Galen's fortunes lay, and with the exception of several extended travels, it was in Rome that Galen would spend the rest of his professional life, ultimately serving as personal physician and confidante to no fewer than four emperors, most notably the emperor and philosopher Marcus Aurelius. Such a high-profile career doubtless contributed greatly to Galen's fame and notoriety, as well as to the popularity of his many treatises, but it served a more important function as well. As court physician Galen had access to the enormous Imperial Archives, which had by this time surpassed even Alexandria as a collection of important documents.

The Sects of Medicine in Galen's Day

Throughout Galen's career the science of medicine was plagued by a bitter theoretical debate between three firmly established sects. Galen himself provides an outline of this debate in several of his surviving works, most notably one entitled *The Sects for Beginners.* The two main antagonists in this debate were the empiricists, who insisted that medicine rely upon the evidence of manifest conditions and upon physicians' cataloguing of experience with such conditions over time, and the rationalists or dogmatists, who insisted that medicine should concern itself with the underlying principles of illness and health, seeing manifest conditions as merely symptoms to be classified analogically. It is an interesting historical aside that this debate marks the first time in intellectual history that this all-too-familiar epistemological controversy would be framed by these two labels: empiricist and rationalist. Finally, there were the methodists, who taught a radical new curriculum, advertising that they could create physicians with as little as six months of training. How could they do this? By rationalizing all sickness and health to a small set of opponent processes such as constriction and dilation.

Galen himself cared nothing for such sectarian battles, believing that in the end what mattered was a critical method for examining data, whatever their source, and ultimately a successful therapeutic methodology. His method of rational inquiry can readily be divided into a number of tenets—namely, the primacy of logical demonstration, the use of ancient sources, a rejection of authority and of dogma, and perhaps most important the need to focus on seeking answers at the level of analysis appropriate to the question under consideration. We turn now to each of these tenets in turn.

Physician and Philosopher

Galen's love of logic, doubtless acquired through his long study in the Hellenistic schools, is reflected in several important treatises he composed on the topic, but treatises unfortunately largely lost to us. However, even in his medical writings directed at a clinical audience, often themselves non-specialists in logical method, he regularly directs his readers to ever greater rigor. Note that this stands in stark contrast to Hippocrates' general distrust of philosophical writing. For just one example, in his work *That the Best Doctor Is Also a Philosopher* he writes:

[The true doctor] must study logical method to know how many diseases there are, by species and by genus, and how in each case, one is to find out what kind of treatment is indicated. The same method also provides the foundations for knowledge of the body's very nature, which is to be understood on three levels. First, the level of the primary elements, which are in a state of total mixture with each other; secondly, the level of the perceptible, which is also called the "homogeneous"; thirdly, that which derives from the organic parts. The use and function for the animal of each of these is also a lesson of the logical method: they too should be learnt by a process of rigorous demonstration, not uncritically. (*The Best Doctor Is Also a Philosopher*, 3.60, p. 33)

In fact, on several occasions Galen recommends a thorough grounding in logic as a necessary prerequisite for any studies of a scientific nature, including medicine. In the section of his great work of moral philosophy *The Affections and Errors of the Soul,* concerned with error, he suggests that those who wish to become more precise thinkers undertake, first, elementary training in geometry or simple logic, in anticipation of later pedagogical doctrines of formal discipline. Toward this end, he says,

[t]hose who wish to become expert in scientific proof should therefore monitor their own progress, practicing first (as I have suggested) on a number of individual questions where the right answer has a self-confirming status which the inquirer can recognize, as is the case in mathematics and geometry, which astronomy and architecture in turn use as their bases. (*The Affections and Errors of the Soul*, II, 4.80, p. 138)

Further, in his works on moral philosophy, he follows the line of many of his Stoic and Epicurean forebears in recommending a process of education in logic as a therapeutic regime that will ultimately yield a happier, more temperate life.

His use of ancient sources is justifiably noteworthy. Galen is everywhere quoting passages of philosophy and poetry throughout his works. He considered Plato the greatest of philosophers and reasserted his tripartite soul, complete with anatomic localization of the different faculties: reason in the head, passion in the heart, desire in the liver. He looked to Aristotle and the peripatetics for his teleological view of physiology. Stoic functionalism permeates his writing, and indeed it is to Galen that we owe the preservation of much stoic philosophy of mind, most notably through his extensive quotations of the work of Chrysippus of Soloi. And, of course, he does comment extensively on the Hippocratic Corpus. Galen was not, however, a passive appropriator of earlier ideas, although he is often dismissed by the modern reader as a mere eclectic. What is interesting to note is that Galen is always careful to quote his sources with enough context to reconstruct historical arguments in as strong a form as possible before subjecting them to critical scrutiny.

Equally important are the attacks he makes on other authors for misuse of quoted material in attempts either to argue from authority or to align oneself with some dogmatic position without recourse to arguments on point or presentation of evidence. For example, a large portion of his work *The Doctrines of Hippocrates and Plato* is given over to a detailed analysis of the writings of Chrysippus the Stoic; it is in fact because of this work that we have any record of much of Chrysippus' writings at all. At one point he chides the great Stoic for abandoning logical demonstration and resorting to extensive quotations from the dramatists to bolster his position:

> For not merely is Euripides or Tyrtaeus or any other poet, or any non-expert at all, insufficient authority for a doctrine in the absence of all proof, but even Hippocrates himself, admittedly the best of all physicians, or Plato, the first of all philosophers, is not sufficient authority. (*The Doctrines of Hippocrates and Plato*, III, 4.29)

His views on sectarianism, mentioned earlier in considering his educational background and his position on the theoretical debates dividing medicine in his day, are worth repeating in the context of his disdain for authority. In his catalogue of his own books Galen tells of an encounter with a young physician named Marialus, who

> had heard very high praise of a public lecture I had given on a set question in anatomy, and of my teachings on that occasion, from all who had followed them; and so he asked one of my friends to which sect I belonged. The response was that I regarded those who termed themselves "Hippocrateans," "Praxagoreans," and so on as slaves, that I personally took whatever was good from each. (*My Own Books*, 1.13, p. 5)

Such an attitude has perhaps contributed to the notion of Galen as a dilettante and to the charge frequently leveled against him that his system is, in fact, a disordered collection of beliefs that do not cohere into a single theoretical framework. Part of the reason for this confusion is doubtless the attempt by later writers, of lesser ability, to synthesize the Galenic corpus into readily digestible primers for the physicians and scholars of the medieval world. Galen's actual writings do not permit of such an easy synthesis because Galen was always careful to acknowledge that different questions require answers at different levels of analysis, and thus it was inappropriate to attempt to fit into one theoretical framework all of one's opinions on a subject as broad as medicine. Such care to find answers at the appropriate level to the question posed appears even within a given domain of inquiry, as, for example, in his work *Mixtures,* where he states:

> In response to the question, "what is the mixture of man?," say or of horse, ox, dog, or any other creatures, no single answer is possible. For it is not admissible to give a single type of answer to questions which admit of several different kinds of interpretation and criteria. (*Mixtures,* I, 6.548, p. 220)

Such room for multiple levels of explanation within a given domain is greatly expanded when one considers that many of the questions that interested Galen—for example, the seat of the soul and its functional description—cross the boundaries of not only levels of analysis but spheres of discourse within learned inquiry. Thus when examining the doctrines of Hippocrates and Plato, he is not surprised that these two men he admired most should approach similar subject matters from different perspectives—Hippocrates from the perspective of bodily organs and Plato from the perspective of the powers of the soul (see *On the doctrines of Hippocrates and Plato,* VI, 8.57–58).

Finally, a further reason for the apparent disunity of the Galenic corpus is that not all the documents we have extant from Galen were intended for the same audience; indeed, many were not intended to be published at all. Galen wrote a great number of treatises for beginners and for non-specialists, as well as those he wrote specifically for use in the training of physicians and those for his professional colleagues. Galen makes this point in *My Own Books,* the catalogue he has left us, but that has not prevented later writers from attempting inappropriate syntheses or from leveling accusations of inconsistency when such proved impossible.

> Since then, as I have stated above, they were written not for publication but to fit the particular attainments and needs of those who had requested them, it follows naturally that some of them are rather extended, while others are compressed; and their styles, and indeed the actual theoretical content, vary in their completeness. (*My Own Books,* 10, p. 4)

Galen on the Soul

Having examined the various tenets that could be said to comprise Galen's methodology, we now turn to examine the results of this methodology when applied to questions of psychology. The questions of a psychological nature that most interested Galen were about the nature of the soul, its seat in the human body, the role of the bodily humors in its function, and finally the proper therapy for disorders of the soul. Turning to each of these in turn, we find that Galen's take on the substance of the soul, as indeed on all substances in general, was primarily functionalist, derived largely from Aristotle's hylomorphism. Galen says in *The Soul's Dependence on the Body:*

> [B]ut first recall the nature of the common substance of all bodies. Now, this common substance (as we have shown) is comprised of two principles, matter and form. Matter is itself conceptually lacking in quality, but contains within it a mixture of four qualities: heat, cold, dryness, and wetness; and these qualities give rise to bronze, iron, gold; and also to flesh, sinew, fat, gristle, and all such entities—those which Plato calls "first-born" and Aristotle "homogeneous." (*The Soul's Dependence on the Body,* 3.773, p. 152)

Further on an Aristotelian bent, and in direct opposition to both the Stoic emphasis on reason and the Epicurean emphasis on hedonism, he argues that the soul is not unitary in function; rather, many faculties can be attributed to the single substance of the soul:

> They [many philosophers] seem to conceive of faculties as things which inhabit "substances" in much the same way as we inhabit our houses, and not to realize that the effective cause of every event is conceived of in relational terms; there is a way of talking of this cause as of a specific object, but the faculty *arises in relation to* the event caused. We therefore attribute as many faculties to a substance as activities. (*The Soul's Dependence on the Body,* 2.769, p. 151)

One might be surprised to learn that a writer who elsewhere is so enamored of Plato's writing would adopt such a functionalist, hylomorphic view of the substance of the soul. Such a view seems to be directly at odds with the notion of an immortal soul found in much of Plato's writing, especially in the *Timeaus* from which Galen quotes frequently and quite approvingly. This tension permeates much of Galen's writing on the subject, and he finds no comfort in the fact that the later Plato ascribes immortality only to the rational soul:

> If, then, the reasoning faculty is a form of the soul, it must be mortal: for it too will be a mixture, namely a mixture within the brain. If, on the other hand, it is immortal, as Plato believes, there is a problem as to why it should depart

when the brain undergoes excessive cooling, heating, drying or moistening. (*The Soul's Dependence on the Body*, 3.774, p. 153)

Equally troubling for Galen are the classical problems of mental causation that have so haunted attempts to make a coherent argument for mind-body dualism in subsequent centuries. His anatomical investigations convinced Galen that the nerves likely carry the impulse to motion from the brain to the muscles, and sensory data from the extremities and from the sense organs of the head back to the brain. Further investigations of the effect of pressure on the exposed brains of patients undergoing skull surgery—and, indeed, of the effectiveness of various drugs and toxins upon mental function—left him with a decidedly materialist bent. Nonetheless, he finds Plato's arguments for immortality, as well as much of the Platonist cosmology, compelling, and thus in the end he chooses to declare agnosticism about the substance of the soul and instead to provide arguments for its tripartite nature and location of physical embodiment. The final answer to the question of the soul's substance does not seem to Galen to be amenable to logical demonstration, and thus he chooses to forgo further comment.

[B]ut I have nowhere presumed to declare the identity of the substance of the soul. Even whether it is entirely incorporeal, whether it is something bodily, whether it is entirely invisible, or whether perishable—I have yet to find anyone who has employed geometric-style proofs on any of these questions (*The Construction of the Embryo*, 6.701–702, p. 201)

On the question of the seat of the soul, Galen is unambiguous. He follows Plato's tripartite division of the soul's basic functions into rational, spirited, and desiderative, as well as his localization of these separate functions respectively in the brain, heart, and liver. In doing so, he is openly rejecting the then more popular localization scheme provided by Aristotle and further refined through the writings of the Stoics, placing all functions of the soul in the heart. Galen gives many reasons throughout several of his treatises for preferring the tripartite system, especially for the location of the rational soul in the brain. His evidence ranged from anatomical investigations, tracing neural pathways, to descriptions of experiments in vivisection and the varied responses of an animal to pressure applied to the heart and brain, as well as to ligation of various vessels, nerves and arteries, proceeding from both organs. In the end, though, he feels his and others' clinical experience of head wounds and other maladies provides the strongest evidence for a link between the tissue of the brain and the rational, perceptive, and volitional functions of the soul. In *The Construction of the Embryo*, for example, he states boldly:

In previous times, when the state of anatomical knowledge was not so well advanced as it is now, there would naturally have been some confusion regarding the source, which supplies perception and motion through the nerves to the parts of the animal. But now that long and consistent clinical experience has moved doctors universally to share the opinion of the anatomists, and no one confronted with cases of mania without fever, of melancholy, of any kind of damage to the faculties of memory or reason, of phrenitis with fever, of lethargy, epilepsy, or apoplexy, would refrain from applying treatment to the head, they alone [the Stoics] are still conducting an enquiry into matters which are perfectly well known to anyone with the slightest curiosity. (*The Construction of the Embryo*, 4.677–678, p. 189)

As for where in the brain the rational soul might be located, in the psychic *pneuma* filling the ventricles or in the neural tissues themselves, Galen is unambiguous. He states quite clearly in his work *On the Doctrines of Hippocrates and Plato* that the seat of the rational soul is to be found in the substance of the brain itself. The *pneuma* in the ventricles, far from being the substance of the soul itself, is instead referred to as the first instrument of the soul. Similarly, the seats of the spirited soul and of the desiderative soul are said to be in the substance of the heart and liver themselves, with arterial blood and venous blood serving as their respective first instruments. Medieval cell doctrine, with its attendant focus on the ventricles of the brain, seem to have more to do with the works of Augustine, and others who may have read poor glosses of Galen's anatomy, than with Galen himself.

The substances of these organs are said to be able to carry out their particular functions because of the unique mixture of the elements within them. For Galen, drawing upon the widespread medical traditions of his time and from the writings of Hippocrates himself, these elements are the simple properties hot, cold, wet, and dry. In his work *Mixtures* he writes that most of the physicians of his day acknowledge that within animal bodies there are at least four common mixtures that seem most prevalent and efficacious. These are the hot and wet blood, the cold and wet phlegm, the hot and dry yellow bile, and the cold and dry black bile we have encountered previously. Strangely, in the history of medicine Galen is often credited with this humoral theory. What is perhaps most surprising about this is that Galen does not claim credit for this doctrine at all, instead ascribing it to common medical theory of his day; indeed, relative to those who came after him, he makes rather little use of it in the explanation of human psychology. In fact, far from being the physical (or if you prefer, psychopharmacological) determinist that such a theory seems to entail, Galen is quite convinced of the ability of humans to make rational choices. His clinical works dealing with what we might characterize as psychological disorders—for example, *The Affections and Errors of the Soul*—are not full of litanies of purgatives to cure melancholy; they are, rather, works of moral philosophy similar in tone and in recommendations to the *Handbook* of Epictetus or the *Meditations* of Marcus Aurelius. The method of rational inquiry and dispassionate analysis is supposed to free one from the dominance of one's temperament or of one's momentary passions.

This is consonant with the one part of the humoral theory that Galen is willing to consider his unique contribution, namely, his focus on balance as the most desirable state. Other theorists, he tells us, have noted that because infants are warm and moist and corpses cold and dry, warmth and moisture must be the most desirable state for the organism. Similarly, they argue that as Hippocrates noted, the incidence of many diseases was least in the spring-time, a warm moist season, and thus these two qualities must be the chief determinants of health. Galen disagrees, arguing that the prime of life is midway between the cradle and the grave, and that the spring is neither as hot as the summer nor as moist as the winter, and thus balance is the key to health. He extends this principle to psychology, saying:

> Such are the bodily characteristics of the well-balanced man. His soul, similarly, should be at an exact balance between boldness and cowardice, hesitation and rashness, pity and envy. Such a person would be good-spirited, affectionate, generous and wise. (*Mixtures* II, 1.576, p. 233)

CONCLUSION

Medicine, with its attendant discipline surgery and its frequent dialogue with philosophy, can be regarded as a third approach to the questions of human nature, its discourse distinct from those of poetry and philosophy. From its birth in the earlier traditions of Near Eastern mysticism, the medical tradition ranges broadly over issues of human life and health, illness and death. No single view of psychology can be said to emerge from this varied tradition, yet there are occasional fragments dealing with issues such as thinking, emotion, consciousness, and madness. In this chapter we have attempted to highlight some of these fragments, with sufficient contexts of their larger theoretical situations. The reader interested in more information is directed to any of the numerous works on Hellenic and Hellenistic medicine that are readily available (some of which are listed in the bibliography).

NOTES

1. As translated by James Longrigg, in *Greek Medicine From the Heroic to the Hellenistic Age: A Source Book*, p. 35.

2. The interested reader is referred to the excellent discussion of the interplay between rational and irrational elements in Greek medicine presented in Grmek (1991).

3. Translation by Kathleen Freeman in *Ancilla to the Pre-Socratic Philosophers*, p. 40ff.

4. As translated by James Longrigg, in *Greek Medicine From the Heroic to the Hellenistic Age: A Source Book*, p. 35.

5. Unless otherwise noted, all quotations from the Hippocratic Corpus are taken from the readily available translation by G. J. Chadwick and W. N. Mann, I. M. Lonie and W. T. Witherington, in G.E.R. Lloyd (ed.), *Hippocratic Writings,* Penguin Classics.

6. Unless otherwise noted, all quotations from Praxagoras have been taken from the comprehensive edition and translation by Fritz Steckerl (1958), *The Fragments of Praxagoras of Cos and His School.*

7. Unless otherwise noted, passages from Galen are taken from the *Selected Works* translated by P. N. Singer for Oxford University Press, 1997. Galen's *On the doctrines of Hippocrates and Plato* is quoted from the only currently available translation, the 1984 Corpus Medicorum Graecorum, vol. 5, pt. 4, translated and edited by P. De Lacy for Akademie-Verlag.

Chapter 7

The Roman Empire:
Christianity and Neoplatonism

As we have seen, Stoicism, Epicurianism, and Skepticism dominated the philosophical scene in the early Roman world. In addition to these formal schools of thought, there was swirl of religions and cults that would strongly influence the one religion that would come to dominate the late Roman Empire: Christianity. Christian thought is the intellectual foundation on which stands much of modern European and Near Eastern philosophy in a wide range of topics, including psychology. Consequently, it is one of the main subjects of this chapter.[1]

Not nearly as well known to the modern reader as Christianity, however, is another philosophical movement that contended with Christianity for dominance in the Roman Empire. As Stoicism and Epicurianism faded from view, a revival of ideas derived mainly from the teachings of Plato took their place. This new form of Platonism emphasized his later metaphysical works and combined authentic Platonic thought with "platonized" interpretations of Aristotle's work. Some schools integrated into this mix strands of Stoicism, as well as Pythagorean and Egyptian interests in numerology and magic. Because of its apparently syncretic nature, this movement was named *Neo*platonism by eighteenth- and nineteenth-century historians of philosophy in order to distinguish it from what they took to be "authentic" Hellenic Platonism. The Neoplatonists, however, considered themselves to be orthodox Platonists. In the past few decades respect for Neoplatonism has been renewed among many scholars of ancient philosophy.

The Roman renewal of Platonism reached its intellectual peak in the work of a third-century philosopher named Plotinus, but it began with the so-called Middle Platonists of the centuries surrounding the birth of Christ. It continued to have influence on into the Middle Ages. Perhaps most important, although pagan Neoplatonism often saw itself as a rival to Christian thought, many significant early Christian thinkers, as we shall see, were themselves reformed Middle Platonists or had been strongly influenced by Platonic ideas. As a result, much of early Christian metaphysical and psychological thought owes its origin to Platonism. This complex set of relationships is spelled out more fully below.

THE INTELLECTUAL CLIMATE OF IMPERIAL ROME

Eastern "Mystery Religions"

In addition to Rome's "official" religion of Jupiter, Juno, and the rest of the pantheon, a number of "mystery" religions, mostly derived from Eastern sources, began to spread throughout the rapidly expanding empire.[2] The "mystery" of these religions is not to be confused with mystic*ism* (the belief in the possibility of union with the divine through meditation or contemplation) but, rather, associated with the secret rites of initiation into the cult that they involved.

The oldest of these cults may well have been that of Cybele (also know as Meter), the "Great Mother," which originated in Phrygia (present-day west-central Turkey). According to Cybele's myth, her lover, Attis, castrated himself as punishment for an infidelity and bled to death under a pine tree. Three days later, it was said, he rose again. Priests of Cybele were similarly required to castrate themselves in homage to the goddess. The spring celebration prescribed the letting of blood by the chief priest and the cutting down of a tree, which was then adorned with violets as symbols of Attis' blood. The initiation rite involved being drenched in the blood of a newly sacrificed bull.

The cult of Isis came from Egypt, where she was queen of the gods. After her husband, Osiris, had been murdered by his brother, Seth, Isis was said to a have searched for and collected the parts of Osiris' body that Seth had scattered across the world. After reassembling them, she became pregnant by them and bore a child, Horus, who sought revenge for his father's murder. Rites of Isis, though less ecstatic than those of Cybele, were viewed with no less awe by many Greeks and Romans. The very antiquity of Egypt (united ca. 3150 BC) and its cultural institutions earned from many other peoples a deep respect. A large temple to Isis was built in Rome itself under the emperorship of Caligula (ruled AD 37–41).

The cult of Mithras was of Indo-Iranian origin. Mithras was a god of light or possibly of the sun itself. His worship became popular among Roman soldiers after about AD 100. The details of the myth are not completely known to us, so secret was the cult, but the story seems to have involved the sacrificing of a wild bull. From the blood of the bull was said to come forth grain and other symbols of fertility. In another story, Mithras is said to have saved humankind from a world-destroying flood unleashed by an evil god. The sun imagery of the Mithraic cult may have been adopted by the cult of *Sol Invictus* (Invincible Sun), which was popular among soldiers of the emperor Constantine in the early fourth century. The traditional birth-date of *Sol Invictus* was December 25, as close to the date of winter solstice as the Romans could get.

It is easy to overstate the case, but clearly some of the details of the myths of the mystery cults provided some of the "raw materials" used by Christians as they developed their religion during the same era. As we shall see, however, part of what helped Christianity ultimately prevail over these other cults was its recruitment of some highly educated scholars who were able to give it a solid philosophical foundation the others lacked. Questions of the origin and nature of the *psyché* were central to these developments.

Middle Platonism

During the two centuries before the birth of Christ, as we have seen, Skepticism's influence began to grow in philosophical circles. It dominated the Athenian Academy, particularly under the leadership of Carneades of Cyrene (213–129 BC), and it seemed able to significantly undermine the arguments of the leading Stoics of the time, such as Chrysippus. As a re-sult, the other philosophical and religious schools of the time began to merge with one another, closing ranks in the face of what was perceived to be a common enemy (see Wallis, 1995, p. 27). The first of these alliances can be seen in the rise of Antiochus of Ascalon (ca. 130–ca. 68 BC) to the head of the Academy around 79 BC (Kidd, 1967, p. 384). Although he is known for bringing Platonic thought back to Plato's old school, which had been domi-nated by Skeptics for over a century, it was his expressed intention to unify Platonic and Stoic thought (Rees, 1967, p. 337). With the publication of Aristotle's school texts by Andronicus in the first century BC (Wallis, 1995, p. 27), Antiochus argued that Aristotle's work, too, could be brought un-der the Platonic umbrella. As this new form of Platonism developed in the early part of the Christian era, it was often infused with elements of a vari-ety of mystical texts bearing Egyptian and Platonic flavorings: the *Chaldaean Oracles, Sibylline Oracles, Asclepius, Corpus Hermeticum,* and the like. Such books offered the promise of salvation, as well as other, more mundane ben-efits, through the use of special magic and ritual (see Copenhaver, 1992, for an excellent account of their origin and use).

In Alexandria a Jewish scholar named Philo (30 BC–AD 45) began work-ing to integrate traditional Jewish scripture with Platonic thought. In one of his most famous works, he attempted to show that Moses had been a philosopher equal in stature to Plato, intimating that Plato may have bor-rowed some of his best ideas from the Hebrew prophet. Philo's position on the origin and nature of the soul was essentially that given by Plato in the *Timaeus:* The rational part of the human soul was created by the Maker. Some of these souls remained bodiless (the angels, according to Philo), but those to be embodied were associated, according to Philo, with the stars. As had Plato, Philo said that the irrational parts of the soul are of the body and die when it does. The rational part of the soul was said to be immortal, however. Although divine in origin, even this rational part of the soul, according to Philo, cannot directly know God, who is described as the "Uncreated One": unnamable, ineffable, and incomprehensible. Only through the mediation of the divine *Nous* (à la Anaxagoras and Aristotle) or *Logos* (à la the Stoics), can one know God.

These modifications to Plato's account strongly foreshadow the developments made famous over two centuries later by the "founder" of Neoplatonism, Plotinus, described later in this chapter. Contrary to most philosophies of his time, however, Philo stressed the absolute freedom of the human will, even in the face of the causal forces of nature (Wolfson, 1967, p. 152). In coming centuries many significant Christian theologians would begin to echo Philo's sentiments in their own attempts to reconcile Christianity and Platonism. The version of Plato's thought put forward by Philo has a strong Pythagorean numerological tinge. The tone of this combination of Judaism, Platonism, and Pythagoreanism is better seen than described:

> [Moses] says that in six days the world was created, not that its Maker required a length of time for His work, for we must think of God as doing all things simultaneously, remembering that "all" includes with the commands which He issues the thought behind them. Six days are mentioned because for the things coming into existence there was need of order. Order involves number, and among numbers[,] by the laws of nature the most suitable to productivity is 6, for if we start with 1 it is the perfect number, being equal to the product of its factors (*i.e.,* 1 × 2 × 3), as well as made up of the sum of them (*i.e.,* 1 + 2 + 3), its half being 3, its third part 2, its sixth part 1. We say that it is in its nature both male and female, and is a result of the distinctive power of either. For among things that are[,] it is the odd that is male and the even female. Now of odd numbers 3 is the starting-point, and of even numbers 2, and the product of these two is 6. For it was requisite that the world, being most perfect of all things that have come into existence, should be constituted in accordance with a perfect number, namely six. (Philo, *On the Account of the World's Creation,* 1966, ch. 3)

Various forms of Platonism gradually became the main bulwark of the Roman pagan establishment against the rising tide of Christianity. The works of these Middle Platonists have not survived, in the main. We know something of Albinus (fl. ca. 150), who worked to assimilate all Aristotle's work to Plato's and who was teacher to Galen of Pergamum (129–199), the greatest of Roman physicians. Another second-century Neoplatonist named Atticus, however, vigorously opposed Albinus' aim, arguing that the teachings of Plato and Aristotle are incompatible (see Wallis, 1995, pp. 31–32). We also know that one Celsus (fl. ca. 178) wrote a Platonic critique of Christianity that has been partially preserved only because its arguments were so powerful that the early Christian theologian Origen (discussed below) composed a refutation of it over seventy years later. Finally, we know of one Numenius of Apamea, who lived in the second century and whose work so closely resembles that of Plotinus in certain respects that Plotinus was accused of having plagiarized it.[3] There were others, too, but we now move on to the movement that Platonists increasingly saw as the greatest threat to the traditional Roman way of life: Christianity.

EARLY CHRISTIANITY

Early Christian thinkers contributed crucially to the developing Roman ideas about the soul and the mind. Their influence on modern psychological thought is so pervasive that we sometimes have trouble recognizing it for what it is because it often operates as unquestioned background to further developments. Also, early Christian psychological thought is frequently overshadowed by the colossal revolution Christianity wrought in European and Near Eastern theology, with which it is inextricably intertwined. One of the most significant Christian contributions to theory of soul and mind, and the one highlighted here, was their bringing of the question of the freedom of the will to the forefront of psychological debate. As we have seen, other philosophers, dating back even to Plato, had raised the question of the freedom of the will,[4] but it usually played a relatively peripheral role in their theories of the *psyché,* the *nous,* and so on. After Philo, however, the early Christians were among the first to regard it as a *crucial* element in the proper discourse about the soul and mind.[5]

Very early Christianity was, of course, mainly confined to the Jewish people of the Levant. Jews were well known, if not very numerous, in the Roman Empire. Their reputation seems to have been, on the whole, somewhat negative. As Chadwick (1993) puts it:

> In the ancient world everyone knew at least three things about the Jews: they would not be associated either directly or indirectly with any pagan cult (which seemed antisocial), they refused to eat not only meat that had been offered in sacrifice to the gods but also all pork (which seemed ridiculous), and they circumcised their male infants (which seemed repulsive). (pp. 18–19)

Yet, Jewish communities that had formed outside of the Levant, as a result of various economic and political factors, often gathered around them circles of interested Gentiles—people drawn by the elegance of monotheism, by Jewish morality, and by the venerability of Jewish texts.

When St. Paul began his famous trek to Greece, the relaxation of traditional Jewish practices seems to have been an important factor in his ability to attract to the Christian cause Gentiles who were already interested in

Judaism. As time went on, the original Jewish community of Christians became a less significant force within the Church, especially after all Jews were
expelled from Judaea by the emperor Hadrian in 135, and the Gentile
Church became the orthodox force in the new religion. As early as the second century, Irenaeus, bishop of Lyon (ca. 130–ca. 200),[6] was able to condemn the Jewish Christians (called Ebionites[7]) as heretics for, among other
things, not believing in the Virgin Birth of Christ.

The Gnostics

Before an official Christian orthodoxy had been established, various
groups of religious communities called "Gnostics" (from the Greek word for
"knowledge," *gnosis*) adopted parts of the Christian story and integrated it
with other religious and philosophical texts. Gnosticism was not a unified
religious movement but a term used to cover many diverse sects. In general,
Gnostics believed that everything spiritual is good and divine, and everything
material, including their own bodies, evil and cursed. Some manifested their
indifference to the material world with extreme licentiousness, believing that
nothing done with mere bodies could taint the purity of their souls. Most,
however, were strict ascetics, denying themselves all bodily pleasures. Their
cosmogony was drawn from both the first books of Genesis and Plato's
Timaeus, although they believed the Demiurge—the maker of the material
world—to have been an ignorant, or even evil, being because he had created (evil) matter. Some identified the Demiurge of the *Timaeus* with the
God of the Old Testament, arguing that the "true" God had revealed himself only in Christ's resurrection. Although the Gnostics talked of Platonic
philosophy, there is little evidence that they actually practiced philosophical
analysis to any great degree. They seem to have regarded Plato's teachings
in much the same way they regarded Scripture—namely, as revelation rather
than as an argument to be examined, criticized, and reworked.

The Gnostics' identification of the God of the Old Testament with the
Demiurge of the *Timaeus* led some of them to expressions of anti-Semitism
because they saw Jews as followers of that "inferior," perhaps even "evil,"
earlier god. This anti-Semitic sentiment, though not its cosmological justification, seeped into "orthodox" Christian communities as well. One group,
the "Ophites," even worshipped the serpent of the Garden of Eden for having first given humans knowledge (*gnosis*) in defiance of the God of the Old
Testament. The "theological dualism" of the Gnostics (the belief in two
Gods, one evil and one good) was to become one of the main points of
contention between the Gnostics and "orthodox" Christians.

The *gnosis,* or knowledge, proclaimed in the Gnostics' name was thought
to be of an intuitive, rather than reasoned, sort, and it was thought to be
available only to an elect few. Each Gnostic sect had its own story of how

the soul, after being freed from its material "prison" by the death of the body, would have to battle its way through the planetary spheres, each inhabited by an evil (material) demon, before reaching heaven. Special magical words and names were taught to members to help their souls on their way.

Two main groups of Gnostics were led by a Platonist, Valentius (fl. 2nd c.) and by an Egyptian priest, Basilides (fl. 2nd c.). A third important group—considered Gnostic by most Christian writers of the time, but who more recent research has shown to be distinctive in several ways—was led by an Asian preacher named Marcion (d. ca. 180). The Valentinians proposed that in addition to the body and soul (*psychê*), some people—namely, the Gnostic elect—have *pneuma* (often translated as "spirit") as well. This *pneuma* was thought to give them their special *gnosis* and guarantee them entry into heaven. Regular Christian faithful, they thought, have only *psychê*, but no *pneuma*. This might allow them an afterlife, but they had no hope of developing *gnosis* through study or practice or somesuch. All such matters, said the Valentinians, were predetermined by God. Finally, those who were not among even the Christian faithful were thought not even to have *psychê*—that is, they were thought to be nothing but animated bodies. For them there need be no regard, and for them no hope of afterlife.

The Gnostics' deterministic belief that the individual has no control over his or her ultimate fate—that one is predestined for salvation or damnation—was a second main point of contention between Gnostics and orthodox Christians. It was a debate that would lead the Christians to stress the importance of the freedom of the will to such a degree that it would become a core tenet of their religious beliefs and, simultaneously, of their psychological theory.

Finally, the Gnostics argued that Christ had been not a man but a pure spiritual being. Only those without *pneuma* had seen him as a man. To the consternation of orthodox Christians, this included the Apostles, who had first reported Christ's essential humanity. The Gnostics argued, or at least intimated, that more enlightened people (such as themselves) would have seen his purely spiritual form.

St. Justin Martyr (ca. 100–ca. 165)

Although many early Christians were dogmatic in their beliefs, some tried to integrate the philosophical approach to knowledge with the developing Christian theology. St. Justin Martyr was one of the first of these. He was born a Greek in Samaria and traveled to Ephesus to be educated. After sampling Stoicism, Aristotelianism, and Pythagoreanism, he settled on learning Platonic philosophy (Justin Martyr, *Dialogue with Trypho,* ch. 2). He reports having been converted to Christianity by a man he met on a beach who could refute the Platonic doctrine of the *psychê*. Despite his conversion, however, he maintained many of his Platonic beliefs, although he now regarded faith rather than reason as the true path to knowledge (Justin Martyr, *Horatory Address to the Greeks,* ch. 36). Still, he regarded pagan myth as the common enemy of both Christianity and Platonic philosophy. He even viewed Socrates as a martyr of a sort, having been executed by pagan authorities for spreading the truth as it had been revealed to him. Justin was a strong advocate of freedom of the will. One of his main criticisms of Gnosticism was that it contained a strict determinism with respect to salvation. Those who have *pneuma* are saved; those without it are not. Justin recognized, however, that without freedom there can be no moral responsibility, and without freedom the message of Jesus has no point, for it can change nothing.

This advocacy of free will was the beginning of a crucial turning point in the history of psychological thought. Although Christians were by no means the first to claim that humans have free will, in their battle against Gnosticism Christians came to make freedom of the will a *central aspect* of their psychological doctrine.

Justin also rejected the Gnostics' claim that Christ was never truly incarnate. He argued, in traditional philosophical fashion, that Christ was fully human, but that immanent within him was the divine *Logos,* the Reason of God. This combination of humanity and divinity was what enabled him to mediate between the spiritual and the material realms. Justin's description of the relationship between "Father" and "Son" initiated one of the first great controversies in Christianity. Are they one person or two? If two, then are there not two gods? If one, then how can Christ have been truly incarnate if God, the Father, is not? Justin said the *Logos* mediates between them, "like one torch lighting another." To many this seemed too close to ditheism (belief in two gods). The battle over the nature of the Trinity—Father, Son, and the Spirit they share—had begun.

Tertullian (ca. 160–ca. 230)

Among the most influential participants in the debate about the Trinity was Tertullian, a fiery Christian theologian from Africa who converted from orthodox Christianity to Montanism.[8] He was the first major Christian to write in Latin rather than in Greek, making his teachings accessible to a much wider audience than those of earlier theologians. With respect to the Trinity, he argued that the Father and Son are one "substance" (*substantia*) but two "persons" (*persona*). By contrast with Justin, however, Tertullian explicitly rejected all attempts to explicate or defend Christian revelation in terms of philosophy. Faith is the only path open to the Christian, he argued. He recognized that if reason were sufficient, then faith would be unnecessary. He claimed to believe the Christian story precisely *because* it is, in a certain sense, absurd. In its very absurdity, Tertullian believed, lies a test of one's faith. That is why faith is so crucial to salvation. Chiding philosophical theologians, he asked rhetorically, "What has Athens to do with Jerusalem?" (Tertullian, *Prescription Against the Heretics,* ch. 7).

Tertullian was the first of the major Christian writers to compose a treatise specifically about the soul (*De Anima*). The work reveals Tertullian's erudition with respect to the philosophical views influential in his time. He expended a great deal of effort attempting specifically to refute the views of Plato, Aristotle, the Stoics, the Epicureans, and the Middle Platonists where their views conflicted with Scripture. He also adopted the arguments of these schools, however, when it served his purpose. Almost paradoxically, despite his emphasis on faith, he felt required to refute the views of his opponents on purely logical grounds where he could. Unfortunately, many of his arguments are so weak as to be convincing only to those already converted to his cause. For instance, he rejected the Stoics' (and many others') assertion that two bodies cannot occupy the same space with the claim that a pregnant woman is a counterexample to this principle (ch. VI, p. 186).[9] Because so many of his original arguments are so poor or based on misinterpretations of his opponents' positions, it may be best to think of Tertullian not so much as a Christian *philosopher* but, rather, as a Christian *polemicist.* Despite this, Tertullian's *De Anima* gives us our first full account of the psychological thought of the early Christians.

First, he argued that the soul (*anima*) is created at birth, rather than existing before the body, as in Plato's *Timaeus.* What is more, it was, he said, created by the "breath (*flatus*) of God" (ch. IV, p. 184). Although the soul was not said to be material, Tertullian held it to be *corporeal,* contra the "Platonists," none of whom he names specifically (ch. VI, p. 185). He also rejected the Platonic view that the senses detect only things material, and the intellect things incorporeal, on the grounds that color and sound are sensed but incorporeal (ch. VI, p. 186). Even if this claim were to be accepted (although it certainly would *not* have been by his pagan contemporaries), it comes into conflict with a proof he soon afterward offered for the soul's being corporeal. Specifically, he claimed that the soul itself is nothing at all "if it is not a bodily substance" (ch. VII, p. 187). This implies, however, that nothing can be said to truly exist unless it is corporeal. But surely he believed sounds and colors to exist, even though he claimed them to be incorporeal.

Given that he believed the soul to be corporeal, the question arose concerning its spatial dimensions. For this information Tertullian relied on the testimony of an unnamed "Montanist sister" who was said to have had visions and to "converse with angels, and sometimes even with the Lord." He cites her report that

a spirit has been in the habit of appearing to me; not, however, a void and empty illusion, but such as would offer itself to be even grasped by the hand, soft and transparent and of an ethereal color, and in form resembling that of a human being in every respect. (ch. IX, p. 188)

The soul (*anima*) was not the only object of psychological interest with which Tertullian dealt. As mentioned, the Gnostics also advocated the existence of a spirit (*pneuma*) that was, at least in some people, said to be superior to the soul. In addition, Greek philosophy had long been concerned with what makes bodies live. Although, according to Christians, the soul departs at the death of the body, there was no evidence, even in Scripture, that the soul is responsible for the vital functions of the body while alive. The bodily function thought to require explanation most crucially was breathing, and Tertullian virtually identified the question of spirit with the question of breath. On the basis that soul (life) and spirit (breath) are never found apart in humans, he argued that "the spirit or breath is an adjunct of the human soul" (ch. X, p. 190). Spirit, he went on to say, is "a term expressive of an *operation* of the soul, not of its nature" (ch. XI, p. 190, italics added). He was careful, however, to distinguish the breath of humans, which keeps them alive, from the "Breath of God," which was thought to have given humans souls in the first place (*Genesis*, Bk. ii, ch. 7).

In addition to the questions of soul and spirit, there was also the question of mind (*animus*[10]), which Tertullian identified with the old Greek problem of *nous*. Anaxagoras and Aristotle said the *nous* was unchangeable and able to apprehend all other things.[11] If true, this would make it superior to the soul (*anima*), which was said, for instance, to suffer the pains of hell (a kind of change) if it were so unfortunate as to end up there or, alternatively, to change its character from evil to good through an act of will (discussed more below). Since the suggestion that anything is superior to the soul was unacceptable to Christians, Tertullian proclaimed "that the mind coalesces with the soul—not indeed as being distinct from it in substance, but as being its natural function and agent" (ch. XII, p. 192). Thus, Tertullian had folded three problems—that of life (and afterlife), that of bodily functions (particularly breath), and that of intellect—into one. To summarize, then, the soul, in his view, was a unified corporeal entity, two functions of which were the spirit and the mind. As was traditional for philosophers of the time, he located this supreme entity in the heart on the basis of biblical passages (ch. XV, p. 194).

There remained for Tertullian the question of the senses. Many philosophers, such as Plato, had argued that as parts of the body rather than the mind, the senses are subject to error and not to be trusted. Tertullian argued, on the contrary, that the senses are, in fact, one with the mind and not prone to error as had been commonly believed. His argument for this conclusion is particularly tortured, but it seems to amount to the claim that whatever is sensed, even if not true to the world, has been authentically *caused* by the world and is therefore not truly in error (ch. XVII, p. 196). This, of course, had never been denied by earlier philosophers. The point had simply been that the senses could not be trusted to reveal veridical information about the world. Such a misinterpretation of the claims of philosophical opponents is not unusual in Tertullian's work, but it is particularly glaring in this passage.

Tertullian's aim in folding the senses into the mind was, of course, to identify them with the soul as well (ch. XVIII). In like fashion, Plato's "lower" parts of the soul (*thumoeides* or courage, and *epithumetikon* or desire) were made parts of the soul as well (ch. XVI), leaving nothing important about humans left over to be explained by natural philosophy (or science). All was to be attributed to divine grace (although he did concede that "local influences," "national peculiarities," "bodily condition," and other "accidental circumstances" can affect how the soul develops, ch. XX, p. 201).

Only after discussing all this did Tertullian touch on that aspect of Christian psychology that was rapidly becoming the most important: freedom of the will. Like his predecessors, he argued the case for freedom against Gnostic determinism, specifically against the Valentinians. By way of freedom, he argued, humans are able to turn away from evil and be, as he put it, "born again and re-made" (ch. XXI, p. 202). Here again we see why the changeability of the soul was so important to early Christians and why, as a result, they were led to reject Gnostic claims of its immutability.

The second half of Tertullian's *De Anima* is devoted to topics that need not detain us greatly here: the refutation of many opponents' positions (including that of the Pythagoreans), the development of the soul as the individual's body grows (both reach maturity at about fourteen years of age), the sources of evil, the natures of sleeping and dreaming (most dreams are natural, but some are sent by God), the details of the separation of the soul from the body at death, and the futility of magic (it can produce only illusion, not substantial change). Still, the influence of his work on the emerging Christian world, particularly in the western Roman Empire, can hardly be overestimated. In particular, the influence of his unshakable faith in the literal truth of every word of the Bible, as well as his utter rejection of all other apparent sources of knowledge (e.g., science and philosophy), can still be seen in some groups of Christians today. Tertullian staked out one extreme in the continuum of beliefs that would be adopted by Christians.

Origen (ca. 185–254)

As popular as Tertullian's writings were, they by no means halted the attempt to integrate Christian teaching and the lessons of Greek philosophy. In the Eastern Empire St. Clement of Alexandria (ca. 150–ca. 215) taught that although all had been created by the Christian God, there was still much that Christians could learn from Plato, Aristotle, and the Stoics. He even hinted, as had Philo before him, that Plato had borrowed some of his ideas from Moses (Chadwick, 1993, p. 96).

Far more influential (and controversial) than Clement, however, was the man who succeeded him as head of the catechetical school at Alexandria, Origen. He may have been taught by Ammonius Saccas, the man who would later tutor the "founder" of Neoplatonism, Plotinus.[12] He never seems to have held Plato and Greek philosophy in as high esteem, however, as did Clement. A popular story about Origen claims that he castrated himself as a young man to ensure his purity. This may well have been an invention of one of his many enemies (Chadwick, 1993, p. 109). During his time in Alexandria, he wrote his most important work, *De Principiis* (*On First Principles*). In 232, having incurred the displeasure of the Demetrius, the bishop of Alexandria, he moved to Caesarea, in present-day Turkey. There he continued to write, including his lengthy response to Celsus' popular critique of Christianity, mentioned earlier. One fascinating aspect of this book is that both men were Platonists, and thus they shared many fundamental beliefs. In the main only issues surrounding Christianity separated them. In 250 Origen was arrested and tortured during the first general Roman persecution of the Christians, under the emperor Decius (ruled 249–251), who spent his short reign attempting to engineer a revival of traditional Roman paganism. Origen died in 253 or 254 at Tyre, where almost 1,000 years later European Crusaders reported visiting his tomb (although nothing of it remains today). His works were intermittently popular during the centuries after his death but were condemned by St. Chrysostom in 400, apparently as part of a personal dispute with one Theophilius of Alexandria. St. Jerome (ca. 347–419), who had been a follower of Origen until about that time, suddenly condemned his works as heresy. The pope of the day agreed to condemn certain passages, although he said he had no knowledge of Origen's works. In 553 one Theodore of Mopsuestia attempted to have Origen's works declared anathema, again as part of a dispute that seems to have had little to do with Origen's actual beliefs; but the pope refused to attend the meeting at which the condemnation took place, and it seems never to have been made official Church doctrine (Prat, 1907).

So what were these ideas that made Origen among the most important and most controversial of early Christian philosophers? Origen was among the first to claim that the most important meaning of the Bible lies not in its literal interpretation (very contrary to Tertullian) but in its *symbolic* meaning. Some took this to mean that he denied the literal truth of the Resurrection, which would have been legitimate grounds for an accusation of heresy, but it is by no means clear that this is what he meant. It seems not to have been so much the denial of literal truth that interested him as the primacy of other levels of truth—social, spiritual, and so on.

Like Justin and Tertullian, Origen also fought Gnosticism on the basis of freedom of the human will. In Origen one can see the concept of free will continue to grow in importance. He was the first to write an entire treatise specifically on the subject (Prat, 1907), but it is now lost. Fortunately, he also devoted large portions of his most important work, *De Principiis*,[13] to a discussion of the soul and its freedom. There he argued that every living thing[14] has a soul (*anima*) because every living thing has imagination (*phantstikê*) and desire (*hormêtikê*),[15] the defining qualities of life in his opinion. He later explains, in strikingly Stoic fashion, that although pieces of wood and stones are "held together by their constitution (*hexis*) alone," animals and plants are "held together by nature and a soul (*psychê*)" (Bk. III, ch. 1, sec. 2). Soul is attributed, however, to metals, fire, and springs of water as well, presumably on account of their ability to move (e.g., metal under the influence of a magnet). In animals the soul can give rise to images (*phantasias*) that "incite effort," such as a spider weaving a web or a bee producing wax. Although Origen conceded that the abilities of animals such as hunting dogs and war horses make it sometimes seem as though they possess reason,[16] only humans have the faculty of reason fully (Bk. III, ch. 1, sec. 3). This allows humans not only to have images of things they desire but also to *judge* the goodness and wickedness of their desire and to reject those desires that are wicked. This ability to make moral judgments and act upon them is just what it means to say that humans have free will, according to Origen.

Origen also gave an account of the origin of the rational souls. He tells a story reminiscent of, though not identical with, that given by Plato in the *Timaeus*. God created a finite number of rational souls. They were identical to begin with (contrary to the Gnostics' claim to being a spiritual elect)—hot and fiery and full of light—but some "cooled" and turned to "slothfulness and a dislike of labor in preserving what is good, and an aversion to and neglect of better things [which] furnished the beginning of a departure from goodness" (Origen, Bk. II, ch. 9, sec. 3). Those that remained good became angels and stars and heavenly bodies. Those that cooled a little became humans. Those that cooled even more became demons (*inferna*), completely alienated from the good. Because they all have free will, however, Origen allowed that even the demons could return to the good and achieve salvation. He stressed (*contra* the Gnostics) that all humans—even those who claim not to be able to control their desires—have free will and can control themselves through education and the exercise of reason.

Christian thought continued to develop after Origen. The fight with Roman authorities was by now in full swing and would not be settled until the end of the fourth century. After the Decian persecution under which Origen suffered would come the "Great Persecution" of Diocletian (ruled 284–305). Then would come the reconciliation of the Roman state with Christianity under Constantine (ruled 306–337), only to be overturned by the attempt of Julian "The Apostate" (361–363) to revive paganism once again. Finally, the Christian emperor Theodosius would outlaw paganism in 391. There were also a series of battles to be fought within Christianity itself, most notably against the sect known as Arianism.[17] Despite condemnations at the Council of Nicaea (325) and the Council of Constantinople (381), Catholicism would not secure its victory over the Arian challenge until after the collapse of the Roman Empire in the West, when the Frankish king (and Catholic convert) Clovis defeated the (Arian) Visigoths at the battle of Vouillé (in present-day France) in 507.

NEOPLATONISM

Middle Platonism, discussed earlier in this chapter, was never a unified movement under strong leadership. As we have seen, it took different forms in different places throughout the empire, variously integrating late Platonic thought with Stoicism, Aristotelianism, mysticism of assorted kinds, Judaism, and even Christianity. In the middle of the third century, however, one Platonist would rise above the others to develop it into a single and integrated vision of the cosmos and humans' place in it. That person was Plotinus, the focus of this section, beginning with a discussion of his life and work. After Plotinus' death, Neoplatonism splintered in many directions. Plotinus' student Porphyry tried to carry the torch his master had passed to him, collecting and editing Plotinus' work into the form we have today. Iamblichus, by contrast, a one-time student of Porphyry's with strong Pythagorean leanings, developed the "theurgic" or magical side of the movement. Theurgy is the attempt to call down divine powers to intervene in earthly matters. We examine the thought of Porphyry and Iamblichus in the second part of this section. Finally, we look at what became of Neoplatonism as Rome struggled toward becoming a Christian empire during and after the rule of Constantine. Two main schools developed, one in Athens and one in Alexandria, and attempted to deal with the rising Christian tide in quite different ways.

Plotinus (205–270)

Plotinus was probably born in upper Egypt, quite possibly to an ethnically Greek family. As did many serious scholars of the day, he studied in Alexandria, apparently moving from teacher to teacher, unhappy with them all. He finally happened upon one Ammonius Saccas, who may also have been the teacher of Origen, a man twenty years' Plotinus' senior. After eleven years under Ammonius' tutelage, he joined a Roman military expedition to Persia, under the command of Emperor Gordian III (ruled 238–244), in order to learn more of Eastern philosophy. Gordian's assassination forced Plotinus to escape with his life back to the West. He eventually ended up in Rome itself, where he opened a school and began writing. The most important of his students was Prophyry, who posthumously collected and organized

Plotinus' writings into the form in which his works are now known, the *Enneads*. It is a collection of six books of nine tractates each (numbers that pleased Porphyry's numerological inclinations[18]) concerning metaphysics, cosmology, psychology, ethics, debates with Gnostics and other opponents, and a wide range of other issues. In time Plotinus earned the ear of a second emperor, Gallienus (ruled 260–268), and was given permission to found a city in Campania, in Italy, based on the precepts of Plato's *Laws*. The plan was never realized, however, and Gallienus' assassination in 268 seems to have forced Plotinus to leave Rome for good. He died of leprosy two years later.

As mentioned, Plotinus considered himself to be an orthodox Platonist. He does not appear to have viewed his own work as having entailed a major transformation of Plato's teachings. He considered himself to be more of an expositor than an innovator. This is quite surprising because, at least at first glance, Plotinus' work seem to focus on a few issues raised primarily in Plato's later metaphysical work, especially the *Parmenidies, Sophist,* and *Philebus*. In these works Plato proposed that some kinds might have priority over others—that they might be arranged in a hierarchy of importance (see ch. 3, note 15, of this volume)—and that the highest kinds might themselves proceed from an even higher realm, sometimes referred to simply as "The One" (*to hen*), which is not an entity unto itself but, rather," beyond being."

Plotinus appears to have developed these ideas into an elaborate metaphysical structure far beyond anything found in Plato's writings. But if so, how could Plotinus have believed himself to have been merely an expositor of Plato's thought? A crucial hint may lie in a comment made by Aristotle in his *Physics*. In Book IV he wrote, "[I]n the *Timaeus* [Plato] gives an account of what receives form which differs from the one he gives in what are called his unwritten doctrines" (290b13–14). There are also several places in the *Metaphysics* in which Aristotle attributes to Plato positions that do not seem to appear in any of Plato's known works. Along with a few comments by Plato to the effect that certain ideas cannot be effectively taught through the written word, but can be conveyed only through face-to-face communication (e.g., *Second Letter,* 314b–c), these have led some to speculate that a portion of Plato's teachings—his most cherished ideas on metaphysics—was known only to those who actually attended the Academy and was intentionally omitted from the books written for public consumption. Among a certain group of modern Platonic scholars—especially those at Tübingen University in Germany—a great deal of attention has been paid to uncovering what the content of these "unwritten doctrines" might have been (see, e.g., Findlay, 1974; Krämer, 1982/1990; Szlezák, 1993/1999). It is now the opinion of some Plotinus specialists that Plato's unwritten doctrines were transmitted to Plotinus and it was mainly these, rather than the written texts we know today, that were the basis of his work.

The controversy over the "unwritten doctrines" is a complex matter far beyond our scope here, but a brief outline may convey the flavor of the debate. Pepple (1997) outlines the primary elements of the "unwritten doctrines" as being the following:

(A) There are two fundamental principles underlying everything: the One and the Indefinite Dyad (Aristotle, *Metaphysics*, 987b20–22, 988a10–15).
(B) These fundamental principles somehow generate everything else, in the following order: numbers, forms, and sensible things (Aristotle, *Metaphysics*, 988a10–15; Theophrastus, *Metaphysics*, 6b10–15).
(C) Forms are generated from the One and the Dyad, sensibles from the forms and the Dyad (Aristotle, *Metaphysics*, 988a10–15).
(D) The One is associated (but apparently not identical) with goodness, the Dyad with evil (Aristotle, *Metaphysics*, 988a14–15 together with 1091b13–14)

These claims obviously require some explication. The One was thought to be the simple, self-sufficient, unique, and perfect source of all. It has no parts or properties; it is eternal and unchanging. It is said to be inherently prior to everything else, the metaphysical foundation on which everything is premised. Being the source of all being, it was said itself to be "beyond being." As such, language was believed to be inadequate to directly describe what the One is, and thus it was the subject both of a "negative theology," describing what it is not, and of indirect description through analogy and metaphor. The One was the primary metaphysical sphere of Plotinus' philosophy (see, e.g., Bussanich, 1996, on the metaphysics of the One).

Everything else was said to "emanate" or "proceed" from the One.[19] The nature of this procession is subtle because it must not imply that the One in any sense diminished or otherwise changed; nor must it suggest that it embarks upon a causal process of some sort. Plotinus often illuminated procession from the One in terms of a series of metaphors:

It must be a radiation from [the One] while it remains unchanged, like the bright light of the sun which, so to speak, runs around it, springing from it continually while it remains unchanged. All things which exist, as long as they remain in being, necessarily produce from their own substances, in dependence on their present power, a surrounding reality directed to what is outside them, a kind of image of the archetypes from which it was produced: fire produces the heat which comes from it; snow does not only keep its cold inside itself. Perfumed things show this particularly clearly. As long as they exist, something is diffused from themselves around them, and what is near them enjoys their existence. And all things when they come to perfection produce; the One is always perfect and therefore produces everlastingly; and its product is less than itself. (*Enneads*, V.1.6, 28–40)

The first such procession from the One was thought to be the Dyad, the primordial twoness or division between things. The Dyad has gone by other names: for example, the Indefinite Two, the Great and the Small, the One-Many (*hen-polla*). In Plotinus' philosophy, because of his emphasis on the primary division between the Knower and the Known (i.e., the object of knowledge) it was called *Nous*, usually translated as "Intellect." This is not a personal or individual intellect, but a universal intellect, related to Aristotle's "Unmoved Mover"—the originator of all change and motion. The intellectual activity of *Nous* was not thought to be "logical" in the sense of a series of connected propositions. Instead, it was regarded as being of a higher, more contemplative character, more on the order of "insight" or "intuition" rather than "reason" narrowly conceived (see Blumenthal, 1996). *Nous* is intimately involved in the generation of "intelligible being"—the Forms—but it does not do it alone. Its capacity is derived from the One. In different essays Plotinus emphasizes the respective roles of *Nous* or the One in the making of the Forms. This has led to controversy over which one is primary cause of the Forms (see, e.g., Bussanich, 1996, pp. 51–55, for a further discussion of these issues). The Forms and the One are not completely distinct from each other (thus "One-Many"), and so *Nous* contemplates the Forms directly.

Just as *Nous* proceeds from the One, so from *Nous* proceeds *Psychê*, usually translated as Soul. Whereas the primary domain of the *Nous* was thought to be intellectual activity, the domain of the *Psychê* was said to be living (*zôon*). As Plotinus put it:

> Let every soul, then first consider this, that it made all living things itself, breathing life into them, those that the earth feeds and those that are nourished by the sea, and the divine start in the sky; it made the sun itself, and this great heaven, and adorned it itself, and drives it round itself, in orderly movement; it is a nature other than the things which it adorns and moves and makes live, and it must necessarily be more honorable than they, for they come into being or pass away when the soul leaves them or grants life to them, but soul exists for ever because "it does not depart from itself." (*Enneads*, V.1.2, 1–10)[20]

Psychê is responsible for a variety of the activities of living things, in addition to discursive thought, and Plotinus sometimes falls into the idiom of speaking of "parts" of *Psychê* in order to articulate his theory. We will use this idiom here as well, for ease of presentation, but one should be wary of taking this talk of "parts" too literally. Ultimately, *Psychê* was thought to be unified. Its "parts" might be better thought of as "powers" (Plotinus used the term *"dynamis"*) than as "pieces."[21]

Psychê was thought to have a "higher part," which mediates between living things and *Nous*, and a "lower part," which was said to be responsible for the very life of living things.[22] Such life manifests itself primarily in movement. This, it should be recognized, is among the most traditional functions of *Psychê* in Greek thought. Usually, however, each individual living thing had been said to have its own *psychê* to control its own movements. Plotinus believed in such individual *psychês*,[23] but he thought the tendency of *Psychê* to break down into the *psychês* of individual beings showed just how far from the perfection of the One *Psychê* had fallen. That which is perfect can never be many; it must be unified. Still, Plotinus did not believe that by the act of differentiation *Psychê* had fallen into irredeemable corruption. To be sure, it was thought to be a step toward "evil" in the sense that it was farther from perfection. Yet, the *psychês* of all living beings were believed to remain related to one another in *Psychê*. Thus the possibility remained open for their ultimate reunification and redemption.

Because the One is not, technically speaking, a being of any kind, it is not correct to collectively call the three foundations of Plotinus' philosophy— the One, *Nous*, and *Psychê*—"objects" or "entities." As a result, it has become traditional to call them "hypostases," a term literally meaning something that supports something else from beneath. Gerson (1994, p. 3) is quick to point out that Plotinus did not use the term. They are sometimes referred to as "spheres" as well (e.g., Gatti, 1996, p. 24).[24]

Having described Plotinus' metaphysics in general terms—the One, *Nous*, and *Psychê*—we are now in a position to lay out his theory of the psychology of individual humans. Some *psychês* were thought to remain relatively pure, such as those of the stars. Others, however, were said to become overly entangled with matter and thus "fall" far from the One; so far, in fact, that they become embodied. As we have intimated, humans and other life forms were thought to be among these. Whether this "fall" was a culpable act on the part of the *psychê* was an issue about which Plotinus seems to have been ambivalent. On the one hand, he described it as being "instinctive" (IV.3.13) and thus without moral implications. On the other, he saw it as an act of revolt against the superior *Nous* and One (IV.3.12) and thus ethically unacceptable. Some *psychês*, according to Plotinus, develop an "emotional attachment" (Wallis, 1995, p. 77) to matter and thus turn their attention to the impermanent physical world, rather than toward the universal and permanent Forms from which they came.

Even for those *psychês* that become embodied, however, their greatest calling remains to return, by means of philosophical contemplation, to their original higher, disembodied status in *Psychê* and then to continue their ascent to *Nous* and, ultimately, the One itself. Such ascension was thought to be extraordinarily difficult, however. Porphyry reports that even Plotinus had achieved unification with the One only a few times during his life. Recognizing that most people would be incapable of such intellectual feats, some later Neoplatonists would increasingly turn to magical rituals that could be practiced by everyone in order to bypass such stringent intellectual demands.

Most normal psychological functions apart from pure reason were said to require the combined activity of *psychê* and body.[25] Plotinus took great pains to show that the composite of *psychê* and body he had in mind was neither the interpenetration of two kinds of matter, as the Stoics claimed, nor a hylomorphic relationship, as Aristotle had proposed (IV.7).[26] Plotinus, by contrast, argued that the *psychê* is an immaterial entity that can combine with a body for a finite period of time but then retain its integrity upon the death of the body.

When writing of the operation of the composite of *psychê* and body, Plotinus sometimes used Plato's tripartite terminology (*logistikon, thumoeides, epithumetikon*) and sometimes Aristotle's vocabulary of nutritive,[27] perceptive, and rational faculties. Ultimately, however, Plotinus believed the *psychê* to be unified, although one's focus could be shifted from one function of the *psychê* to another as required by the discussion. One cannot, however, easily ignore the fact that the internal strains of Plotinus' theory are very apparent in his account of the composite *psychê*-body. On the one hand, he must have it that the *psychê*, being an ideal entity, is essentially unchangeable. On the other hand, normal psychological functions such as emotion, perception, and cognition seem to crucially involve change of some sort.[28] At some points he argued that the *psychê* has only an idea of what the body feels; that only the body truly changes. At other times he entertained the possibility of a changeable part of the *psychê* in its extreme "lower" regions, but he quickly reverted to the *psychê*'s essential incorruptibility. At still other times he talked of the possibility of a "detachable" part of the lower *psychê* that fuses with the body temporarily but is then redeemed when it returns to the *psychê* proper.

The *psychê* was conceived of as being incorporeal, and thus it was thought to have no particular location in the body.[29] It was said, paradoxically, to be simultaneously present everywhere within the body and also nowhere. Plotinus likens the relationship of the *psychê* and the body to that of a light that is present throughout a sphere without itself taking up any space. Metaphors of light, such as this one, played a crucial role in the elucidation of Neoplatonic metaphysics. The relationship between matter and Forms was called "illumination" (VI.5.8). As we saw above, the One itself was sometimes compared with the Sun, which was thought to be at the center of everything (metaphysically, if not physically), dispensing its life-giving and seemingly inexhaustible power to all in its embrace. When Neoplatonism was revived in the European Renaissance, over a millennium later, showing the sun to be physically at the center of the universe was high on the agendas of many Renaissance thinkers, not least of whom was Nicholas Copernicus, famed proponent of heliocentrism.

Among those activities thought to require a composite of *psychê* and body were the "affections" (*pathê*). These include pleasure and pain, emotions, and hunger, thirst, and other desires. Pleasure and pain are primarily physical, but since they can take place only in a *living* body, *psychê* was thought to be involved to at least a minimal degree. In emotion there was thought to be more direct involvement of the *psychê*. In shame, for instance, an idea that something shameful has occurred was said to arise in the *psychê*, and this produces a change in the blood that results in blushing and the various other bodily correlates of shame. That is to say, the shame is *known* in the *psychê* but *felt* in the body. In desire as well, the process is begun in the *psychê* and somehow transferred to the body (see III.6 for these examples).

Perception, too, was said to require the *psychê*-body composite. Plotinus was among the first philosophers to clearly mark out the difference between sensation and perception proper. He did this by first arguing against the then-popular theory that perception is the reception of an imprint (as into, e.g., wax) of the form of an object directly on to the *psychê*. If it were, it would violate his principle that the *psychê* is unchangeable. Instead, he argued, an imprint of the object's form is left on the *psychê*-body composite. The *psychê*, then, in effect compares the Forms to which it has access through *Psychê* to the imprint left on the sensory organs of the body and makes a judgment about its identity (perception). Plotinus argued that because perception involves judgment, it is an *activity* rather than a mere "affection." Interestingly, what we have is a theory of *looking*, rather than the traditional passive theories of *seeing*. Plotinus also broke with most of his philosophical brethren in accepting recent medical discoveries showing that nerves travel from the eyes to the brain, instead of to the heart. As a result, he argued, the perceptive faculty is in the head rather than the heart (IV.3.23).

Memory is another faculty of the *psychê* that Plotinus discussed at some length. It poses special problems for his theory. On the one hand, he insisted that it belongs to the *psychê* rather than the body (IV.3.19). Memory is, after all, memory of knowledge, and true knowledge must be of the Forms, not of the impermanent world. On the other hand, he recognized that many memories result from the perception of physical events, and he struggled to account for this fact without violating his principles that *psychê* is unchangeable and that knowledge, being eternal, belongs to the "higher" realm. In effect, he proposed two kinds of memory, grounded in two sorts of imagination, which work in tandem as long as the body lives. The "lower" form of memory is directed at the practical world of everyday life, remembering physical events and their accompanying affections. He likened it to the shades found in the Hades of Homer's poems. The "higher" form of memory was said to have corresponding intellectual images, which are not "tainted" by accidents or affections. By this conduit, from lower to higher imagination, information was said to pass from the senses to discursive reason.[30]

There is an immediate problem here, however. Because images as traditionally conceived are copies of perceptions (see, e.g., Aristotle's *De Anima*), Plotinus was left trying to explain the intellectual images of the higher form of memory. In a move reminiscent of the Stoic theory of mind, Plotinus avers that the "higher" images are verbal (*logoi*), rather than pictorial, in nature. "Higher" acts of memory recall these verbal images rather than the pictorial ones (see Wallis, 1995, pp. 79–80, for a more detailed discussion of these issues). When the *psychê* leaves the body at death, only these intellectual images are retained; the "lower" images are left behind.

One may ask why Plotinus believed *any* memories to be retained by the *psychê* upon the death of the body. After all, in its pure state *psychê* has access to the essential Forms, and memories are of accidental events of the impermanent material world. The reason for this has to do with Plotinus' theory of reincarnation, which was derived almost directly from the *Timaeus*. The *psychês* of people who live well (i.e., in accord with the Good) are reincarnated as humans again. Those of people who live badly are reincarnated as animals or even plants. In order for the *psychê* to be judged good or bad, however, it must retain something of its character after the death of the body. This character is retained in the form of memories, even if of a "purified" intellectual form. Without these, all *psychês* would be the same and there would be no basis on which to judge some good and some evil.

This is a problem that would come to haunt Islamic and Christian philosophers for centuries to come. If the soul leaves the body purified of the evil with which it was involved when embodied, then it cannot be condemned for a taint it no longer possesses. If this were true, then under the Christian and Islamic accounts of life after death, all souls, being pure, should go to paradise. This just wouldn't do for most Islamic and Christian thinkers, for it implies that earthly acts have no impact whatsoever on salvation. If, instead, souls carry after death the taint of sins they committed while embodied, it must manifest itself in some way. What sort of "mark" does it make on the soul, and how does it get there (given the hypothesized separation between the material and ideal realms)?

Finally, the last of the faculties of the individual's *psychê* is that of discursive reason. This faculty is even more fully removed from the *psychê*-body composite, more fully in the camp of the *psychê* proper, than memory. Reason receives the images of perception and memory and is able to render judgment on their validity by comparing them with the images of the Forms available to the *psychê*. Although perception was said to be an act of judgment, what reason does is of a higher order. Perception renders judgment only in the sense of identifying the objects of sense. Reason, by contrast, is able to render judgments about the goodness and beauty of an object, as well as the justice of given acts. To do this it must have some sort of access to the Forms. Thus, it is able to make abstract judgments that are not possible at the level of mere perception. This allows reason to follow a course of philosophical inquiry. Reason is, for Plotinus, far and away the most important of the faculties of the *psychê*. It is what makes humans rational, and when properly deployed it looks upward, away from the impermanence and corruption of the material world to the essential beauty and goodness of the ideal realm.

In addition to being acknowledged for his detailed account of the *psychê* and its faculties, Plotinus is often recognized for being among the first to contribute a significant theory of the "self" to psychological thought (see Dodds, 1960). Gerson (1995, pp. 139–146) explains Plotinus' theory by distinguishing between what he calls the endowed self and the ideal self. The endowed self is that entity about whom one can speak of as continuing from one psychological event to another. For example, suppose you were hungry yesterday but later ate and became full. Then today you found yourself hungry again. There is a sense in which it is the same self that was hungry on each occasion. This self is the endowed self. It mediates, in some way, between the pure cognitive part of the *psyché* and the part that is combined with the body.

The ideal self, by contrast, is the self that one can envision becoming without wholly changing into someone else. For example, perhaps you would like to become a scholar but recognize that you will have to change in certain ways if you are to attain that goal. Even so, these changes would not destroy the present self and replace it with an utterly new one; there is a continuity between the present self and the ideal self you wish to become. We in the modern world have a tendency to think of the ideal self as something we build for ourselves based on our own personal dreams and ambitions. For Plotinus, however, the ideal self is the same for everyone and resides, as a Form, in *Nous*. The ultimate goal of everyone is to return to the disembodied state and ascend to *Nous* (and, ultimately, to the One). To believe otherwise, according to Plotinus, is to be distracted from the truth by impermanent physical matters; it is to be irrational.

Finally, we come once again to the issue of personal freedom. In one sense Plotinus can be seen as trying to carve out a middle path between the ruthless determinism of the Gnostics, on the one hand, and the radical voluntarism of the orthodox Christians, on the other. Far more important to Plotinus than these two groups, however, were the positions on freedom laid out by Plato and by Aristotle. We will briefly review these before describing Plotinus' attempt to synthesize them.

On several occasions (e.g., *Meno*, 77b–78b; *Timaeus*, 86d) Plato argued that no one can freely choose what is wrong. Instead, such people choose what they believe to be the right course of action, but they are wrong. They are misled by irrational desires, ignorance of the facts, or faulty reasoning. According to Plato, we would not want to say that a person misled by irrationality, ignorance, or stupidity is acting freely. Such a person is being led astray by these factors. For instance, a thief believes that material gain will be for the good (his or her own, in particular), but he or she does not understand what is truly good and does not rationally factor in all the evils that will result from, and ultimately overbalance, the good of his or her material gain. Thus, the truly free person, according to Plato, is the one who can free him- or herself from irrational desire, ignorance, and intellectual error and come to a rational conclusion about what action best serves the good. That is, only the rational person is truly free. This conclusion has been criticized for many reasons. Perhaps chief among these is that it leads to the seemingly paradoxical conclusion that the "truly free" person can "freely" come to only one conclusion—that which is maximally rational. This seems, from at least one perspective, more like determined behavior than free behavior.

In Book III of the *Ethics,* Aristotle lays out a position more appealing to the modern mind. He first distinguishes between actions that are involuntary and those that are voluntary. Of the involuntary, there are those that are compelled through force (e.g., being pushed or coerced) and those that come from ignorance (e.g., throwing away valuables contained in a box that you believed to contain only trash). Of the voluntary, there are those that involve choice and those that do not. In this context choice means something like reasoned deliberation. "We call actions done on the spur of the moment voluntary," says Aristotle, "but not the result of choice" (*Ethics,* 1111b). Under this scheme people can freely choose to do the wrong thing, as for instance when a thief decides to mug someone on an impulsive desire for quick money.

Although Plotinus used Aristotle's theory as his basic framework (see VI.8), he aimed to show, in line with Plato, that one can never freely choose an evil course of action; one can only freely choose good. The choice of an evil course of action—almost defined as one involved with the material world—is the result of the *psychê*'s entanglement with the body. Freedom from the body results in the freedom of the *psychê*. Plotinus summarizes the position quite succinctly:

> Now when the *psychê* is without a body it is in absolute control of itself and free, and outside the causation of the physical universe; but when it is brought into a body it is no longer in all ways in control, as it forms part of an order with other things. Chances direct, for the most part, all the things around it, among which it has fallen when it comes to this middle point, so that it does some thing because of these, but sometimes it masters them itself and leads them where it wishes. The better *psychê* has power over more, the worse over less. (III.1.8)[31]

There is a suggestion here that the power of physical causation and the power of reason are perpetually, or at least frequently, at loggerheads. Plotinus' conception of causation is broader than ours, however. Within the domain of causation he would include the power of desire, not just for food and drink but also for things like wealth and political power. To be free, therefore, is to overcome these desires with reason, and he is convinced that reason will ultimately lead one to contemplation of the Forms. The "desire" to contemplate the Forms is not like other desires. It is of a different order—a "rational" desire—and therefore not to be shunned by the rational person.

As with Plato, however, the final conclusion is that to be fully free is to be supremely rational, and that to act for evil is, *ipso facto*, to be caught in the grip of irrationality. Plotinus argues that when a choice appears before us, this is not evidence of our freedom but, on the contrary, evidence that we have fallen away from rationality, which would have instantaneously told us which alternative was the right one. Thus, we are free, but perhaps only to make a single choice. All others decisions would show that we had lost our freedom.

To reiterate Plotinus' guiding principle, because the One encompasses everything ultimately, there can be no turning away from it. Everything is guided by its participation in the One. There is simply no alternative. Freedom consists in knowingly and willingly embracing its Good. Paradoxically, the appearance of plausible alternatives shows that we have slipped away from rationality because the proper exercise of reason would show us the proper course immediately.

In Plotinus we have an Idealism of the highest order. It extends even beyond Plato's written works in its belief that the world of the mind—construed very broadly—is more real and more important than the world of matter. Things of the physical realm of being are no more than images and projections of the Ideal realm. His theory of the *psyche*, therefore, focused far more sharply on how we are able to gain access to the Ideal realm than on those issues that are the bread and butter of contemporary psychology, such as perception (of the physical world), learning (about the physical world and relations within it), social relations, child development, and so on. To Plotinus, the matters that most interest us in the modern world were either peripheral or simply misguided. To one such as him, the most important psychological questions were concerned with what best enables the individual *psyche* to grasp the Forms and ultimately to reunify with the One.

Although Plotinus was the greatest of the Neoplatonic philosophers, he was by no means the only one. After his death Neoplatonism splintered off in many directions. Two of the most important of his successors were his student and biographer Porphyry and the Syrian scholar Iamblichus. Later two major "schools" of Neoplatonism arose as well, one in Athens and another in Alexandria. It is to the development of these thinkers and schools that we now turn.

Neoplatonism after Plotinus

As we have seen, Plotinus struggled intellectually to maintain the uneasy balance between the distinctness of the One, *Nous,* and *Psyche* and their ultimate unity. The tensions within the theory were bound to eventually give way, and they began to do so almost immediately upon his death. On the one hand, his most important student, Porphyry, was led to emphasize the essential unity of the hypostases, "telescoping" them into the One.[32] The other most important Neoplatonist of the second half of the third century, Iamblichus, moved in the other direction, emphasizing the differences between the hypostases and multiplying them in number by dividing each into its own sets of distinct parts or types. We elaborate on these developments in this section.

Porphyry (232–305), was born in the city of Tyre (in present-day Lebanon), and began his serious studies in Athens with Longinus (ca. 220–273),[33] a one-time student of Ammonius Saccas (as, it will be recalled, were Plotinus and possibly Origen). In 262 Porphyry went to Rome to study with Plotinus, with whom he stayed for six years. Upon the closure of Plotinus' school in 268, Porphyry moved to Sicily, where he stayed for a number of years. At some point late in his life he returned to Rome, publishing the collection of Plotinus' works we now have, the *Enneads,* just before he died. Because his professional life took place mostly in the Western Empire, his most significant influence on Neoplatonic (and Christian) thought was in the West. It has sometimes been said that in the West Plotinus himself has been "read through Porphyrean spectacles" (Wallis, 1995, p. 96). His most important works were his (1) *Sentences Leading to the Intelligible World,* a collection of aphorisms on a range of metaphysical topics; (2) *Against the Christians,* a work of Biblical criticism which has been said to have "remained unequaled until modern times" (Wallis, 1995, p. 101); and (3) important commentaries on several works by Plato and Aristotle, of which only the introduction to the critique of Aristotle's *Categories* remains complete. This work is commonly known as *Isagoge,* the Greek word for "introduction." There also exist fragments of his commentary on the *Timaeus,* as well as what might be his commentary on the *Parmenides.*[34] He also wrote a *Life of Pythagoras,* a book advocating vegetarianism (*De Abstinentia*), and a series of allegorical interpretations of traditional Hellenic myths, the latter in line with the tenets of Neoplatonism. Of this last group, only the interpretation of the cave of the Nymphs in the *Odyssey* remains.

In many ways Porphyry may be said to have been an "orthodox" Plotinian. He believed that Plato had shown the way to knowledge, although he accepted more of Aristotle's logic than had Plotinus. He also basically accepted Plotinus' triad of hypostases, although he questioned the full reality of *Nous* and *Psychê* because of their dependence on the One. Further, he agreed that reunification with the One is the primary goal of life and that this could be achieved through philosophical activity. In other ways, however, he opened the door to the more extreme forms of Neoplatonism. He accepted mystical religious works into Neoplatonic education and philosophy. It has been suggested that this development filled a void in the Neoplatonic strategy against Christianity—namely, that the Christians had their holy book, full of divine revelations, to hand, whereas the Neoplatonists had no such authoritative text to which they could turn.

The most important of these Neoplatonic "holy books" was the *Chaldaean Oracles,* a book of obscurely worded revelation and instruction. Much of its content is reminiscent of the work of Numenius of Apamea, the second-century Middle Platonist from whom Plotinus seems to have drawn ideas. Who copied whom, or if they both worked from earlier sources is a matter of debate. Although Plotinus ignored the *Chaldaean Oracles,* Porphyry cited it as an authoritative text. It seems to have been composed during the second half of the second century, possibly on the basis of older texts, by two men named Julian who were father and son. The son is said to have once worked magic with the weather to assist the Roman army (cited in Copenahver, 1992, pp. xxiv–xxv). The text has much in common, at least loosely, with the Neoplatonic view of the cosmos. It claims that the cosmos is ruled by a Supreme Intellect "beyond the reach of intelligence," which had given rise to a second Intellect identified with the Demiurge. This second Intellect was said to have created the material world, which was regarded as an evil "cloak" or "tomb" from which the human *psyché* must escape. Within the Supreme Intellect was also said to have emerged a female power known as Hecate,[35] identified with the *psyché* of the world, who acted as a line of "communication" between the sensible and Intelligible realms.[36]

It is easy to see how, with a bit of work, these principles might have influenced Plotinus' ideas of the One, *Nous,* and *Psyché*. What is more, what did not fit with orthodox Neoplatonism was interpreted in such as way as to bring it in line with such beliefs. For instance, Intelligence was described as a kind of fire in the *Oracles,* which contravened the Neoplatonic contention that it is immaterial (recall that fire was traditionally considered to be one of the four basic material substances). To bring this claim to heel, the fire mentioned was interpreted by Porphyry as being of a "dematerialized" kind, making it simply "light" instead, a common metaphor for Intelligence in Neoplatonic circles.[37]

In a stunning parallel with Christian theology, the *Chaldaean Oracles* referred to the Supreme Intellect as "Father," and also as as a "trinity-in-unity." Later Christian Neoplatonists, such as Marius Victorinus, Synesius of Cyrene, and Nemesius of Emesa,[38] may have grabbed hold of such opportunities in their efforts to integrate the two competing schools of thought.

The prime importance of the *Chaldaean Oracles* to Neoplatonism was its introduction of theurgy, a kind of magic, to the movement. The word "theurgy" seems, in part, to have originated as a play on words, distinguishing itself from "theology," on the one hand, and "*theoria*" (i.e., philosophical contemplation), on the other. It means something like "divine work," but it is important to understand that theurgy was distinguished from Christian "miracle-working" by claiming its basis in the natural workings of the cosmos itself, not in the intervention of an anthropomorphic God outside the cosmic order, as they believed the Christians held.[39] By way of theurgy the *Chaldaean Oracles* taught a straightforward path to eternal salvation through magical ritual. This is something that neither the Christian texts nor the pagan competitors to the *Chaldaean Oracles,* such as the now better-known *Corpus Hermeticum,*[40] could offer. The power of theurgy was said to be based on the principle, articulated first by Plotinus, that each part of the universe is contained in every other part as well. Plotinus believed this to be the basis of the success of astrology and the like, but he did not believe such magic could work beyond the sensible realm. Thus, for Plotinus, the philosopher, who operates in the Intelligible realm, neither needs magic nor is susceptible to its powers. Later Neoplatonists went far beyond the bounds set by Plotinus, however. Because there was thought to be a "sympathy" among all parts of the cosmos, by properly manipulating the right parts nearby, it was thought one could create effects that "resonate" throughout the cosmos. If true, this might be the basis of a very powerful magic indeed.

Although Porphyry believed in the potential power of theurgy, his attitude was one of respectful distance. He saw its powers as potentially dangerous and liable to misuse if they were to fall into the wrong hands. Moreover, he believed that the final stages of union with the One still lay in philosophical contemplation, not in ritual magic. Iamblichus, however, was not so cautious. He raised theurgy to a level *above* that of philosophy, and it is to his work we now turn.

Iamblichus (ca. 250–ca. 326) was born in Chalcis in Syria and studied with Porphyry for a time.[41] He was much more strongly influenced by Pythagoreanism and by Eastern "mystery" cults than was Porphyry. He also had a great deal more influence than Porphyry on the course Neoplatonism would take in the late Roman period, in the Eastern Empire in particular. Iamblichus' student Aedesius founded a school devoted mainly to theurgy in Pergamum (in present-day Turkey), and one of Aedesius' students, in turn, Maximus of Ephesus, would become the driving force behind Emperor Julian's effort to restore paganism to its status as official religion of Rome in the early 360s. Also, the late Athenian Academy and its most illustrious head, Proclus, owed more to Iamblichus' formulation of Neoplatonic problems than to Porphyry's. The later Alexandrian school was indebted to him as well.

Unfortunately, none of Iamblichus' major metaphysical works have survived, so it is often difficult to tell where Iamblichus' beliefs end and where the developments of his followers begin. Given this caveat, however, we will try to outline the main differences between Iamblichus and other major Neoplatonists. Whereas Porphyry, as we have seen, tended to emphasize the unity of the three hypostases, Iamblichus emphasized more heavily their distinctness. Indeed, he made new distinctions within hypostases that Plotinus had not. Damascius[42] says that Iamblichus went so far as to propose an entity transcending even the One, which he called "the Ineffable." *Psychê* was declared to be a completely self-subsistent hypostasis, dependent on *Nous* for its origin, but not a mere "projection" of *Nous*, as Porphyry had suggested. As for the *psychês* of individuals, Iamblichus divided them into a number of distinct orders. The Demiurge's *psychê* and the World *psychê* were said to be of a different kind from the human *psychê*. He also disagreed with Plotinus that there is an "unfallen" portion of the human *psychê*. It is all essentially separated from and inferior to the other hypostases. The *psychês* of humans were, in turn, said to be essentially different from, and essentially superior to, those of other animals. Thus, reincarnation of *psychês* of evil humans as non-human animals, an article of faith among other Platonists, was declared by Iamblichus to be impossible.

Contrary to perhaps the most significant psychological tenet proposed by Plotinus, Iamblichus doubted that the human *psychê* could *ever* return to *Nous* and contemplate the Forms directly through the practice of philosophy. The *psychê*, he said, is normally able only to contemplate *Logoi*—"images" or "projections" of the Forms themselves. The *psychê* is, thus, permanently separated from *Nous*, with a single exception: It may rise to the level of Intellect, and beyond, through the power of theurgy. It is here that Iamblichus broke most decisively with Neoplatonic tradition. If one statement can characterize Plato and all his followers, it is that the path to knowledge, and whatever salvation knowledge affords, is the path of philosophy—not science, not religion (of the ordinary kinds), not *doxa*. Iamblichus, however, raised magical ritual to a level higher than philosophy itself.

Almost paradoxically, Iamblichus can be seen as the point of departure for the long process of separation between psychology and metaphysics that we know today. This is not to say that he regarded psychology as a natural science. It would be a long while before that development would be completed. Nevertheless, whereas all previous philosophers had believed there to be something "cosmological" about the *psychê*, Iamblichus here said, perhaps for the first time, that the *psychê* is forever (barring magic) separated from the cosmological mysteries, if there be any, and therefore operates on its own principles (see Lloyd, 1967b). As such it must be studied on its own merits, not as surrogate for, or pale reflection of, the cosmos as a whole.

Neoplatonism in a Christian Empire

During the last twenty years of Porphyry's life, Neoplatonism was in ascendance. Diocletian (ruled 284–305) was emperor, and the "Great Persecution" of the Christians was under way. The last twenty years of Iamblichus' life, however, was a different time. Under the leadership of the emperor Constantine (sole emperor 306–337), Rome became an officially Christian state. Pagan Neoplatonism, though not outlawed, suffered severe setbacks.

In 325 Constantine called a meeting of all the bishops of the empire in the city of Nicaea to hammer out an agreement as to what would constitute orthodox Christianity. The main issue dividing Christians at this time was the nature of Christ—had he been divine or was he a mere mortal?—and they worked out the creed to which all Christians would thereafter be required to adhere. Arius (ca. 250–336), a popular Alexandrian priest, argued that Christ could not have been truly divine, for this would undercut the immutability of God himself. Instead, Arius argued, Christ had been a being created out of nothing, directly by God himself. The bishops saw this as an attack on the significance of Christ (i.e., the claim that God himself had not come to earth and walked among us), and they wrote a creed proclaiming that "the Son is of one substance with the Father"—that is, they are both wholly divine.[43] Arianism was condemned as a heresy, and Christianity started down the road toward a new unity. A reconciliation between orthodoxy and Arianism was nearing completion when Arius died in Constantinople in 336. His death scuttled the agreement, however, and the fight with Arianism would continue on into the sixth century.

Although the emperor Julian (sole emperor 361–363) returned to persecuting Christians and attempted to revive paganism during his short reign, the empire was soon restored to its Christian course and paganism was finally outlawed outright by the emperor Theodosius (ruled Eastern Empire 379–395) in 391. Meanwhile, in the West, Rome itself was sacked by the Visigoth Alaric in 410 and finally captured by Odoacer in 476.

These were the conditions under which the Athenian and Alexandrian schools of Neoplatonism existed. The Alexandrian school seems to have suffered most. Christian Patriarchs periodically launched violent attacks upon its pagan members. The most famous of these is the lynching of the influential woman scholar Hypatia. As a result, Alexandrian Neoplatonists tended to refrain from commentaries on Plato's religiously sensitive cosmological and metaphysical works. They focused their efforts on the ethical works and on Aristotle's logic and physics, although in a highly Neoplatonized form. Under them the assimilation of Aristotle's work to the Platonic framework found its most extreme form. By the late fifth century the school had been taken over by Christian leaders. In 610 its last official leader, Stephanus, moved to Constantinople to head up the new Imperial Academy. In 642 the Alexandrian school was finally closed by the conquering Muslims.

The Athenian Academy seems to have been afforded more freedom. It was much more determinedly pagan than its sister school in Alexandria, however, and its most famous leader, Proclus (410–485), was once forced into exile for a year to avoid charges of impiety. Interestingly, Athens seems to have had a number of Jewish scholars during this time as well. Proclus' work was the most original of any of the late Athenians. Its most striking feature is its exponential multiplication of metaphysical entities (up to fifteen). Despite its complexity, however, Proclus' approach was relentlessly logical. His most important work, *Elements of Theology,* is organized as a set of over two hundred propositions, each rigorously deduced from those that go before. It is, in effect, the axiomatic method of Euclid of Alexandria (fl. ca. 300 BC), the famed geometer, applied to the study of metaphysics. For all this, Proclus' contribution to the study of the *psychē* must be regarded as modest at best. After Proclus the Athenian school went into decline. In the 520s it made something of a recovery under the leadership of Damascius, but it was closed by order of the Christian emperor Justinian in 529. The Athenian scholars moved en masse to Persia at the invitation of that country's king, but they returned a short while later, disappointed at their inability to establish a viable school there.

With this development Christianity became the only intellectual option in Europe and the Near East. Neoplatonism did not really die, however. It continued on not only in the thought of the Christians who had conquered it in Europe but also in the philosophy of the Muslims who would sweep across western Asia and North Africa in the 600s.

CONCLUSION

In this book we have traveled a long way conceptually from the earliest ideas about the *psyché*, presented in Homer's *Iliad*. There the *psyché* was a vaporous "double" that left the person's body when he or she died for a dreary afterlife in Hades. Terms such as *thumos, phrenes*, and *noos* carried more of what we would consider to be the psychological burden than did *psyché*. Through pre-Socratic times, however, *psyché* began to acquire a more psychological character. It began to take on cognitive functions in the living person, and speculation on the *psyché*'s material nature became an important point of debate. With Socrates the *psyché* grew further, acquiring moral characteristics. In Plato's work it became a complex structure, being elaborated into a number of parts responsible for a variety of psychological functions. These parts were thought to be independent enough to come into conflict with each other. The works of Aristotle, the Stoics, the Epicurians, and the medical schools represented a variety of attempts to understand the *psyche* from more a naturalistic perspective. Philosophical and medical approaches began to conflict with each, but they also fruitfully cooperated at times as well. This was especially true in the work of Galen. By the time of the Roman Empire, however, competition between Christianity and Neoplatonism brought back to prominence the idea that the *psyché* is closely involved with the divine and the supernatural.

Belief in the divine nature of the soul would, of course, dominate much of medieval psychological thought in the Islamic and Christian worlds, but the medical approach to certain aspects of the mind continued to be taught alongside the religious views (see, e.g., Kemp, 1990, 1996). This, however, is a separate story requiring separate volumes of its own.

NOTES

1. See Dodds (1965) for a very readable introduction to the thought of this period.

2. See Burkert (1987) for an excellent short introduction. For a more extended treatment, see also Ferguson (1970).

3. See Dodds, 1960, on both Numenius and Ammonius.

4. See, e.g., Book III of Aristotle's *Ethics.*

5. An anonymous reviewer of a grant proposal related to this work argued that freedom of the will is not an issue to which the Christians have especially original claim because the question had been debated by others previously, and it was, of course, central to many legal codes in the ancient world (namely, no free will implies no moral responsibility). We disagree with little of this. Our main point here is that the Christians were the first to make freedom a *central* aspect of their *psychological* theory—so central that they were the first to compose whole treatises specifically on the topic (e.g., Origen, St. Agustine).

6. Irenaeus was the first to establish and defend the canonical version of the New Testament essentially in the form known today.

7. Although the term "Ebionite" was thought by Tertullian and some later theologians to be derived from the name of some early leader, Ebion, it seems instead to come from a Hebrew term meaning "the poor" (see Chadwick, 1993, p. 23).

8. Montanists, led by Montanus of Phrygia, were ecstatic Christians who believed that the second coming of Christ was very near, at which point all good Christians would be physically, bodily resurrected. Their prophecies were not recognized by the wider Church, but they did have some influence on its development. Women played a much more prominent role in Montanism than in the mainstream Christianity of the time.

9. With respect to references to Tertullian's *De Anima,* the chapter numbers will apply to any edition. The page numbers, however, apply only to the Holmes translation, full detail of which are given in the references section.

10. It is crucially important to distinguish the Latin word translated as "soul," *anima,* from the Latin word translated as "mind," *animus.* Although they are just feminine and masculine versions of the same word, their meanings are very different.

11. We are speaking, in the case of Aristotle, of the enigmatic "active intellect."

12. Eusebius, the most important historian of the early Church, cites Porphyry, the most important of Plotinus' students, as having said this. There seems to have been another Origen, however, a pagan, who was tutored by Ammonius. Eusebeus may have confused the two. Merlan (1967a, p. 352) believes that both Origens were students of Ammonius. Popkin (1967, p. 552) is convinced that they were one and the same man. Wallis (1995), however, states that "the only point that seems certain is that the two Origens were different people" (p. 38). In short, very little is certain about this intriguing story.

13. Most of Origen's original Greek text has been lost. A complete Latin translation was composed by Rufinus about 400. Rufinus believed the Greek text with which he worked to be incomplete, and it is clear from the Greek fragments we still have that he added interpretive material. To what degree he knew these additions to be correct, and to what degree he was attempting to protect himself from the Origenist controversy then underway, is not entirely clear. All Book II passages cited here are from the Latin, as that is all we have. All Book III passages cited here are from the original Greek.

14. He seems here to be referring only to animals.

15. Although this passage is from the Latin text, Rufinus uses the Greek terms here. He later translates them into Latin as *sensibilis et mobilis.* The Crombie translation,

which is being used here, appends a note to these that reads "Erasmus remarks that *phantastikê* may be rendered *imaginitiva,* which is the understanding; *hormêtikê, impulsiva,* which refers to the affections."

16. Rufinus tries to soften this point considerably in his Latin translation.

17. Arians held the belief that Jesus simply could not have been both human and divine. He had to have been either one or the other, and Arius argued he had been fully human.

18. He apparently had to arbitrarily cut Plotinus' major work on the *psychê* into two parts to achieve the correct total of fifty-four essays. Hereafter, all references to Plotinus give the Ennead as a Roman numeral and the tractate as an Arabic numeral (i.e., IV.3 means Ennead IV, tractate 3). Sometimes a second Arabic numeral will be appended to denote a particular chapter within a tractate.

19. There is controversy over the use of the term "emanation." Plotinus says simply that the One overflows, and that what is perfect must reproduce itself (see, e.g., V.1.6; V.2.1). See Wallis, 1995, pp. 61–69, on the nature of "emanation," as well as Gatti, 1996, p. 31, on why the traditionally used "emanation" might be, strictly speaking, inappropriate. Bussanich (1996, p. 46) offers "procession" instead.

20. Quoted final clause from Plato's *Phaedrus,* 245 C9.

21. The major works on *Psychê* are to be found in *Enneads,* IV. Much of the present account follows those of Gerson, 1994, and Wallis, 1995. See also Blumenthal, 1993.

22. See, e.g., Blumenthal, 1971, 1996.

23. Here, and through the rest of this section, we use the capitalized *Psychê* to denote Plotinus' third hypostasis, the emanation of *Nous.* By contrast, we use the lowercase *psychê* to denote the "souls" of individuals. Keeping the two distinct is important if the reader is to understand the description that follows of the relationship between the two that is proposed by Plotinus.

24. The classic introduction to the hypostases is *Ennead* V.1.

25. See Blumethal (1971) for an extensive discussion of the matter, from which the following account has, in part, been derived.

26. It will be recalled that Aristotle had argued that the *psychê* is just the form of the living thing and cannot exist apart from its matter, the body.

27. Plotinus more often uses the term "vegetative" rather than "nutritive," but for the sake of consistency with the earlier chapter on Aristotle, we have chosen to use "nutritive" here.

28. See III.6 for Plotinus' discussion of this, as well as chapter 5 of Blumenthal (1971) for a good analysis.

29. Plotinus occasionally slips into the quasi-Platonic convention of placing sensation in the head, anger in the heart, and desire in the liver, but he seems in these places to be speaking of parts of the body that are active when these faculties are in use, not locations of the *psychê* per se.

30. This interpretation is directly attributable to Blumenthal (1971, pp. 89–90), and is in direct opposition to Inge's (1929, vol. 1, p. 226) classic claim that higher memory and imagination belong to discursive reason.

31. The translation of this passage is from Gerson (1995, p. 158), although "soul" has been replaced with the original *"psychê"* throughout.

32. This term is from Lloyd (1967a, p. 288).

33. A long tradition attributes the famed literary-critical work *On the Sublime* to Longinus, but this is apparently mistaken (Wallis, 1995, p. 38).

34. See the argument presented by Hadot (1968).

35. Note that *Psyché* was always regarded as female in Greek philosophy.

36. See Copenhaver (1992, pp. xxiv–xxvi) for a brief description of the *Oralces*.

37. This example is cited in Wallis (1995, p. 105).

38. Marius (fl. ca. 350) was an African-born pagan philosopher who taught in Rome. His conversion to Christianity apparently came as a shock to his followers (Chadwick, 1986, p. 9). He produced the Latin translations of Plotinus' *Enneads* and Porphyry's *Isagoge* that St. Augustine would later read. The latter, in particular, would become a standard text in the Latin West for the next millennium (see Clark, 1981). Synesius (ca. 370–ca. 413) was a mathematician and scientist who became bishop of Ptolemais, on the North African coast, in 410. He is known to have been a student of Hypatia of Alexandria (ca. 370–ca. 415), the woman pagan philosopher and mathematician, perhaps best known for having been stoned to death by a mob of radical Christian monks. Nemesius (fl. ca. 400) was a bishop and one of the foremost physicians of his day.

39. See Wallis, 1995, p. 108.

40. See Copenhaver (1992) for an introductory essay on the origins and influence of the *Hermetica*.

41. See Blumenthal and Clark (1993) for a series of articles on Iamblichus' thought and influence.

42. Damascius was the last head of the Athenian Academy, which closed in 529.

43. The creed of 325 is not identical to the "Nicaean Creed" used in the Church today. The contemporary creed seems to have been the product of the Council of Constantinople in 381, under the emperor Theodosius.

References

Annas, J. E. (1992). *Hellenistic philosophy of mind*. Berkeley: University of California Press.

Armstrong, D. M. (1968). *A materialist theory of mind*. London: Routledge Press.

Bambrough, R. (1963). General introduction. In J. L. Creed & A. E. Wardman (Eds. & Trans.), *The philosophy of Aristotle* (pp. 11–30). New York: New American Library.

Barnes, J. (1979). Aristotle's concept of mind. In J. Barnes, M. Schofield, & R. Sorabji (Eds.), *Articles on Aristotle: Vol. 4. Psychology and aesthetics* (pp. 32–41). London: Duckworth. (Originally published in *Proceedings of the Aristotelian Society*, 1971–1972.)

Barnes, J. (1982). *The presocratic philosophers* (Rev. ed.). London: Routledge & Kegan Paul.

Barnes, J. (1987). *Early Greek philosophy*. London: Penguin.

Barnes, J. (1995). Metaphysics. In J. Barnes (Ed.), *The Cambridge companion to Aristotle* (pp. 66–108). Cambridge, UK: Cambridge University Press.

Blumenthal, H. J. (1971). *Plotinus' psychology: His doctrines of the embodied soul*. The Hague: Martinus Nijhoff.

Blumenthal, H. J. (1993). *Soul and intellect: Studies in Plotinus and later Neoplatonism*. Aldershot, Eng.: Variorum.

Blumenthal, H. J. (1996). On soul and intellect. In L. P. Gerson (Ed.), *The Cambridge companion to Plotinus* (pp. 82–104). Cambridge, UK: Cambridge University Press.

Blumenthal, H. J. & Clark, E. G. (Eds.) (1993). *The divine Iamblichus: Philosopher and man of gods*. London: Bristol Classical Press.

Blumenthal, H. J. & Markus, R. A. (Eds.) (1981). *Neoplatonism and early Christian thought: Essays in honour of A. H. Armstrong*. London: Variorum.

Brandwood, L. (1990). *The chronology of Plato's dialogues*. Cambridge, UK: Cambridge University Press.

Bremmer, J. (1983). *The early Greek concept of the soul*. Princeton, NJ: Princeton University Press.

Burkert, W. (1987). *Ancient mystery cults.* Cambridge, MA: Harvard University Press.

Burnet, J (1930). *Early Greek philosophy* (4th ed.). New York: Macmillan. (Original edition published 1892.)

Bussanich, J. (1996). Plotinus's metaphysics of the One. In L. P. Gerson (Ed.), *The Cambridge companion to Plotinus* (pp. 38–65). Cambridge, UK: Cambridge University Press.

Chadwick, H. (1986). *Augustine.* Oxford: Oxford University Press.

Chadwick, H. (1993). *The early Church* (Rev. ed.). London: Penguin.

Cherniss, H. (1957). Timaeus 38A8–B5. *Journal of Hellenic Studies, 77,* 18–23.

Clark, M. T. (1981). The Neoplatonism of Marius Victorinus the Christian. In H. J. Blumenthal & R. A. Markus (Eds.), *Neoplatonism and early Christian thought: Essays in honour of A. H. Armstrong* (pp. 153–159). London: Variorum.

Copenhaver, B. P. (1992). Introduction. In B. P. Copenhaver (Ed.), *Hermetica: The Greek* Corpus hermeticum *and the Latin* Asclepius *in a new English translation with noted and introduction* (pp. xiii–lxxxiii). Cambridge: Cambridge University Press.

Cornford, F. M. (1941). *The* Republic *of Plato.* Oxford: Oxford University Press.

Cornford, F. M. (1991). *From religion to philosophy: A study in the origins of Western speculation.* Princeton, NJ: Princeton University Press. (Original work published 1912.)

Cox, D. R. & Brandwood, L. (1959). On a discriminatory problem connected with the works of Plato. *Journal of the Royal Statistical Society* (Series B), *22,* 195–200.

Diels, H. & Kranz, W. (1951). *Die Fragmente der Vorsokratiker* [The fragments of the pre-Socratics] (6th ed.). Berlin: Weidmann.

DiFilippo, J. G. (1993). Reply to André Laks on Anaxagoras. *Southern Journal of Philosophy, 31,* 39–48.

Dodds, E. R. (1951). *The Greeks and the irrational.* Berkeley, CA: University of California Press.

Dodds, E. R. (1960). Numenius and Ammonius. In (no editor), *Les sources de Plotin* [Plotinus' sources] (pp. 3–32). Geneva: Vanduvres.

Dodds, E. R. (1965). *Pagan and Christian in an Age of Anxiety.* Cambridge: Cambridge University Press.

Durrant, M. (Ed.) (1993). *Aristotle's* De anima *in focus.* London: Routledge.

Edmonds, J. M. (1928). *Lyra Graeca.* (2nd ed., 3 Vols.). Loeb Classical Library. Cambridge: Harvard University Press.

Ehrenberg, V. (1968). *From Solon to Socrates: Greek history and civilization during the 6th and 5th centuries BC.* London: Methuen.

Epictetus (1983). *The Handbook of Epictetus* (N. P. White, Trans.). Indianapolis: Hackett Publishing Co.

Everson, S. (1995). Psychology. In J. Barnes (Ed.), *The Cambridge companion to Aristotle* (pp. 168–194). Cambridge: Cambridge University Press.

Feigl, H. (1970). Mind-body, *not* a pseudo-problem. In C. V. Borst (Ed.), *The mind-brain identity theory* (pp. 33–42). London: Macmillan. (Original work published 1960.)

Ferguson, J. (1970). *The religions of the Roman Empire.* Ithaca, NY: Cornell University Press.

Findlay, J. M. (1974). *Plato: The written and unwritten doctrines*. London, New York: Humanities Press.

Flew, A. (Ed.) (1983). *A dictionary of philosophy* (2nd ed.). London: Macmillan.

Fodor, J. A. (1968). *Psychological explanation: An introduction to the philosophy of psychology*. New York: Random House.

Fodor, J. A. (1975). *The language of thought*. Cambridge, MA: Harvard University Press.

Fodor, J. A. (1981). *Representations: Philosophical essays on the foundations of cognitive science*. Cambridge, MA: MIT Press.

Gadamer, H.-G. (1989). *Truth and method* (2nd ed., J. Weinshaeimer & D. G. Marshall, Trans.). New York: Crossroad. (Original work published 1960.)

Galen. (1963). *On the passions and errors of the soul* (P. W. Harkins, Trans., Introduction and interpretation by Walther Riese). Columbus, OH: Ohio State University Press.

Galen. (1984). *On the doctrines of Hippocrates and Plato*. Corpus Medicorum Graecorum, vol. 5, pt. 4 (P. De Lacy, Trans. and Ed.). Berlin: Akademie-Verlag

Galen. (1997). *Selected works*. (P. N. Singer, Trans.). Oxford: Oxford University Press.

Gallop, D. (Ed.) (1984). *Parmenides of Elea: Fragments*. Toronto, ON: University of Toronto Press.

Gaskin, J. (Ed.) (1995). *The Epicurean philosophers*. Rutland, VT: Everyman.

Gatti, M. L. (1996). Plotinus: The Platonic tradition and the foundation of Neoplatonism. In L. P. Gerson (Ed.), *The Cambridge companion to Plotinus* (pp. 10–37). Cambridge, UK: Cambridge University Press.

Gerber, D. E. (Ed. and trans.) (1999). *Greeki Iambic poetry*. Cambridge, MA: Harvard University Press.

Gergen, K. J. (1985). The social constructionist movement in modern psychology. *American Psychologist, 40*, 266–275.

Gergen, K. J. (1991). *The saturated self: Dilemmas of identity in contemporary life*. New York: Basic Books.

Gergen, K. J. (1994). *Realities and relationships: Soundings in social construction*. Cambridge, MA: Harvard University Press.

Gergen, K. J. (2001). Psychological science in a postmodern context. *American Psychologist, 56*, 803–813.

Gerson, L. P. (1994). *Plotinus*. London: Routledge.

Gibson, J. J. (1966). *The sense considered as perceptual systems*. Boston: Houghton Mifflin.

Gibson, J. J. (1979). *The ecological approach to visual perception*. Boston: Houghton-Mifflin.

Grant, R. M. (1967). Origen. In P. Edwards (Ed.), *Encyclopedia of philosophy* (Vol. 5, pp. 551–552). New York: Macmillan & Free Press.

Green, C. D. (1998). The thoroughly modern Aristotle: Was he *really* a functionalist? *History of Psychology, 1*, 8–20.

Grmek, M.D. (1991). *Diseases in the ancient Greek world* (M. Muellner & L. Muellner, Trans.). Baltimore, MD: Johns Hopkins University Press.

Hadot, P. (1968). *Porphyre et Victorinus* [Porphyry and Victorinus] (2 vols.). Paris: Etudes Augustiniennes.

Heidegger, M. (1992). *Parmenides* (A. Schuwer & R. Rojcewicz, Trans.). Blooming-
ton, IN: University of Indiana Press. (Original work published 1982.)

Hippocrates. (1978). *Hippocratic writings* (G.E.R. Lloyd, Ed.; J. Chadwick, & W.
N. Mann, with I. M. Lonie & E. T. Withington, Trans.). New York: Penguin Books.

Hobbes, Thomas. (1994). *Human Nature and De Corpore Politico* (J.C.A. Gaskin,
Ed.). Oxford: Oxford University Press. (Original work published 1695).

Homer. (1946). The Odyssey. (E. V. Rieu, Trans.). Harmondsworth, Eng.: Penguin Books.

Homer. (1950). *The Iliad.* (E. V. Rieu, Trans.) Harmondsworth, Eng.: Penguin
Books.

Inge, W. R. (1929). *The philosophy of Plotinus* (2 vols.). London: Longmans, Green.

Inwood, B. & Gerson, L. P. (Eds.) (1988). *Hellenistic philosophy: Introductory readings.* Indianapolis: Hackett Publishing Co.

Irwin, T. H. (1991). Aristotle's philosophy of mind. In S. Everson (Ed.), *Companions to ancient thought: Vol. 2. Psychology* (pp. 56–83). Cambridge: Cambridge
University Press.

Jaeger, W. (1934). *Aristotle, Fundamentals of his development* (R. Robinson, Trans.).
Oxford: Oxford University Press. (Original work published 1923.)

Janssens, P. A. (1970). *Paleopathology.* London: Curwin Press.

Jaynes, J. (1976). *The origin of consciousness in the breakdown of the bicameral mind.*
Boston: Houghton-Mifflin.

Johansen, T. K. (1998). *Aristotle on the sense-organs.* Cambridge, UK: Cambridge
University Press.

Kagan, D. (1969). *The outbreak of the Peloponnesian War.* Ithaca, NY: Cornell University Press.

Kagan, D. (1974). *The Archidamian War.* Ithaca, NY: Cornell University Press.

Kagan, D. (1991). *Pericles of Athens and the birth of democracy.* New York: Touch-
stone.

Kahn, C. H. (1979). *The art and thought of Heraclitus.* Cambridge: Cambridge
University Press.

Kemp, Simon. (1990). *Medieval psychology.* New York: Greenwood Press.

Kemp, Simon. (1996). *Cognitive psychology in the middle ages.* Westport, CT: Greenwood Press.

Kerferd, G. B. (1967a). Theophrastus. In P. Edwards (Ed.), *Encyclopedia of philosophy*
(Vol. 8, pp. 99–100). New York: Macmillan & Free Press.

Kerferd, G. B. (1967b). Aristotle. In P. Edwards (Ed.), *Encyclopedia of philosophy*
(Vol. 1, pp. 151–162). New York: Macmillan & Free Press.

Kidd, I. G. (1967). Greek academy. In P. Edwards (Ed.), *Encyclopedia of philosophy*
(Vol. 3, pp. 382–384). New York: Macmillan & Free Press.

Kirk, G. S. & Raven, J. E. (1957). *The presocratic philosophers.* Cambridge: Cambridge University Press.

Kirk, G. S., Raven, J. E., & Schofield, M. (1983). *The presocratic philosophers* (2nd
ed.). Cambridge: Cambridge University Press.

Krämer, H. J. (1990). *Plato and the foundations of metaphysics. A work on the theory
of the principles and unwritten doctrines of Plato with a collection of the fundamental documents* (J. R. Catan, Trans.). Albany, NY: State University of
New York Press. (Original work published 1982.)

Laks, A. (1993). Mind's crisis. On Anaxagoras. *Southern Journal of Philosophy, 31,* 19–38.

Lawson-Tancred, H. (1986). Introduction. In Aristotle, *De anima* (H. Lawson-Tancred, Trans., pp. 11–116). London: Penguin.

Ledger, G. R. (1989). *Re-counting Plato: A computer analysis of Plato's style.* Oxford: Oxford University Press.

Lee, D. (1974). Translator's introduction. In Plato, *The republic* (D. Lee, Trans., 2nd ed., pp. 11–58). Harmondsworth, Eng.: Penguin.

Lloyd, A. C. (1967a). The later Neoplatonists. In A. H Armstrong (Ed.), *The Cambridge history of later Greek and early medieval philosophy* (pp. 269–325). Cambridge: Cambridge University Press.

Lloyd, A. C. (1967b). Iamblichus. In P. Edwards (Ed.), *Encyclopedia of philosophy* (Vol. 4, p. 105). New York: Macmillan & Free Press.

Long, A. A. & Sedley, D. N. (Eds.) (1987). *The Hellenistic philosophers* (Vol. 1). Cambridge, UK: Cambridge University Press.

Longrigg, J. (1998). *Greek medicine from the heroic to the Hellenistic age: A source book.* New York: Routledge.

Lovibond, S. (1991). Plato's theory of mind. In S. Everson (Ed.), *Companions to ancient thought: Vol. 2. Psychology* (pp. 35–55). Cambridge: Cambridge University Press.

Majno, G. (1991). *The healing hand: Man and wound in the ancient world.* Cambridge, MA: Harvard University Press. (Originally published 1975.)

Marcovich, M. (1967). *Heraclitus, of Ephesus.* Mérida, Venezuela: Los Andes University Press.

Marcus Aurelius (1964). *Marcus Aurelius' Meditations* (M. Staniforth, Trans.). London: Penguin Books.

McKirahan, R. D. (1994). *Philosophy before Socrates: An introduction with texts and commentary.* Indianapolis, IN: Hackett.

Merlan, P. (1967a). Plotinus. In P. Edwards (Ed.), *Encyclopedia of philosophy* (Vol. 6, pp. 351–359). New York: Macmillan & Free Press.

Merlan, P. (1967b). Neoplatonism. In P. Edwards (Ed.), *Encyclopedia of philosophy* (Vol. 5, pp. 473–476). New York: Macmillan & Free Press.

Murray, David J. (1988). *A History of Western Psychology* (2nd ed.). Englewood Cliffs, NJ: Prentice-Hall.

Nunn, John F. (1996). *Ancient Egyptian medicine.* London, Norman, OK: University of Oklahoma Press.

Nussbaum, M. C. (1972). *Psychê* in Heraclitus. *Phonesis, 17,* 1–16, 153–170.

Nussbaum, M. C. (1994). *The therapy of desire: Theory and practice in Hellenistic ethics.* Princeton, NJ: Princeton University Press.

Nussbaum, M. C. & Rorty, A. O. (Eds.) (1992). *Essays on Aristotle's De anima.* Oxford: Clarendon Press.

O'Brien, D. (1981). Plotinus and the Gnostics on the generation of matter. In H. J. Blumenthal & R. A. Markus (Eds.), *Neoplatonism and early Christian thought: Essays in honour of A. H. Armstrong* (pp. 108–123). London: Variorum.

Origen. (1885). *De principiis* (F. Crombie, Trans.). In A. Roberts & J. Donaldson (Eds.), *The ante-Nicene Fathers: Translations of the writings of the Fathers down to A.D. 325* (Vol. 4). Buffalo, NY: Christian Literature Publishing.

Ostenfeld, E. (1987). *Ancient Greek psychology and the modern mind-body debate.*
    Aarhus, Denmark: Aarhus University Press.
Owen, G.E.L. (1953). The place of the *Timaeus* in Plato's dialogues. *Classical Quar-
    terly,* N.S. *3,* 79–95.
Pepple, J. (1997, Feb. 7). The unwritten doctrines: Plato's answer to Speusippus.
    Retrieved November 27, 2000, from *http://www2.kenyon.edu/people/pepplej.*
Philo Judaeus of Alexandria. (1966). *On the account of the world's creation given by
    Moses* (F. H. Coson & G. H. Whitaker, Trans.). In J. L. Saunders (Ed.), Greek
    and Roman philosophy after Aristotle (pp. 200–227). New York: Macmillan
    & Free Press.
Philoponus, John (1991). *On Aristotle on the intellect* (W. Charlton, Trans.). London:
    Duckworth. (Original work written ca. 550.)
Plato. (1937). *Plato's cosmology: The* Timaeus *of Plato* (F. M. Cornford, Trans.). New
    York: Harcourt Brace.
Plotinus. (1984). *Enneads.* (A. H. Armstrong, Trans.). Cambridge, MA: Harvard
    University Press.
Popkin, Richard H. (1967). Origen. In P. Edwards (Ed.), *Encyclopedia of philoso-
    phy.* (Vol. 5, pp. 551–552). New York: Macmillan & Free Press.
Prat, Ferdinand (1907). *Origene, le theologien et l'exegete.* Paris: Bloud.
Putnam, H. (1975). Minds and machines. In H. Putnam, *Mind, language, and
    reality: Philosophical papers* (Vol. 2). Cambridge: Cambridge University Press.
    (Original work published 1960.)
Putnam, H. (1975). Philosophy and our mental life. *Philosophical papers: Vol. 2. Mind,
    language, and reality* (pp. 291–303). Cambridge: Cambridge University Press.
Radice, B. (1973). Alexander the Great. In *Who's who in the ancient world* (Rev. ed.,
    pp. 54–56). Harmondsworth, Eng.: Penguin.
Rees, D. A. (1967). Platonism and the Platonic tradition. In P. Edwards (Ed.),
    Encyclopedia of philosophy (Vol. 6, pp. 333–340). New York: Macmillan & Free
    Press.
Robinson, D. N. (1986). *An intellectual history of psychology* (Rev. ed.). Madison,
    WI: University of Wisconsin Press.
Robinson, D. N. (1989). *Aristotle's psychology.* New York: Columbia University Press.
Robinson, H. M. (1978). Mind and body in Aristotle. *Classical Quarterly, N.S. 28,*
    105–124.
Robinson, H. M. (1983). Aristotelian dualism. In J. Annas (Ed.), *Oxford studies in
    ancient philosophy* (Vol. 1, pp. 123–144). Oxford: Clarendon Press.
Robinson, J. M. (1968). *An introduction to early Greek philosophy: The chief frag-
    ments and ancient testimony, with connecting commentary.* Boston: Houghton
    Mifflin.
Robinson, T. M. (Ed.) (1987). *Heraclitus: Fragments.* Toronto, ON: University of
    Toronto Press.
Robinson, T. M. (1992). Plato and the computer. *Ancient Philosophy, 12,* 375–382.
Robinson, T. M. (1995). *Plato's psychology* (2nd ed.). Toronto, ON: University of
    Toronto Press.
Roney, L. (1990). *Chaucer's Knight's Tale and Theories of Scholastic Psychology.*
    Tampa: University of South Florida Press, 1990.
Rorty, R. (1970). Incorrigibility as the mark of the mental. *Journal of Philosophy,
    67,* 399–424 .

Rorty, R. (1979). *Philosophy and the mirror of nature*. Princeton, NJ: Princeton University Press.

Rosen, S. (1988). *The quarrel between philosophy and poetry*. New York & London: Routledge.

Russell, B. (1945). *A history of Western philosophy*. New York: George Allen & Unwin.

Ryle, G. (1949). *A concept of mind*. New York: Barnes & Noble.

Sajama, S. & Kamppinen, M. (1987). *A historical introduction to phenomenology*. Beckenham, Eng.: Croom Helm.

Sampson, E. E. (1985). The decentralization of identity: Toward a revised concept of personal and social order. *American Psychologist, 40*, 1203–1211.

Sanford, D. H. (1989). *If P, then Q: Conditionals and the foundations of reasoning*. London: Routledge.

Sappho. (1965). *Sappho* (W. Barnstone, Ed. and Trans.). New York: New York University Press.

Schofield, M. (1991). Heraclitus' theory of soul and its antecedents. In S. Everson (Ed.), *Companions to ancient thought 2: Psychology* (pp. 13–34). Cambridge: Cambridge University Press.

Schwyzer, H.-R. (1960). "Bewusst" und "Unbewusst" bei Plotin ["Conscious" and "unconscious" in Plotinus. In (no editor), *Les sources de Plotin* [Plotinus' sources]. Geneva: Vanduvres.

Searle, J. R. (1980). Minds, brains, and programs. *Behvaioral and Brain Sciences, 3*, 417–424.

Shields, C. (1990). The first functionalist. In J-C. Smith (Ed.), *Historical foundations of cognitive science* (pp. 19–33). Dordrecht, The Netherlands: Kluwer.

Simon, B. (1978). *Mind and madness in ancient Greece: The classical roots of modern psychiatry*. Ithaca, NY: Cornell University Press.

Smart, J.J.C. (1970). Sensation and brain processes. In C. V. Borst (Ed.), *The mind-brain identity theory* (pp. 52–66). London: Macmillan. (Original work published 1959.)

Snell, B. (1982). *The discovery of the mind in Greek philosophy and literature*. New York: Dover. (Original work published 1953.)

Sober, E. (1993). *Philosophy of biology*. Boulder, CO: Westview Press.

Sorabji, R. (1974). Body and soul in Aristotle. *Philosophy, 49*, 63–89.

Sorabji, R. (1988). *Matter, space, and motion: Theories in antiquity and their sequel*. Ithaca, NY: Cornell University Press.

Sorabji, R. (1992). Intentionality and physiological processes: Aristotle's theory of sense-perception. In M. C. Nussbaum & A. O. Rorty (Eds.), *Essays on Aristotle's* De anima (pp. 195–226). Oxford: Clarendon Press.

Steckerl, F. (1958). *The fragments of Praxagoras of Cos and his school*. Leiden, The Netherlands: E. J. Brill.

Szlezák, T. A. (1999). *Reading Plato* (G. Zanker, Trans.). London: Routledge. (Original work published 1993.)

Talbert, R. J. A. (Ed.) (1985). *Atlas of classical history*. London: Routledge.

Taylor, A. E. (1928). *A commentary on Plato's* Timaeus. Oxford: Oxford University Press.

Tertullian (1885). A treatise on the soul (P. Holmes, Trans.). In A. Roberts & J. Donaldson (Eds.), *The ante-Nicene Fathers: Translations of the writings of the Fathers down to A.D. 325* (Vol. 3). Buffalo, NY: Christian Literature Publishing.

Tertullian. (1966). *Prescription against the heretics*. In J. L. Saunders (Ed.), Greek and Roman Philosophy after Aristotle (pp. 343–351). New York: Macmillan & Free Press.

Thomson, R. Campbell. (1903-1904). *The devils and evil spirits of Babylonia* (2 vols.). London: Luzak.

Toulmin, S. & Goodfield, J. (1962). *The architecture of matter*. Chicago: University of Chicago Press.

Tourney, G. (1965). Freud and the Greeks: A study of the influence of classical Greek mythology and philosophy upon the development of Freudian thought. *Journal of the History of the Behavioral Sciences, 1,* 67–85.

Vlastos, G. (1991). *Socrates: Ironist and moral philosopher*. Ithaca, NY: Cornell University Press.

Von Staden, H. (1989). *Herophilus: The art of medicine in early Alexandria*. Cambridge: Cambridge University Press.

Wallis, R. T. (1995). *Neoplatonism* (2nd ed.). London: Hackett.

Wishart, D. & Leach, S. V. (1970). A multivariate analysis of Platonic prose rhythm. *Computer Studies in the Humanities and Verbal Behavior, 3* (2), 90–99.

Wolfson, H. A. (1967). Philo Judaeus. In P. Edwards (Ed.), *Encyclopedia of philosophy* (Vol. 6, pp. 151–155). New York: Macmillan & Free Press.

Young, C. M. (1994). Plato and computer dating. In J. Annas (Ed.), *Oxford studies in ancient philosophy,* (Vol. 12, pp. 227–250). Oxford: Clarendon Press.

Index

About the Authors

CHRISTOPHER D. GREEN is Associate Professor of the History and Theory of Psychology at York University in Toronto.

PHILIP R. GROFF is the Manager of Research Development and Evaluation at SMARTRISK. He has taught in the psychology departments of the University of Toronto, York University, and the Ontario Institute for Studies in Education.